AGRARIAN SYSTEM OF THE SIKHS

Agrarian System of the Sikhs

LATE EIGHTEENTH AND EARLY NINETEENTH CENTURY

INDU BANGA

MANOHAR
2026

First published 1978
Reprinted 2026

ISBN 978-93-88540-19-3

Published by
Ajay Kumar Jain *for*
Manohar Publishers & Distributors
4753/23 Ansari Road, Daryaganj
New Delhi 110 002

Printed at
Replika Press Pvt. Ltd.

Dedicated
to my father, C.L. Banga
and
to my mother, Sita Banga

Foreword

The Sikhs during the phase of their political struggle in the 18th century and of the state power during the first half of the 19th century had developed political and social institutions which were appreciably different from those developed in any other part of the country. Dr. Banga has discussed with great ability the nature and development of many of these institutions, especially the *Rākhī*, the *Gurmata*, the *Dal Khālsa* and the *Misl*.

The Sikh movement started with a special appeal to the trading classes. Nevertheless, it struck deep roots in the peasantry, simultaneously developing its own feudal relations. These feudal relationships affected land rights and the relations of the state with various agrarian classes through the functioning of the land revenue administration. They are of special interest to the students of social and economic history. There was no sharp break with the agrarian relations and the mode of agricultural production as it existed in the Mughal times and yet, as Dr. Banga has shown, the land system under the Sikhs developed its own characteristic features. By the use of detailed original source material, much of which had not been utilized before, Dr. Banga's work has become invaluable for a meaningful study of agrarian relations in the Punjab from the middle of the 18th to the middle of the 19th century.

New Delhi
16 June 1978

S. Nurul Hasan

Preface

This book is the revised version of my Ph.D. thesis submitted at Guru Nanak Dev University, Amritsar, in 1974. It covers the period of Sikh rule in the Panjab during the late 18th and early 19th centuries. Besides a brief exposition of the political and institutional developments of the period, which had a bearing on the agrarian system, the foci of this study are the vassal chiefs, the *jāgīrdārs*, the *dharmarth* grantees, the peasants, land revenue, revenue administration and land tenures. On the whole, the book breaks a fresh ground in regional history, more specifically in the history of the Panjab.

Nevertheless, this study is better viewed in relation to the socio-economic history of medieval India. Despite the recent interest in trade and industry, and in urbanization, the major thrust in the socio-economic history of medieval India has been in the area of agrarian history as, for instance, in the works of W.H. Moreland and Irfan Habib. The questions which these historians have posed and answered relate basically to the produce from land and its division between the cultivator and the state. It is in this context that the rates and methods of assessment and the modes of collection acquire meaning and significance. The machinery devised by the state for these purposes comes in for serious attention. However, the state did not collect all its share directly, and hence the importance attached to the role of the intermediaries. Also, the revenues due from land were assigned to a large number of its employees in *jāgīr*, and hence the relevance of the *jāgīrdārī* system for socio-economic history. Similarly, the state alienated its share by way of reward or charity. The most important of such grantees were individuals and institutions connected with religion, and hence the importance of *madad-i-ma'ash* or *dharmarth* grants. Above all, the question of the condition of the peasant is closely related to the share he gets from the produce, the nature and character of the administration, and the attitude of the intermediaries as well as the administrators. Studied in this manner, agrarian matters cover not merely the produce from land and land revenue but also embrace the social strata, like the ruling classes, the peasantry and the intermediary categories.

The present study too is concerned with questions raised and answered by the historians of medieval India, but on a much smaller scale. Regional studies serve two basic purposes: they serve as a check on generalizations made about larger areas; and, collectively in the process, they advance our knowledge of the country as a whole. The question of change and continuity may partially serve the first of these purposes. If the second purpose is eventually served to some degree, I shall feel gratified.

New questions arising from a new conceptual framework impart new significance to known and familiar evidence. Contemporary chronicles, news-letters, official orders, travel accounts, gazetteers, reports, manuals and the like begin to tell a new story when properly questioned. All such familiar sources have been used in the present work. Two sources may be mentioned as of peculiar importance : the *Khālsa Darbār Records* in the Punjab State Archives, Patiala; and the *Foreign/ Political Consultation* volumes in the National Archives of India, New Delhi. The former contain detailed information on nearly all aspects of the agrarian history of the early 19th century; the latter contain thousands of entries based on orders issued by the Sikh rulers during the late 18th and early 19th centuries. It may only be added that these entries do not make much sense without a certain degree of familiarity with the official orders in Persian.

The book is marked by numerous longish footnotes, detailing evidence in support of a point or its elaboration. They are obviously meant for those who may have a special interest in the subject. The text, consequently, is free from argumentation. The general reader as well as the specialist, I hope, would welcome this arrangement in a book which treats of a little known subject. Most of the non-English words and terms are explained where they occur for the first time; a comprehensive glossary is given at the end. Diacritics are used where deemed necessary, and the *Persian English Dictionary* by Steingass has been used for transliteration. Full detail of works cited is given only in the bibliography. The maps of the 'area of Sikh dominions' and the 'vassal principalities in the hills' may be treated as an integral part of the work.

Lastly, I acknowledge with pleasure my gratitude to Professor J.S. Grewal for his guidance, help and interest at all stages of this study. I am immensely thankful to Professor S. Nurul Hasan, Professor N.G. Barrier and Dr. John C.B. Webster for their valuable suggestions for revision and presentation, and to Professor G.S. Gosal for his help in preparing the maps. I am grateful to Professor S. Nurul Hasan for his Foreword. The Publishers of this book have been extremely accommodating and helpful and I am thankful to Mr. Ramesh Jain for his cooperation and patience. Personally, I am deeply indebted to Mrs. H. Grewal and Miss Navjot Kaur who remained a source of help and strength to me in many ways.

This book is dedicated to my parents as a small return for their affection, sympathy and encouragement.

June 1, 1978 Indu Banga
Amritsar

Contents

1

Land and the People

The conquests of Ranjit Singh and 'the fixed colonies of the Sikh people' covered the vassal principalities in the hills, the former Mughal provinces of Lahore and Kashmir, more than half of Multan, nearly a third of Delhi and a considerable part of the province of Kabul.[1] During the period of Sikh rule most of the area covered by the principalities of vassal chiefs in the hills remained outside the direct control of the Sikh rulers. Over the trans-Indus territories, Sikh rule lasted for only fifteen to twenty years, and in Kashmir and Multan, for twenty-five to thirty years. Only over the Satlej-Jamna Divide and the former province of Lahore did the sovereign Sikh rule last for nearly half a century to ninety years. Forming the core dominions of the Sikhs, these territories were by far the most important also in terms of population and produce.[2]

The large number of hill principalities was a reflection of the physical configuration of the Himalayan ranges cut by the

[1] J.D. Cunningham, *A History of the Sikhs*, 1.

[2] Information on the land and the people of the Sikh dominions is available, not readily though, in the Imperial Gazetteer of India, the district and state gazetteers, settlement reports, the census reports of 1855 and 1868, the accounts of contemporary and near contemporary observers and early British administrators, contemporary chronicles and the detailed sheets of the Survey of India, in addition to the published works of Denzil Ibbetson, H.A. Rose, Frederic Drew, Hutchison & Vogel, David Ross, James Douie, H.K. Trevaskis, Dudley Stamp and O.H.K. Spate. All these works are listed in the Bibliography, and on these, at any rate, is based the brief description of the area of the Sikh dominions.

main rivers and their tributaries into numerous large and small valleys flanked by lofty or low mountains. Rajput princes of ancient lineage formed the ruling class of this area, with the Katoches between the Satlej and the Ravi, the Jamwāls between the Ravi and the Chenab, and the Chhibāls between the Ravi and the Jehlam, as the dominant groups. Next in importance to the ruling families were the land-owning Thākurs.[3] The agriculturist Ghīraths and Kanets, the pastoral Gaddīs and Gujjars, the trading Khatrīs and Banīas, the professional Brāhmans and several categories of artisans and craftsmen, formed the bulk of the hill population, confined largely to valleys and concentrated particularly in capital towns.[4]

The trans-Indus territories consisted of the valleys of Peshawar and Kohat, the lowland of Bannu and the flood-plain of the Indus between Kalabagh and the Panjnad. Due mainly to the Kabul river, the Peshawar valley appeared to form 'a great oasis' in the arid trans-Indus.[5] The Bannu lowland too was well watered by the Kurram, the Tochi and several other streams. The valley of Kohat was much broken by ridges. The Derajat, which included the flood-plain of the Indus, were almost completely devoid of rainfall. Nevertheless, the trans-Indus territories contained the highest proportion of land-owning and agriculturist population in the Sikh dominions.[6] Numerous Pathan tribes were dominant in Peshawar, Kohat and Bannu. In Dera Ismail Khan also their proportion was considerable, but several Jat clans formed nearly half of the population in the Derajat, followed closely by the Baloches in Dera Ghazi Khan. Besides some minor agriculturist tribes and

[3] The Thākurs who had 'nearly all the land in proprietorship' have been regarded as 'the peasantry of the mountains' as the Jats were of the Panjab plains: Frederic Drew, *Jummoo and Kashmir Territories*, 107.

[4] Some of these towns which had also been the seat of the ruling chiefs were Bilaspur, Suket, Mandi, Kulu (Sultanpur), Siba, Guler, Kangra, Nurpur, Chamba, Bhadarwah, Bandralta (Ramnagar), Mankot (Ramkot), Basohli, Jammu, Rajauri, Chenini, Jasrota and Manawar.

[5] The relative prosperity of the valley was reflected in the size of the city of Peshawar which was next only to Amritsar and Lahore in the entire Sikh dominions.

[6] The proportion of the land-owners and agriculturists in Peshawar and Dera Ghazi Khan was over 74 per cent: Ibbeston, *Panjab Castes*, 26-27 & 28-29.

'foreign' Muslim land-owners, Hindu and Muslim traders and shopkeepers, and Muslim artisans and craftsmen formed the rest of the population in the trans-Indus.[7]

In the areas beyond the hill principalities of the Panjab, Kashmir was the most important Sikh conquest. The valleys of the Indus and the Shayok, accounting for the Buddhist Ladakh and the Muslim Baltistan, remained outside the administrative pale of the province of Kashmir.[8] Within the province, the Kashmir valley formed its most productive part, consisting of a 120-mile long alluvial plain of width varying from one to sixteen miles and intersected by the Jehlam and its many tributaries. On the banks of the Jehlam, between Gingal and Muzaffarabad, and in the lower parts of the Kishanganga valley, lived the tribal people known as the Khakhā and the Bambā. Lower down the Jehlam, the Gakhkhars formed the dominant tribe. The agriculturists in the valley of Kashmir, the craftsmen connected with its celebrated shawl trade, and the menial groups were all Muslim. If we add to these all *shaikhs* and *sayyids*, and some traders and shopkeepers, we account for the majority of Muslim population in Kashmir. Among the non-Muslims, Kashmiri *pandits* were the most important and their chief occupation was service in civil administration. Much of the population of Kashmir was concentrated in towns.[9]

The province of Multan consisted largely of the lower portions of the Bari, the Rachna and the Sindh Sagar Doabs, covering the areas of Dipalpur, Multan, Jhang and Muzaffargarh, where cultivation was confined mostly to the riverain tracts. The upland between the river valleys, destitute of 'living brooks and shady groves', was generally used as

[7] The percentage of the vagrant tribes and the menials and the artisans in the trans-Indus was below 20. The proportion of the mercantile classes too in this region was the lowest, about 4 per cent : ibid, 28-29 & 30.

[8] Ladakh and Baltistan had been subdued by the Dogra soldiers of Gulab Singh, respectively in 1834 and 1842, and were therefore controlled by him as a vassal of the Lahore Darbar and not by the then governors of Kashmir.

[9] Besides Srinagar, Gilgit, Skardu (Baltistan) and Leh (Ladakh), the important towns of Kashmir were Anantnag, Baramula, Sopor, Uri, Garhi and Muzaffarabad on the Jehlam, and Darband, Tarbela and Ghazi on the Indus, while Mansera, Dhamtaur, Nara and Haripur were between those rivers.

pasture for cattle and other animals. The land-owning and agriculturist population formed only about 40 per cent of the total, largely because of the preponderance of semi-nomadic tribes. Besides Baloches, the dominant tribes were those of the Daudpotras, Khattars, Khokhars and the Kharals. There was a small percentage of 'foreign' Muslims and Arāins also. In towns and cities, the Hindu trader and shopkeeper was as conspicuous as the Muslim artisan or craftsman.

The core dominions of the Sikhs, bounded by the Himalayas in the north and the Rajputana desert in the south, the river Jamna in the east and the river Indus in the west, covered the Satlej-Jamna Divide, the Bist Jalandhar and Chaj Doabs, and the upper portions of the Bari, the Rachna and the Sindh Sagar Doabs. With the exception of the upper Sindh Sagar, the entire area between the Jamna and the Jehlam presented one uniformly level plain. A submontane zone parallel to the Shivaliks, separating the plains from the hills, was traversed by innumerable *chos* or intermittent streams. The Ghaggar passed through the middle of the Satlej-Jamna Divide before losing itself in the sands near Sirsa. The valleys of the five rivers were lowlands full of fine alluvial deposits.[10] The uplands between the river valleys were comparatively dry and unproductive and presented a more formidable barrier than the rivers.[11]

The Jalandhar Doab, traversed by two perennial streams, called Beins, did not recede sufficiently from the hills to include any desert tract and was known as 'the garden' of the Panjab during the Sikh times.[12] The upland of the upper Bari Doab,

[10] These lowlands, generally called *bet*, were several miles wide depressions along the river banks. Enriched by yearly inundation during the rainy season, they were tracts of great natural fertility, and water for irrigation was obtained at a few feet from the surface. Shifts in the *bet* areas corresponded to the occasional changes in the courses of the rivers in flood.

[11] The uplands, generally known as the *bār*, were a feature common to all the *doābs* and were locally known by different names : Mājha, Ganji Bār and Nīlī Bār in the Bari Doab, Sāndal Bār in the Rachna Doab, Kirāna Bār in the Chaj Doab, and the Thal in the lower Sindh Sagar.

[12] Jalandhar Doab is the smallest of the five *doābs*. Situated between the rivers Satlej and the Beas, it forms nearly an equilateral triangle with its base resting upon the sub-Himalayan hills. Cultivation depended

particularly the tract around Lahore and Amritsar, known as the Mājha, was fairly culturable.[13] However, the region in the south of Lahore, known as Nakkā, assumed the appearance of a barren steppe, covered with low bushes or grass.[14] In the upper Rachna Doab, Sāndal Bār covered the greater part of the upland which could boast only of hardy bushes. The Kirāna Bār in the Chaj Doab covered its largest portion, supporting excellent grass but only in good seasons. The Thal in the Sindh Sagar Doab was a high platform more or less completely covered by sand dunes, giving the appearance of a sandy rolling prairie, covered with grass in years of relatively good rainfall but little better than a desert in seasons of drought. Its scanty population subsisted largely on flocks and herds, wandering from place to place in search of grass.

The upper portions of the Sindh Sagar Doab were sharply marked off from the plains of the Panjab by the Salt Range. The highest point of the Range reached nearly 5000 feet and several peaks ranged between 2000 and 3000 feet. Perhaps the most massive deposits of rocksalt in the world were found in the Salt Range. They were worked at several places like Kalabagh and Khewra. The spurs of the Salt Range to the

largely on rainfall but it was protected by thousands of wells not only in the *bet* area but also in the uplands.

[13] According to Ahmad Shah, the term Mājha was used for the tract between Amritsar and Qasur on the one hand, and between Lahore and Bhairowal on the other: *Tārīkh-i-Hind* (cited hereafter as *Tārīkh*), 181-85.

Notwithstanding this local use of the term, it came to be applied, wrongly though, to the Central Panjab just as the term Mālwa came to be applied to the whole tract across the Satlej. Locally, the term Mālwa was used for the area covered by the district of Ludhiana, a large part of the district of Ferozepur and portions of the states of Patiala and Nabha.

[14] In the middle of the Bari Doab, in much of the Dipalpur area or the Montgomery district, the central plateau was almost entirely uncultivated and the soil was generally inferior. The country around Pakpatan was better, but only slightly. Cultivation was confined to either the riverain tracts or the area covered by inundation canals. The entire plateau was divided locally into the Ganjī Bār and Nilī Bār. Below Dipalpur and Pakpatan, the Bari Doab widens still more to form the 'desert plateau' of Multan, from river to river, where cultivation was possible only in the flood-plains of the river.

north merged into the Pothuhār Plateau which covered the larger parts of Rawalpindi and Jehlam. The Soan transversed the plateau to join the Indus above Kalabagh. A strip of some 20 miles by 10 along the Indus in the north-east of Attock, known as Chhachh, was the most favoured area in the Sindh Sagar Doab.

Diversity of rainfall received from the monsoons both from the Arabian Sea and the Bay of Bengal cut across the Doabs and divided them into horizontal zones, running parallel to the hills.[15] The submontane in Ambala, Hoshiarpur, Gurdaspur, Sialkot, Gujrat and Rawalpindi received from 30 to 40 inches of rain. Below the submontane in Karnal, Ludhiana, Jalandhar, Amritsar, Lahore, Gujranwala, Jehlam and Attock, the annual rainfall varied from 20 to 30 inches. The remaining area with less than 20 inches constituted semi-desert belts, the rainfall decreasing with distance from the hills.[16]

Various means of irrigation mitigated the lack or inadequacy of rainfall with varying success in different parts of the Sikh dominions. The simplest method was to cut channels from natural streams, as in Chhachh and the Satlej-Jamna Divide above Ambala. *Sailāba* or autumnal riverflood, could be used at least for sowing. Similarly, inundation canals and embankments could afford partial supply of water. All these means had to be combined with wells for proper rearing of crops in areas of inadequate rainfall, as in the Derajat, Muzaffargarh, Multan, Jhang, Dipalpur and Pakpatan. Only two areas were served by perennial canals: the upper Bari Doab by the famous Shah Nahr, and the middle portion of the Bari Doab by the Khanwah canal.[17] Much of the upper Satlej-Jamna Divide, the

[15] These zones receded west and south westwards of the hills. The belt receiving rainfall of less than 10 inches ran southwest at right angles to the Shivaliks and was outside the ordinary sphere of the monsoon. It included the Derajat, Multan, Muzaffargarh and the Thal, and also the Sāndal Bār, the Ganjī and the Nīlī Bār.

[16] Patiala, Nabha, Bhatinda, Faridkot, Ferozepur and Shahpur are situated in this belt. The rainfall in this belt was capricious and varied from place to place and year to year. An inch of rainfall here could be literally worth lakhs.

[17] Perennial canals which had been excavated in Mughal times for purposes of irrigation went out of use in the beginning of Sikh rule

Jalandhar Doab and the upper Bari and upper Rachna Doabs were served more or less adequately by wells. All the same, large tracts of land in the Panjab plains remained uncultivated during the Sikh period because of the inadequacy of irrigational facilities.[18]

The seasonal rhythm made it possible for the cultivator to gather at least two sets of harvests in a year. The *rabī'* or spring crops were generally sown in October-November and reaped in April-May. The *kharīf* or autumn crops were generally sown in July and reaped in October. The principal *rabī'* crops were wheat, barley and gram; the principal *kharīf* crops were maize, rice, millets and cotton. Sugarcane, included in the *kharīf*, though it took a whole year to ripen, was also among the principal crops. The principal crops were grown practically throughout the Sikh dominions. However, a varying number of additional crops were grown in different parts, both in the *rabī'* and the *kharīf* season.[19] Several areas were known for

since no single ruler controlled territories large enough to cover a whole canal. The famous Shah Nahr in the upper Bari Doab which had been excavated in the time of Shah Jahan, was renovated in part through Ranjit Singh's orders and, passing through Dina Nagar, Dharmkot and Majitha, it branched off to Lahore while some of its water was brought to Amritsar by a fresh channel. It was capable of irrigating 70,000 *bighas* of land. Partly because of the Shah Nahr and partly because of the large number of wells, upper Bari Doab was probably the best irrigated tract in the Sikh dominions. In any case, irrigated land was the rule here and unirrigated land was the exception: 'R. Napier's Report on the Shah Nahr or Husli Canal', *Foreign/Secret Consultation*, 28 April 1848, No. 62.

The *ta'alluqa* of Dipalpur, consisting of seventy-two 'estates', was chiefly irrigated by the Khanwah canal which had been excavated first in the time of Akbar and renovated in the 1840s. This canal irrigated 30 'estates' of Hujra Shah Muqim also: 'SSR Lower Bari Doab', ibid., No. 64, paras 51-52.

[18] According to one contemporary estimate, only half the land in the Sindh Sagar Doab was under cultivation, and in the Chaj Doab, where it was more than one-half, there were 'vast tracts of jungle, extending for miles and miles without a beegha of cultivation'. What was needed in this case was 'solely good irrigation': L. Bowring to John Lawrence, ibid., No. 65.

[19] The *rabī'* crops also included pulses, vegetables, poppy, tobacco, pepper, *zīra*, safflower and fodder. Besides pulses, vegetables and fodder, the *kharīf* produce included *til*, hemp and chillies. It may be

good varieties of rice, Kashmir having as many as seventy-five.[20] Fruit bearing trees and orchards and herbs were common in the hills, the submontane and the Peshawar valley. Indigo was grown in Muzaffargarh and Jalandhar, and saffron in Kashmir.

The proportion of the land-owning and agriculturist population in different parts of the core dominions of the Sikhs ranged from 35 to 75 per cent.[21] The most numerous among them were the Jats, consisting of over eighty clans. Their proportion in different parts ranged from 30 to 60 per cent.[22] Like the rest of the people, they were predominantly Muslim in the west and predominantly Hindu in the east. The Sikhs formed a considerable proportion of the Jats only in the central parts. Besides the Rajputs in the submontane, the Pathans in Hazara and the Baloches in Muzaffargarh, several tribes were dominant in certain areas, like the Gakhkhars and the Awāns in the upper Sindh Sagar, and the Gujjars in the upper portions of the Divide and the Doabs. Minor agriculturist tribes were

added that in spite of the climate and physical differences, products from land, on the whole, were much the same throughout.

[20] Mir Ahmad, *Dastūr al-'Amal-i-Kashmir*, f133 a.

[21] Nearly 75 per cent cent in the trans-Indus, this proportion was around 55 per cent in the upper Singh Sagar and the upper Rachna Doabs. In the Jalandhar Doab and also around Ludhiana it was above 50 per cent and in the territories of Patiala and Nabha in the Satlej-Jamna Divide, about 48 per cent. In the majority of the other districts, the proportion of the land-owners in the total population was above 40 per cent. In Amritsar, however, it was only slightly over 35 per cent. It is interesting to note that the vagrant tribes, the menials and the artisans in Amritsar formed more than 40 per cent of the total population. Their percentage in the trans-Indus was below 20 and in most of the districts of the Panjab proper and the Satlej-Jamna Divide, they formed about 30 per cent of the population : Ibbetson, *Panjab Castes*, 28-29.

[22] In fact, even across the Indus in the Derajat the Jats accounted for nearly 45 per cent of the population, and they were more numerous than the Pathans and the Baloches put together. At places in the Jalandhar Doab, the Jats formed over 60 per cent of the population and in Muzaffargarh and Rohtak they were over 30 per cent. In most of the districts they formed nearly a quarter of the total population, but in Ambala and Karnal, their proportion was 16 per cent and 15 per cent, respectively. However, the majority of the Sikh rulers were Jats, and the Sikh Jats came to constitute the largest proportion of the nobility during the Sikh times: ibid., 26-29 & 126-31.

important in certain areas, like the Arains in the upper portions of the Divide and most of the Doabs, the Sainīs in the Jalandhar and the upper Bari Doabs, the Māhtons in the Jalandhar Doab, and the Bāghbāns in the upper Sindh Sagar. Several categories of Hindu and Muslim artisans and menials were indirectly connected with agriculture. A small proportion of the land-owners and agriculturists were found in every town.

The people of towns and cities, on the whole, had nothing directly to do with agriculture. They were very largely connected with trade and manufacture. There were two large cities in the core dominions of the Sikhs : Amritsar and Lahore. With a total population of nearly three lakhs, they were important centres of commerce and manufacture. The capital towns of the Sikh chiefs attracted traders and craftsmen in sufficient numbers to give a considerable impetus to urbanization. The total number of towns in the entire Sikh dominions was nearly 120.[23] The number of large villages which could also be termed small towns ran into thousands. By far the largest number of villages and towns were clustered in the river valleys and in the upper portions of the Satlej-Jamna Divide and the Doabs. The Satlej-Jamna Divide, the Jalandhar Doab, the upper Bari and the upper Rachna Doabs could boast of a larger number of towns and villages than the rest of the Sikh dominions put together.[24]

In fact, the meridian through Lahore divided even the core areas of the Sikh dominions into two very dissimilar tracts. The tract east of Lahore formed only a quarter of the plain

[23] The number of towns with a population of over 20,000 however, was rather small: Multan, Jammu, Batala, Jalandhar, Ludhiana, Ambala, Sialkot, for example. However, the number of towns with a population ranging from 10,000 to 20,000 was more than 20. Also, there were over 50 towns with 5,000 to 10,000 inhabitants. This information is based on the Panjab Census of 1855.

[24] This region had a density of 250 to 300 persons per square mile, and over a hundred large and small towns. Some of the most important besides those mentioned already were Kaithal, Thanesar, Jagadhari, Sadhaura, Shahabad, Patiala, Nabha, Hoshiarpur, Kapurthala, Kartarpur, Rahon, Qasur, Wazirabad, Gujranwala, and Chiniot. Only a few important towns, such as Gujrat, Jalalpur, Rawalpindi and Pind Dadan Khan were outside this region. This information is based on the Panjab Census of 1855.

area but accounted for half the cultivated area and nearly half the population. The western tract, which formed nearly half of the entire plain area under Sikh rule, contained only one-fifth of the people and one quarter of the cultivated area. Whether instinctively or out of a deliberate design, the Sikhs struggled the hardest to occupy the most fertile regions.

2

The Rulers

Establishment of the Sikh rule in the latter half of the eighteenth century was in fact its re-establishment. In the second decade of the century, Banda Bahadur had conquered territories, struck coin and given new administration to many parts of the Panjab.[1] When he was executed at Delhi in 1716, the fortunes of the Sikhs were at the lowest ebb. Within half a century, however, they declared their sovereign rule over the Panjab and used those very inscriptions on coins which had been used by Banda on his coin and seal.[2] His example, it is evident, was never forgotten by the followers of Guru Gobind Singh.[3]

[1] For detail, see Ganda Singh, *Life of Banda Singh Bahadur*, 40, 50, 72, 76, 82-84, 101 & 112.

[2] Ibid., 82 & *facsimile* facing 153. See also, Ganesh Das, *Chār Bāgh-i-Panjab* (cited hereafter as *Chār Bāgh*), 103 & 133.

[3] Ahmad Shah of Batala refers to 'Nawab' Kapur Singh's association with a group of Singhs who had been the companions of Banda. He also refers to Khushal Singh, the founder of the *dera* with which were later associated the Ramgarhias, as one of the 'Singhs' of Banda: *Tārīkh-i-Hind* (cited hereafter as *Tārīkh*), 404, 412 & 414. Aliuddin too refers to the contemporaries of Banda who remained active in the Panjab during the reign of Muhammad Shah : *'Ibratnāma*, 283-84.

Some of the old associates of Banda appear never to have submitted to the Mughal governor of Lahore. That the Singhs were politically ambitious in the 1720s is evident from a letter of Mata Sahib Devi, w/o Guru Gobind Singh, written in 1726, to a *jamā'atdār (jathādār)*, Bhai Alam Singh, which contains a reference to the sword and the victory of the Sikhs in the future: Ganda Singh (ed.), *Hukamnāmay*,

For ten years after Banda's death, his captor Abdus Samad Khan remained the governor of Lahore.[4] Strong measures of suppression are attributed to him. Nevertheless, many old Singhs survived all measures of persecution. Bhai Mani Singh, a veteran follower of the tenth Guru, resolved the dispute between the followers of Banda and the Khālsa of Guru Gobind Singh, around 1720.[5] The Har Mandir at Amritsar came under the control of the latter during the governorship of Abdus Samad Khan. Also, it is highly probable that by now, some of the followers of Guru Gobind Singh had started organizing resistance to the officials of the Mughal governor of Lahore. By 1726, Abdus Samad Khan was transferred to the province of Multan and his place was taken by his energetic son, Zakariya Khan.

Zakariya Khan had a long tenure of governorship from 1726 to 1745. On all accounts he was a very capable and powerful governor.[6] On assuming office at Lahore he adopted a vigorous policy of repression against those Sikhs who refused to accept his authority. In the beginning he appears to have been optimistic about his success through sheer physical force.[7] In the early 1730s, however, he tried to pacify the leaders by offering

No. 75, pp. 210-11. Significantly, the terms used by Mata Sahib Devi are the same as appear on Banda's seal: *tegh* and *deg* and *fateh*, meaning sword, bounty and victory. See also, 36 n 101.

[4] Abdus Samad Khan had the merit of dealing successfully with Banda. Some near contemporary evidence suggests that he had lured Banda and his companions out of their fortified position in Gurdas Nangal on the promise of safety (*amān*) : Gurbakhsh Singh, 'Banda's Fall : An Unconditional Surrender or Negotiated Settlement', *Proceedings Punjab History Conference* (*1972*), 45-59.

[5] J.S. Grewal, 'Eighteenth-Century Sikh Polity', *From Guru Nanak to Maharaja Ranjit Singh* (cited hereafter as *Guru Nanak to Ranjit Singh*), 97-98.

[6] Zakariya Khan was intimately connected with Qamruddin Khan who was one of the powerful courtiers at Delhi in the reign of Muhammad Shah : Satish Chandra, *Parties and Politics at the Mughal Court*, (*1707-1740*), 209-10. See also, Ganesh Das, *Chār Bāgh*, 69; Indubhusan Banerjee, 'A Short History of the Origin and Rise of the Sikhs', Supplement to the *Indian Historical Quarterly*, Vol. XVIII, No. 1, 10.

[7] Ganesh Das, *Chār Bāgh*, 124.

them a large grant of revenue-free land not far from Amritsar.[8] The beginning of a regular kind of organization of Sikh volunteers into bands (*jathās*) is generally attributed to this phase of their activity.[9] In any case, Zakariya Khan's hopes of pacifying the Sikhs through conciliatory measures were not realized, for they continued to thwart the authority of Mughal officials. Zakariya Khan felt obliged to resume the grant and to revert to his earlier policy ot extirpation. His measures became more thorough and vigorous and, thwarted in his designs, he became desperate and even more aggressive. In the late 1730s, he ordered the execution of the venerable Bhai Mani Singh, apparently the rallying force behind the increasing numbers of the politically active Sikhs.[10] The execution of Bhai Mani Singh only hardened them in their attitude of defiance and resistance.

Nadir Shah's presence in Hindustan in 1738-39 kept Zakariya Khan's attention diverted from the administration of the Panjab and the Sikhs avenged themselves upon his officials and supporters to weaken his administration.[11] Nadir Shah noticed the rather obtrusive activity of the Sikhs in the Panjab and advised Zakariya Khan to be heedful of their ambition and strength.[12] During the last five years of his governorship,

[8] Ratan Singh Bhangu, *Prāchīn Panth Parkāsh*, 211-14; Giani Gian Singh, *Tawārīkh Gurū Khālsā*, 117-18. *Cf.* N.K. Sinha, *Rise of the Sikh Power*, 5 n 8; Teja Singh & Ganda Singh, *A Short History of the Sikhs* (cited hereafter as *Short History*), I, 121; H.R. Gupta, *Studies in the Later Mughal History of the Panjab (1707-1793)*, (cited hereafter as *Studies*), 54.

[9] Ratan Singh Bhangu, *Prāchīn Panth Parkāsh*, 214-17; Giani Gian Singh, *Tawārīkh Gurū Khālsā*, 119. *Cf.* Sinha, *Rise of the Sikh Power*, 5 n 9; Teja Singh & Ganda Singh, *Short History*, 122; Gupta, *Studies*, 54.

[10] Ratan Singh Bhangu, *Prāchīn Panth Parkāsh*, 222-28; Giani Gian Singh, *Tawārīkh Gurū Khālsā*, 124-27; Sohan Lal, *Umdat-ut-Tawārīkh* (cited hereafter as *Umdat*), I, 108, The context in which Bhai Mani Singh was executed is well brought out by Gurtej Singh: 'Bhai Mani Singh : In Historical Perspective', *Proceedings Punjab History Conference (1968)*, 120-27.

[11] Ratan Singh Bhangu, *Prāchīn Panth Parkāsh*, 231-33; Giani Gian Singh, *Tawārīkh Gurū Khālsā*, 136-38.

[12] Ahmad Shah, *Tārīkh*, 315. The conversation between Nadir Shah and Zakariya Khan is reported by the author as follows:

Zakariya Khan's supreme aim was to re-establish order in the face of opposition from the Sikhs who tried to paralyze his administration as a prerequisite to the establishment of their own rule.[13] At the time of Zakariya Khan's death in July 1745, the issue was still unresolved.

For over two and a half years after Zakariya Khan's death, the Mughal governors of Lahore either remained uncertain of their position or embroiled themselves in mutual struggle.[14] They were not able to give their primary attention to the Sikhs whose numbers consequently increased during these years and so did the number of their *jathās* under old and new leaders.[15] What was even more important, the leaders of these *jathās* decided to take collective action, whenever possible or necessary both in offence and defence. Muin-ul-Mulk was appointed to

Nadir Shah—Have you got any troublesome characters in the country?

Zakariya Khan—None, except a group of Hindu *faqīrs*, who assemble twice to bathe in a tank which they regard as a place of pilgrimage.

Nadir Shah—Where do they live?

Zakariya Khan—Their homes are in their saddles.

Nadir Shah—Take care, the day is not distant when these rebels will take possession of your country.

See also, Ratan Singh Bhangu, *Prāchīn Panth Parkāsh*, 231-32; Giani Gian Singh, *Tawārīkh Gurū Khālsā*, 139-40.

13 Ganesh Das explicitly refers to the 'claims' of the Sikhs to 'rulership' (*da'wā-i-riyāsat*): *Chār Bāgh*, 124. See also, Gupta, *A History of the Sikhs*, I, 12 & n 1.

14 It had not been possible to find a successor to Zakariya Khan. The position of his elder son Yahiya Khan, who could get a formal appointment only about a year after his father's death, was contested by his younger brother Shah Nawaz Khan. In March 1747, by ousting Yahiya Khan from Lahore, Shah Nawaz Khan became the *de facto* governor of the province and even toyed with the idea of independence. But Ahmad Shah Abdali invaded the Panjab in January 1748 and defeated Shah Nawaz Khan.

15 According to Aliuddin, after the death of Muhammad Shah in 1748 there were thirty-eight Sikh *sardārs* of the 'fifth generation' (*girch*). Apparently, each of these *sardārs* had his own band of followers. *'Ibratnāma*, 284-85.

the governorship of Lahore in April 1948. In order to establish his control over the province, he had to contend with the rising ambition of the Sikhs and their increasing potential for offence. Like Zakariya Khan, he tried the alternative policies of repression and conciliation. And, like Zakariya Khan, he failed.[16] Muin-ul-Mulk's failure against the Sikhs was virtually the failure of Ahmad Shah Abdali.[17]

In fact, within six weeks of Muin-ul-Mulk's reappointment by Ahmad Shah Abdali as the governor of Lahore, we find a Sikh *sardār* named Hakumat Singh issuing orders in his own name to the *'āmils* of the *pargana* of Kahnuwan in the upper Bari Doab.[18] After the death of Muin-ul-Mulk in November 1753, the number of such *sardārs* rapidly increased and many had come to exercise influence over substantial chunks of territory. Meanwhile, the *sūbadarī* of Lahore had become a bone of contention between several aspirants and each candidate sought help or recognition from either the Afghan or the Mughal emperor.[19] Therewas no governor of the stature of

[16] The first sack of the suburbs of Lahore is said to have taken place in the time of Muin-ul-Mulk : Aliuddin, *'Ibratnāma*, 241. The fact of the increasing numbers of the politically active Sikhs in spite of Muin-ul-Mulk's measures against them is embodied in the popular saying:

Mīr Mannū asān dī dātrī
Asān Mīr Mannū de soè
Jiyon Mīr Mannū Wadhdā
Gharīn gharīn asīn hoe

These lines may be freely rendered as:

'Mir Mannu is the sickle and we are the grass. The more he mows us down, the more numerous we grow'.

[17] Muin-ul-Mulk had been reappointed as the governor of Lahore on behalf of Ahmad Shah Abdali : *ibid.*, 243. For more than a year and a half before his death in November 1753, Muin-ul-Mulk had given his full attention to the Sikhs as Ahmad Shah's representative. See also, the author's 'Ahmad Shah Abdali's Designs over the Panjab', *Proceedings Indian History Congress* (*1967*), 185-90.

[18] It may also be pointed out that Hakumat Singh uses his personal seal on this document. His orders refer to the *qarār-i-qadīm* and the *'amal-i-pādshāhān*, both of which refer to the arrangements made under the former rule of the Mughals : B.N. Goswamy & J.S. Grewal, *Mughal and Sikh Rulers and the Vaishnavas of Pindori* (cited hereafter as *Pindori Documents*), Document XVIII.

[19] See, for example, Aliuddin, *'Ibratnāma*, 145 & 153.

Zakariya Khan or Muin-ul-Mulk and none had the time or the capacity to check the rising power of the Sikhs. In 1754, for example, Mughlani Begam's nominee, Khwaja Mirza Khan, had to fight many engagements with the Sikhs for establishing his hold over Eminabad.[20] Qasim Khan, who was appointed to the *pargana* of Patti, close to Lahore, was not allowed by the Sikhs even to join his post.[21] At the beginning of 1755, Hakumat Singh was again in occupation of the *pargana* of Kahnuwan.[22]

Ahmad Shah Abdali's decision to appoint his son Taimur Shah to the governorship of Lahore did not improve the situation.[23] Jahan Khan, the veteran Afghan general, was sent against the Sikhs towards the close of that year and he was nearly overpowered by them before he was saved by the timely arrival of fresh contingents.[24] At the close of 1757, Tahmas Khan, a contemporary, observed that 'peace and order which had been established in that country was disrupted and the Sikhs rose in armed revolt on all sides'.[25] In the beginning of 1758, they defeated Sa'adat Khan Afridi who was holding

[20] *Tahmāsnāma* (Eng. tr.), 26.
Mughlani Begam, the widow of Muin-ul-Mulk, was the *de facto* governor of Lahore at this time.

[21] Ibid., 23-24. Qasim Khan had even tried to enlist the support of over eight thousand Sikhs by friendly negotiations, giving them thousands of rupees worth of muskets, bows, arrows and other arms. But all this was of no avail and he returned disgusted to Lahore.

[22] *Pindori Documents*, XIX.

[23] In the beginning of 1757, coins were struck in the name of Ahmad Shah Abdali at Delhi, and in addition to the provinces of Lahore and Multan, the *sarkār* of Sarhind was also formally ceded to him: Ganda Singh, *Ahmad Shah Durrani*, 168 & 169.

[24] See *Tahmāsnāma*, ff 78a-b & 79a. It is interesting to note that the initiative for this battle was taken by the Sikhs.

[25] Ibid., ff 79b & 80a:

از همان ساعت صورت امن و شکل بندوبستکه
دران ملک اسلوب یافته بود برهم خورد و
از چهار طرف هنگامه و فساد سکهان برپا شدن گرفت

Jalandhar on behalf of Taimur Shah.[26] Henceforth, 'in whatever direction the army was sent, it came back defeated' and matters came to 'such a pass that the Sikhs attacked even the city of Lahore; in thousands every night they sacked the *muhallas* outside the city wall'.[27]

At this stage, the Marathas appeared on the scene, to be ousted shortly afterwards. Taimur Shah left Lahore in April 1758 and the Marathas reached the Indus by October. Then, for over two years, Ahmad Shah was engaged in a decisive struggle against the Marathas which culminated in the battle of Panipat in January 1761, and the Marathas were eliminated from the politics of the Panjab.[28]

Ahmad Shah soon realized that his more formidable rivals in the Panjab were the Sikhs who had increased their power and prestige precisely when he was preoccupied with the Marathas.[29] After Ahmad Shah's return to Kabul in May 1761, Khwaja Mirza Khan of the four *parganas* (*chahār mahāl*) of Aurangabad, Pasrur, Sialkot and Gujrat fell before the Sikhs. The *faujdārs* of Jalandhar were driven away and even the governor of Lahore was defeated near Gujranwala in September 1761. The Sikhs now 'ranged round all the territory between

[26] *Tahmāsnāma*, ff 111 b & 112 a.

[27] Ibid., f 80 a :

از ین پس هر طرف که فوج میرفت منهزم گشته
می آمد که نوبت بگرد لاهور رسید و هر شب هزاره
هزار سکهان بر شهر میریختند و محله هائے بیرون
شهرپناه را تاخت و تاراج میکردند

[28] For detail, see, T.S. Shejwalkar, *Panipat : 1761*; Sinha, *Rise of the Sikh Power*, 26-30. See also, H.R. Gupta (ed.), *Marathas and Panipat*, 91-101, 118-32, 157-69 & 220-36.

[29] In 1760, for example, the Sikhs had attacked Lahore and obliged its Afghan governor to pay 30,000 rupees: Aliuddin, '*Ibratnāma*, 259.

Rustam Khan, who was holding the *chahār mahāl* went out to chastise the Sikhs but only to be captured by them. He had to pay Rs. 22,000 as ransom : *Tahmāsnāma*, f 106 b.

the Indus and the Satlej and took possession of it'.[30] Finding all his administrators dislodged from their positions by the Sikhs, Ahmad Shah spent the year 1762 in the Panjab to subdue them once for all. In February, he struck a hard blow against them near Malerkotla and killed thousands in a single action.[31] He failed nonetheless in his grand objective. In May 1762, the Sikhs defeated the Afghan governor of Sarhind. In August, they fought against Ahmad Shah himself near Amritsar; the battle remained indecisive and Ahmad Shah retired to Lahore. During his march back to Kabul in December, he was closely pursued by the Sikhs.

The Afghan governors and *faujdārs* were unlikely to succeed where their master had failed. In fact, they found themselves powerless against the Sikhs. Saadat Yar Khan, the *faujdār* of the Jalandhar Doab, was overwhelmed; Zain Khan, the governor of Sarhind was defeated and slain and his territories were partitioned.[32] Kabuli Mal at Lahore, was obliged

[30] *Tahmāsnāma*, f 112a.

[31] Ibid., ff 113a-b & 114a-b. The figure of the killed given by Tahmas Khan is 25,000. For some other estimates, see Gupta, *A History of the Sikhs*, I, 174 n 1.

[32] Bute Shah, *Tārīkh-i-Panjab* (cited hereafter as *Tārīkh*), (SHR 1288), 458. After Zain Khan's death in Sammat 1820 (A.D. 1763) the Sikhs sacked the city of Sarhind and started occupying territories. The manner of this occupation is graphically described by Bute Shah and often quoted by later historians. The original description is as follows :

فیمابین خودها چنان شیوه قرار دادند که هرکس از سنگهان
چیزے از چیز هاے خود مثل پارچه و تازیانه وغیره
در هر مکانے و موضع بیند از دمکان و موضع ازان آباد
شد و هرچند که آنکس صاحب یک اسپ باشد و
دیگرے مالک سپاه بود متعرض و مزاحم احوال آنکس
نه شود

to take dictation from a nominee of Sardar Hari Singh Bhangi.[33] Sarbuland Khan, who had been deputed to deal with Sardar Charhat Singh in the north-western Panjab, was himself taken prisoner.[34] Ahmad Shah's allies too were worsted by the Sikhs. The Afghan stronghold of Qasur was sacked. Bhikhan Khan of Malerkotla was defeated and slain. In the Jamna-Gangetic Doab, the territory of Najibuddaula was laid waste.[35] Before the beginning of 1765, Ahmad Shah felt obliged to come personally to deal with the Sikhs.

The year of Ahmad Shah's invasion of the Panjab marked actually the formal declaration of Sikh sovereignty. He was allowed to reach Lahore without opposition but his further march was effectively obstructed by the Sikh *sardārs* in combination. In February 1765, he decided to return without having struck a blow. His authority was restricted to his camp. He was on the defensive.[36] The Afghan army recrossed the rivers from Sarhind to Attock virtually as a retreat. Within a few weeks of Ahmad Shah's departure from Lahore, the *sardārs* occupied the city and partitioned it among themselves. A coin was struck at Lahore to proclaim the sovereign status of the Sikh *sardārs*.[37] Qazi Nur Muhammad, who had accompanied Ahmad Shah on this expedition, regretfully observed that the Sikhs were fearlessly enjoying territories from Sarhind to the Derajat, including Lahore and Multan.[38]

[33] Kabuli Mal was the governor of Lahore on behalf of Ahmad Shah Abdali. In the beginning of 1763, he was forced by the Sikhs to punish those residents of the city who had earlier sided with Ahmad Shah: Aliuddin, *'Ibratnāma*, 126.

[34] Ganesh Das, *Chār Bāgh*, 131-32. Sarbuland Khan had to pay a ransom of two lakhs of rupees to Charhat Singh to secure his release.

[35] *Tahmāsnāma*, f 123b. Najibuddaula is said to have been Ahmad Shah's 'plenipotentiary' in India. There are several references in the *Tahmāsnāma* to the ravages of the Sikhs in his territories in the *doāb*: ff 134a, 149b, 150b, 143 a-b & 155a.

[36] Qazi Nur Muhammad, *Jangnāma*, 176-78. Significantly, pitched battles were fought on the banks of the rivers Satlej and Beas.

[37] Ganesh Das, *Chār Bāgh*, 128 & 130.

[38] The original reads as follows:

According to a contemporary, the territories of the Sikhs in the late 1770s included whole of the former Mughal province of Lahore, three-fourths of the province of Multan and one-third of the province of Shahjahanabad.[39] This statement is surely suggestive of the extent of Sikh dominions in the 1770s. Some of the veteran Sikh *sardārs* had established themselves in the province of Lahore. Jassa Singh Ahluwalia, for instance, occupied territories in the Jalandhar and Bari Doabs and also across the Satlej, with his headquarters at Kapurthala. Jassa Singh Ramgarhia too had his possessions in these two *doābs*, generally residing at Sri Hargobindpur in the upper Bari Doab. Jai Singh Kanhiya occupied territories in the upper Bari Doab, particularly around Batala. Hari Singh Bhangi and his sons occupied Amritsar and the surrounding area. Gujjar Singh Bhangi had a share in Lahore and occupied Gujrat and some other *parganas* in the upper Chaj Doab. Charhat Singh Sukarchakia came into possession of several *parganas* in Rachna, Chaj and Sindh Sagar Doabs, with his capital at Gujranwala.

These well-known names by no means exhaust the list of the Sikh *sardārs* who established themselves in the Mughal province of Lahore. There were many others: Baghel Singh, Tara Singh Dallewalia and Budh Singh Faizullapuria in the Jalandhar Doab; Lehna Singh, Sobha Singh, Haqiqat Singh, Amar Singh Kingra, Amar Singh Bagga, Hakumat Singh, Sudh Singh, Sahib Singh and Tara Singh Pathankotia in the upper Bari Doab; Jassa Singh Dulu, Jodh Singh Saurianwala, Nidhan Singh Daskewala, Gurbakhsh Singh Waraich, Sahib Singh Sialkotia, Natha Singh Shahid, Jiwan Singh, Bhag Singh Hallowalia, Bhag Singh Muraliwala, Nahar Singh Chamiariwala and Sudh

ز سرہند لاہور ملتان زمین - ای دبرجات آن سگان لعین
نمودند تقسیم آن ملک را - خورند و ندارند از کس رجا

Jangnāma, 177.

[39] *Haqīqat-i-Binā-wa-'Urūj-i-Firqa-i-Sikhān* (anon.), 46.

Singh Chhina in the upper Rachna Doab; and Milkha Singh at Rawalpindi across the Jehlam.[40]

The number of Sikh *sardārs* in the Mughal provinces of Multan and Delhi was equally large. The city of Multan and a very large part of the province were conquered by Jhanda Singh and Ganda Singh Bhangi who placed these conquests in the charge of Rai Singh. There were several *sardārs* in the rest of the lower Bari Doab: Lal Singh in Maruf and Kanganpur; Qamar Singh in Dipalpur and Satghara; Ran Singh, Sahai Singh and Tara Singh in Jethpur, Chunian, Faridabad, Malka Hans, Sayyidwala, Kamalia and Pakpatan.

The *sardārs* in the Delhi province were of two categories: those who originally came from the province of Lahore and those who belonged to the province of Delhi itself. The upper portions of the Satlej-Jamna Divide were largely occupied by the former and the lower portions by the latter. Some of the important *sardārs* of the first category, besides Jassa Singh Ahluwalia and Tara Singh Dallewalia, were Baghel Singh, Gurbakhsh Singh Shahid, Gurbakhsh Singh Kalsi, Hari Singh Sialba, Rai Singh Buria, Khushal Singh of Banur, Karam Singh of Shahabad, Nanu Singh of Jagadhari, Desu Singh of Kaithal and Bhanga Singh of Thanesar. Among the important *sardārs* of the second category were Alha Singh of Patiala and his grandson, Amar Singh, Gajpat Singh of Jind, Hamir Singh of Nabha and Hamir Singh of Faridkot.

The Sikh dominions in the last quarter of the eighteenth century were remarkable more for internal strife than expansion.[41] Besides some minor annexations in the submontane areas, the *sardārs* like Jassa Singh Ramgarhia, Jai Singh Kanhiya, Gujjar Singh Bhangi and Jhanda Singh Bhangi

[40] *Khālsa Darbār Records*, Bundle 5, Vols. I, III, V, IX, X & XI. This information on the individual chiefs is corroborated by the *Foreign/Political Consultations* of the 1850's which contain, among other things, numerous statements of revenue-free grants given by these chiefs.

[41] No significant extension of territory is on record during this period. In fact, Multan was lost by Rai Singh Bhangi in the late 1770s and the conquest of Kangra by Jai Singh Kanhiya proved to be a transitory gain.

collected tribute from the hill principalities.[42] Before long, however, they were fighting among themselves for supremacy. In 1774, Charhat Singh Sukarchakia and Jai Singh Kanhiya supported Brij Raj Dev against his father, Raja Ranjit Dev of Jammu, who in turn was supported by his overlord, Jhanda Singh Bhangi.[43] During this conflict, both Charhat Singh Sukarchakia and Jhanda Singh Bhangi died. Soon afterwards, the Kanhiyas and the Bhangis fought over Pathankot.[44] In 1776, Jassa Singh Ramgarhia was dislodged from his territories by Jassa Singh Ahluwalia and Jai Singh Kanhiya.[45] In 1782, the Bhangis and the Kanhiyas clashed once more over the affairs of Jammu. When they patched up their differences and turned against Brij Raj Dev, he received assistance from Mahan Singh Sukarchakia who, however, raided Jammu later on, appropriating immense booty. Around 1785, Mahan Singh joined hands with Jassa Singh Ramgarhia to defeat his erstwhile ally, Jai Singh Kanhiya, in a battle near Batala in which Gurbakhsh Singh, the eldest son of Jai Singh, was killed.[46] Around 1790, Mahan Singh was trying to wrest some of the territories of Sahib Singh Bhangi.[47] When Mahan Singh died in 1791, the issue of ascendancy between the House of Gujjar Singh Bhangi and the House of Charhat Singh Sukarchakia was still unresolved.

It was left for Ranjit Singh to settle the issue of supremacy and to unite numerous principalities into a single whole. The occupation of Lahore in 1799, largely at the cost of the Bhangis, signalized the beginning of that process. Amritsar was soon wrested from the descendants of Hari Singh Bhangi.[48] Patti was taken over from Budh Singh Faizullapuria in 1811.[49] The Nakai chiefs were dislodged from the lower

[42] See, for example, Aliuddin, *'Ibratnāma*, 301-02 & 462-64; Ahmad Shah, *Tārīkh*, 407-08, 410 & 411-12.

[43] Ahmad Shah, *Tārīkh*, 407-08; Bute Shah, *Tārīkh*, V, f 178b.

[44] Ahmad Shah, *Tārīkh*, 408-09; Aliuddin, *'Ibratnāma*, 294-95.

[45] Ahmad Shah, *Tārīkh*, 418-20.

[46] Bute Shah, *Tārīkh*, V, ff 181a-b & 182a-b.

[47] Ibid., V, f 185a. See also, Ahmad Shah, *Tārīkh*, 411; Ganesh Das, *Chār Bāgh*, 136-37.

[48] Aliuddin, *'Ibratnāma*, 297; Bute Shah, *Tārīkh*, V, ff 166b & 167a-b.

[49] Ahmad Shah, *Tārīkh*, 412; Lepel H. Griffin & Charles Francis Massy,

Bari Doab.[50] In the following year, several other chiefs of the Bari Doab lost their possessions.[51] In 1816, after the death of Jodh Singh, son of Jassa Singh Ramgarhia, his territories in Sri Hargobindpur and Qadian were taken over.[52] On Sada Kaur's imprisonment in 1821, the remnants of the possessions of Jai Singh Kanhiya were annexed to the kingdom of Lahore.[53]

In the Rachna Doab, Bhag Singh Hallowalia's territories like Zafarwal, Qila Sobha Singh, Sukanwind and Hallowal were confiscated and the widow of Nahar Singh was made to part with the *parganas* of Pasrur and Chamiari.[54] Nidhan Singh lost all his possessions, including Daska and Wadala.[55] Similarly, Sialkot was wrested from Jiwan Singh, Akalgarh from the wife of Dal Singh, Chiniot from Jassa Singh Dulu, and Wazirabad from the son of Jodh Singh.[56] Karam Singh Chhina retained a part of his territories but only on condition of service and so did Jodh Singh Kalalwala.[57] This was only a prelude to the total annexation of their territories.

Chiefs and Families of Note in the Punjab (cited hereafter as *Chiefs and Families*), II, 158.

[50] Munshi Bakhtawar Lal, *Tārīkh-i-Zila'-i-Montgomery* (cited hereafter as *Tārīkh-i-Montgomery*), 11; Aliuddin, *'Ibratnāma*, 341.

[51] Some of these were Budh Singh, son of Amar Singh Bagga, Nidhan Singh, son of Jai Singh Kanhiya, Jaimal Singh, son of Haqiqat Singh Kanhiya and Rup Singh, son of Amar Singh Kingra: Ahmad Shah, *Tārīkh*, 450-54 & 462; Griffin & Massy, *Chiefs and Families*, II, 19, 39 & 44; *Foreign/Secret Proceedings*, 3 April 1850, No. 280.

[52] Ahmad Shah, *Tārīkh*, 414.

[53] In the month of Asuj, 1878 (A.D. 1821) the Maharaja imprisoned Sada Kaur and took over her entire territory. Sardar Desa Singh Majithia was appointed to take over all her forts and all of them with the exception of Atalgarh were occupied without a fight. Desa Singh kept Sada Kaur in detention while settling her territory: Ahmad Shah, *Tārīkh*, 482-83.

[54] Bute Shah, *Tārīkh* (SHR 1288), 529-30 & 530-31; Munshi Amin Chand, *History of the Sialkot District* (cited hereafter as *History of Sialkot*), 9-11 & 12-13. See also, Ahmad Shah, *Tārīkh*, 462.

[55] Munshi Amin Chand, *History of Sialkot*, 8-9; Griffin & Massy, *Chiefs and Families*, II, 52.

[56] Bute Shah, *Tārīkh*, V, ff 149 a-b, 164a & 166a; Ahmad Shah, *Tārīkh*, 448, 455 & 468.

[57] Griffin & Massy, *Panjab Chiefs*, I, 313; also, *Chiefs and Families*, II, 57.

For the rest, in the Chaj Doab, Ranjit Singh ejected his most formidable adversary, Sahib Singh Bhangi, from all his territories by 1810 and occupied Jalalpur, Manawar, Sodhran, Islamgarh and Gujrat.[58] In the Sindh Sagar, Jiwan Singh, son of Milkha Singh, was ejected from Rawalpindi.[59] In the Jalandhar Doab, Budh Singh Faizullapuria was ousted from Jalandhar proper, and the Ramgarhia possessions like Begowal, Urmar-Tanda, Banga, Dasuha and parts of Hoshiarpur were also taken over.[60] The possessions of Tara Singh Dallewalia like Lohian, Nakodar, Nawan Shahr and Rahon, had already been annexed to the kingdom of Lahore in 1807 after Tara Singh's death.[61] The widows of Baghel Singh were deprived of part of Hoshiarpur, Nur Mahal, Sham Chaurasi and Hariana.[62] The only Sikh chief to retain his territories in the former Mughal province of Lahore was Fateh Singh, the second successor of Jassa Singh Ahluwalia.[63]

In the province of Delhi, Ranjit Singh's success in uniting the Sikh dominions into one single whole was partial and temporary. In 1807, the Dallewalia territories on the east of the Satlej were taken over.[64] The chiefs of Patiala, Nabha, Jind, Kaithal, Buria, Shahabad, Kalsia and Ambala offered *nazrāna* to Ranjit Singh and some of them received lands on conditions suggestive of vassalage.[65] Tribute was levied from

[58] Aliuddin, *'Ibratnāma*, 305; Ganesh Das, *Chār Bāgh*, 152; Ahmad Shah, *Tārīkh*, 411-12 & 460; *Punjab Government Records (1808-1815)*, II, 169.

[59] Griffin & Massy, *Panjab Chiefs*, I, 135.

[60] Ahmad Shah, *Tārīkh*, 412 & 421-22.

[61] Aliuddin, *'Ibratnāma*, 333-34 & 381; Griffin & Massy, *Chiefs and Families*, I, 170.

[62] Bute Shah, *Tārīkh* (SHR 1288), 552-61.

[63] In 1802, Ranjit Singh and Fateh Singh Ahluwalia had entered into a treaty of friendship and cooperation : Sohan Lal, *Umdat* II, 50-51. With the passage of time, however, the Ahluwalia chief was reduced to the status of a vassal, receiving orders from the Maharaja who was probably contemplating the annexation of his territories when the latter sought the intervention of the British in 1826 : Griffin, *Minor Phulkian Families*, 488-90.

[64] Aliuddin, *'Ibratnāma*, 333-34; Griffin, *Minor Phulkian Families*, 606-07.

[65] Raja Ram Tota, *Iqbālnāma*, f 22 b. It is significant to note here that

many *pattīdārs* also.[66] Ranjit Singh's suzerainty over the Sikh chiefs of the Satlej-Jamna Divide was an accomplished fact by 1808. Also, he had deprived the Rajput Muslim chief of Raikot of his possessions in Ludhiana, Kot Jagraon, Baddowal, Bassi, Talwandi and Sahnewal.[67] However, the Treaty of Amritsar signed with the British in 1809, obliged Ranjit Singh to relinquish everything except possessions worth over 4 lakhs of rupees a year in Baddowal, Nurpur, Sahnewal, Bharatgarh and Bahlolpur.[68]

Besides uniting the territories of the Sikh chiefs of the province of Lahore under his own sway, Ranjit Singh recovered the lost Sikh territories in the province of Multan. In 1818. Nawab Muzaffar Khan was finally defeated and killed and, after about forty years of Afghan rule, Ranjit Singh's administration was established in the core areas of the Mughal province of Multan.[69] Ranjit Singh's penetration into the Panjab hills was also much more effective than that of his predecessors. Many hill principalities were subverted and others were brought under his political control. Some of the important chiefships to accept his overlordship were Chamba, Mandi, Kulu, Jammu and Rajauri and those subjugated by him included, among others, Kangra, Bhimbar and Punchh. Pockets

Ranjit Singh, in giving a twenty-one piece *khil'at* and sword and shield to Raja Sahib Singh of Patiala was quite consciously following the practice of the 'emperors of the olden times': ibid., ff 21b-22a. *Cf.* B.J. Hasrat, *Anglo-Sikh Relations (1799-1849)*, 57 & n 2.

[66] Diwan Amar Nath in his long list of the '*zamīndārs*' who paid tribute to Ranjit Singh, is actually referring to the *pattīdārs* who were autonomous in the administration of their territories. *Cf.* Sinha, *Ranjit Singh*, 23. See also, chapter VI, 132-38.

[67] Griffin, *Rajas of the Punjab*, 87-88; also, *Minor Phulkian Families*, 604-08.

[68] *Foreign Political Consultation*, 31 December 1847, No. 1829. See also, Griffin, *Minor Phulkian Families*, 607, Appendix A.

[69] Ganesh Das, *Chār Bāgh*, 307-09. For the comparatively well-known account of the conquest of Multan and its dependancies, see G.L. Chopra, *Panjab as a Sovereign State* (cited hereafter as *Sovereign State*), 10-13; Sinha, *Ranjit Singh*, 15 & 56-58; Khushwant Singh, *Ranjit Singh*, 52-53, 100, 120 & 123-24; S.M. Latif, *History of the Panjab*, 410-13.

of autonomous authority in the plains too were either wiped out or subordinated.[70]

Ranjit Singh extended the Sikh dominions far beyond the limits dreamt of by his eighteenth-century predecessors. The Afghan province of Kashmir, an area of more than 20,000 square miles and worth more than 25 lakhs of rupees a year, was conquered in 1819.[71] By 1820, he had started leading expeditions across the Indus.[72] For ten years, he remained content with realizing tribute. By 1831, however, he had decided to administer these territories directly. Dera Ghazi Khan was the first to be annexed to the kingdom of Lahore. The administration of Peshawar, Bannu, Tank and Dera Ismail Khan was taken over between 1832 and 1836. By 1837, Ranjit Singh had constructed a strong fortress at Jamrud on the mouth of the Khaibar.

Ranjit Singh's successors maintained the integrity of his dominions till 1845, and even added a few small territories.[73] But after the Anglo-Sikh War of 1845-46, the Jalandhar Doab was taken over by the British; also the chiefs of several vassal territories of the Sikh empire became vassals of the British; some of the autonomous chiefs were placed under Raja Gulab Singh who was given Jammu and Kashmir as a vassal of the British; and, at Lahore, was posted a British Resident. Not only the territorial limits but also the character of the kingdom of Lahore changed considerably after 1845 till it was fully annexed to the British empire in 1849.

Looking at the establishment of Sikh rule in retrospect, we find that piecemeal subjugation was effected, haltingly but assuredly, during the third quarter of the eighteenth century. During the last quarter, there was little expansion of Sikh dominions; the *sardārs* quarrelled as much among themselves as with others; but the administration of their territories

[70] For detail, see chapter III.

[71] For detail, see Chopra, *Sovereign State*, 13-17; Sinha, *Ranjit Singh*, 45-48, 53-55, 59-60 & 152-53; Khushwant Singh, *Ranjit Singh*, 131-34.

[72] For detail, see Chopra, *Sovereign State*, 17-21; Sinha, *Ranjit Singh*, 61-63 & 107; Khushwant Singh, *Ranjit Singh*, 129-31.

[73] The hill principalities of Kulu, Mandi and Rajauri were annexed respectively in 1839, 1840 and 1841. See chapter III, 45, nn 28-30.

became more or less settled. During the first two decades of the nineteenth century, the Sikh principalities between the rivers Satlej and Jamna came under British protection and the Sikh principalities in the Panjab proper came under Ranjit Singh's control; the Sikh dominions vastly expanded with the conquest of Multan and Kashmir and the subjugation of Rajput principalities in the Panjab hills. Territories across the river Indus came under Ranjit Singh's rule in the 1820s and were directly administered by his officials in the 1830s. His legacy was preserved by his successors for over five years. The longest period of sovereign Sikh rule extended from 1765 to 1845, and that too only in the former Mughal province of Lahore which, thus, formed the core area of Sikh dominions.

For a better understanding of this political process and the nature of Sikh rule we may now turn to the 'political institutions' which are believed to have been evolved by the Sikhs, notably the *rākhī*, the *gurmata*, the *dal khālsa* and the *misl*.

Rākhī has been conceived generally as a definite phase in the political career of the Sikhs, as a step that 'supplied them with the idea of raising themselves into territorial chieftains'.[74] This view does find support in Aliuddin's conception of the phase of *nazrāna-gīrī* or *amān* (the Persian equivalent of *rākhī*) as a prelude to the phase of annexation.[75] However, Bute Shah refers to Charhat Singh's conquest of one area and assertion of *rākhī* over another at the same time.[76] *Rākhī* did serve as a prelude to territorial occupation but not as a phase. Territorial occupation and *rākhī* could be established by one and the same chief at one and the same time in two different areas. *Rākhī* was thus a transitional arrangement existing

[74] Gupta, *A History of the Sikhs*, I, 99; also, 98 & 134.

[75] *'Ibratnāma*, 371; See also, James Browne, *Early European Accounts of the Sikhs* (ed. Ganda Singh), 16. That *rākhī* was a phase before the occupation of territory is suggested also in some recent works: see, for example, Sita Ram Kohli, 'Organization of the Khalsa Army', *Maharaja Ranjit Singh: First Death Centenary Memorial* (ed. Ganda Singh), (cited hereafter as *Maharaja Ranjit Singh*), 63-64; Teja Singh & Ganda Singh, *Short History*, 153.

[76] *Tārīkh*, V, ff 176 a-b.

side by side with territorial occupation. The areas once brought under *rākhī* were often, but not always, actually occupied and directly administered sooner or later.

Without justification, *rākhī* has been equated with *chauth* and interpreted as blackmail or tribute.[77] Some of the Sikh chiefs did levy *kharāj* from independent or semi-autonomous chiefs. But it is wrong to apply the word *rākhī* to cover such situations. The term blackmail may be used with some justification only for those outlying territories into which the Sikh *sardārs* led excursions from time to time without eventually occupying them.[78] *Rākhī*, which literally means protection, signified essentially the Sikh chief's claim to a part of the produce from land in return for protection afforded against all other claimants.[79]

[77] See, for example, Cunningham, *A History of the Sikhs*, 95 n 1; H.T. Prinsep, *Origin of the Sikh Power in the Punjab* (cited hereafter as *Origin of the Sikh Power*), 26; Sinha, *Rise of the Sikh Power*, 115.

[78] A good example is afforded by the territories across the river Jamna. The Sikhs led more than a dozen excursions into these territories but no part of the upper *doāb* was ever occupied by them. Therefore, the nature of their interest in these territories turned out to be different from what it had been in the Panjab proper. Thus, whereas, the term blackmail would not be applicable to those areas in which the Sikh chiefs afforded effective protection to the peasants before bringing those areas under direct administration, there may be some justification for its use in connection with the territories across the Jamna where 'as regularly as the crops were cut, the border chieftains crossed over, and levied blackmail from almost every village in a systematic manner. Their requisitions were termed *rukhee*, sometimes euphemistically *kumblee*, i.e., "blanket money" ': G.R.C. Williams, "Historical Sketches : The Sikhs in the Upper Doab", *Selections from the Calcutta Review*, III, No. 10, 234 ; also, 228-59 & 332-54.

[79] It may be pointed out that there is no definite contemporary or near contemporary evidence on the share of produce collected as *rākhī*. According to the Marathi sources, it was one-fourth of the annual revenues: *Delhi Yethil Rāj Karnen*, I, 254 & 278. James Browne, writing in the early 1780s observed that the amount collected as *rākhī* was about one-fifth of the revenue due to the government: *Early European Accounts* (ed. Ganda Singh), 16. The amount of *rākhī*, according to Cunningham, varied from one-fifth to one-half of the government share of the produce : *A History of the Sikhs*, 95n. Kohli also subscribes to this view : 'Organization of the Khalsa Army', *Maharaja Ranjit Singh*, 64. According to a recent estimate, however,

Gurmata literally is 'a resolution endorsed by the Guru', for the Guru was believed to be present in the Khālsa deliberating in the presence of the Gurū Granth Sāhib.[80] It cannot be equated with any 'council' or 'a general meeting' of the Sikhs.[81] That *gurmatas* gave unity and direction to the activities of a large number of Sikh *sardārs* during the third quarter of the eighteenth century may be readily conceded, but neither the meetings of the *sarbat khālsa*, literally the entire body of the Khālsa, nor the resolutions adopted in such meetings give any indication of institutionalization. It can indeed be asserted that these decisions related almost invariably to matters of defence.[82] It can be visualized that the Sikh *sardārs* participating in the *gurmatas* were bound to gain from executing them, but there is no reason to believe that these resolutions were formally binding on the *sardārs*. The limited scope of the *gurmatas* and the incomplete participation even of the important *sardārs* may be illustrated with reference to an event which has been regarded as one of the most important in the history of the re-establishment of Sikh rule in the Panjab, namely, the occupation of Lahore by the Sikhs in 1765. Notwithstanding references to a *gurmata*, Lahore was occupied by only three *sardārs*: Lehna Singh Bhangi, Gujjar Singh Bhangi and Sobha Singh Kanhiya. What

it was one-fifth of the 'income of the people' : Gupta, *A History of the Sikhs*, I, 134. On the whole, the rate of *rākhī* is stated to be one-fifth of the revenue.

[80] Ganda Singh (ed.), *Early European Accounts of the Sikhs*, 16 n 9. Dr Ganda Singh goes on to add, '*Mata* generally means opinion or resolution and it is called *Gurmata*, opinion or resolution endorsed by the Guru, because the Guru is believed to be always presiding over the deliberations of the *Khālsa* held in the presence of the Holy Book, the *Guru Granth Sahib*'.

[81] *Cf.* Prinsep, *Origin of the Sikh Power*, 26; Cunningham, *A History of the Sikhs*, 94 & 119.

[82] The traveller George Forster observed in the early 1780s that in the 'grand convention' called *gurmata* 'the army met to transact the more important affairs of the nation : as the declaration of war or peace, forming alliances and detaching parties on the service of the year'; *A Journey from Bengal to England and through the Northern Parts of India, Kashmir, etc. (1782-1784)*, cited hereafter as *Journey (1782-1784)*, I, 286-87.

is more, they did not occupy it jointly. The city and the adjoining territory were partitioned among the three *sardārs*, each of whom established his own administration in his own jurisdiction.[83] Indeed, as has been observed recentlv, 'the decisions which the Sikh leaders at Amritsar took from time to time were *ad hoc* deliberations of voluntary gatherings and their scope was confined to matters concerning the preservation and augmentation of the striking power'.[84] The *gurmata* obviously stopped short of territorial occupation, government and administration.[85] In 1805, Malcolm observed with reference to a *gurmata* that 'every shadow of the concord which once formed the strength of the Sikh nation seemed to be extinguished'.[86] The great days of *gurmatas*, in fact, had been over more than thirty years ago.[87]

The great days of the *dal khālsa* too were practically over by the beginning of the last quarter of the eighteenth century. It is tempting to use the term 'national army' of the Sikhs for the *dal khālsa* but to pose such an equation is to misjudge its character.[88] There is no denying the fact that on numerous occasions several *sardārs* joined their forces for a collective action. On such occasions, there is a possibility of

[83] Ganesh Das, *Chār Bāgh*, 128.

[84] Grewal, 'Eighteenth-Century Sikh Polity', *Guru Nanak to Ranjit Singh*, 98-99. It may be added that the term *gurmata* was applied to any decision taken anywhere by the *sardārs* present on the occasion.

[85] *Cf.* Teja Singh, 'Historical Barkground', *Maharaja Ranjit Singh*, 11: 'All this land was held in joint ownership by the whole Sikh nation, called the *Sarbat Khalsa*'.

[86] John Malcolm,' 'Sketch of the Sikhs', *The Sikh Religion—a Symposium*, 117.

[87] Forster, for example, makes the following observation during his visit to the Panjab in the early 1780s: 'From the spirit of independence so invariably infused amongst them, their mutual jealousy and the rapacious roving temper, the sicques at this day are seldom seen cooperating in national concert, but actuated by the influence of an individual ambition or private distrust, they pursue such plans as only coincide with these motives: *Journey* (*1782-1784*), I, 291. Elsewhere, Forster states that the priestly class among the Sikhs 'did not possess any influence in the temporal regulation of the state': ibid., 287.

[88] *Cf.* Gupta, *A History of the Sikhs*, I, 53-57; Kohli, 'Organization of the Khalsa Army', *Maharaja Ranjit Singh*, 64.

the entire force having been placed under the general direction of a single person. It is equally probable that each individual *sardār* remained in command of his followers. It must be pointed out however, that an *ad hoc* collective action by several *sardārs* did not make their force a single unit. The *dal khālsa* appears essentially to be very much similar to the *gurmata*. The frequency of joint action by a combination of Sikh *sardārs* accounts for the vital role which is commonly attributed to the *dal khālsa* but the *dal khālsa* did not become anything more than an *ad hoc* combination of the forces of more than one *sardār* for the limited purpose of offence or defence. The *gurmata* and the *dal khālsa*, during the third quarter of the eighteenth century, were the obverse and the reverse of the same political coin.

The working of the *gurmata* and the *dal khālsa* provides an essential clue to the working of the 'organization' now generally conceived as the *misl*.[89] During the process of territorial occupation, smaller leaders of horsemen voluntarily accepted the command of a prominent leader for the purposes of offence and defence. This organization was often strengthened by the ties of kinship but never institutionalized.[90] Ahmad Shah of

[89] *Cf.* Cunningham, *A History of the Sikhs*, 96-97 & 119; Gupta, *A History of the Sikhs*, I, 51-53; Sinha, *Rise of the Sikh Power*, 110.

[90] The ties of kinship were decidedly effective at least in two *misls*: the Ramgarhias and the Bhangis. All the associates of Jassa Singh Ramgarhia —Khushal Singh, Mali Singh, Tara Singh, Mehtab Singh, Sahib Singh, Gulab Singh, Diwan Singh, Jodh Singh and Bir Singh—were either his brothers or nephews or sons: see, Prithipal Singh Kapur, *Sardar Jassa Singh Ramgarhia*, Appendix II.

The most important of the Bhangi *sardārs* can also be traced to two families who associated with each other closely:

I. Bhuma Singh

Hari Singh (nephew and adopted son)

Jhanda Singh

Ganda Singh
|
Desu Singh
|
Gulab Singh
|
Gurdit Singh

Batala, on whose 'authority' many a description of the '*misldārī* system' has been attempted, refers to *sardār* and *misldār* in terms which make the latter clearly subordinate to the former.[91] In other words, a number of *misldārs* were subordinate to a single *sardār*. However, the relationship of *sardārī* and *misldārī* remained all important up to the point of territorial

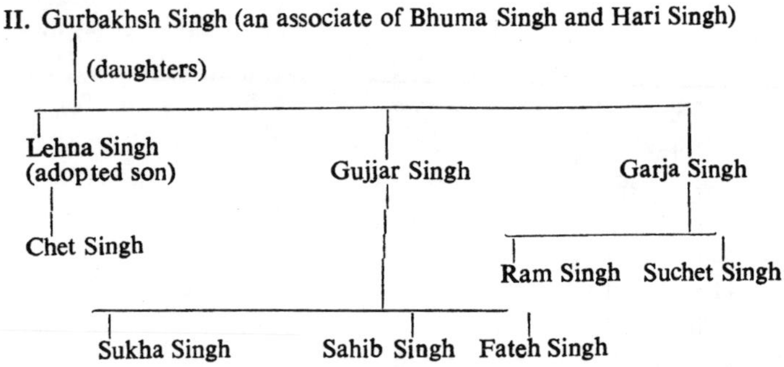

Latif, *History of the Panjab*, 296-306. *Cf.* Giani Gian Singh, *Tawārīkh Gurū Khālsā*, 225.

But the ties of kinship did not always account for the close association of a number of *sardārs*. The collective action of the *sardārs* known as the Kanhiyas, Karorasinghias and the Dallewalias, for example, could not be accounted for in terms of kinship. The Ahluwalias and the Sukarchakias on the other hand, were practically confined to one family and under the leadership of one man at a time.

The case of the Nakais is perhaps the most interesting of all. The Nakai '*misl*' is supposed to have consisted mainly of the two houses of Bharwal and Sayyidwala. 'Between the families there was no relationship but they were near neighbours and were engaged in perpetual quarrels': Griffin & Massy, *Chiefs and Families*, I, 233. At no stage in their history do these rival Houses of the Nakais seem to have associated with each other. In what sense then did they belong to the same *misl*? *Cf.* Aliuddin, *'Ibratnāma*, 334-35 & 339-40; Munshi Bakhtawar Lal, *Tārīkh-i-Montgomery* 10-11.

[91] The point becomes absolutely clear if the contemporary usage of the word *misl* is kept in mind. The term *misl* was used by the contemporaries invariably for a group of soldiers. The *misldār*, therefore, was the commandant of such a group : see, for example, *Khālsa Darbār Records*, Bundle 3, Vol. III, 339, 340, 341, 371 & 373. See also, Kohli, 'Organization of the Khalsa Army', *Maharaja Ranjit Singh*, 82-83; Ram Sukh Rao, *Srī Fateh Singh Partāp Prabhākar*, ff 68b, 85a *et passim*. *Cf.* Fauja Singh, *Military System of the Sikhs*, 12-13; Chopra, *Sovereign State*, 2-3. Chopra, however, seems to grasp the essentials of the situation elsewhere: ibid., 64.

occupation, when the *misldār* got a share in the territory conquered. This relationship had some significance even later but only for the purposes of offence and defence against outsiders;[92] it stopped short of government and administration within the territory as well of the *misldār* as of the *sardār*. This conception of *misldārī* takes into account the available empirical evidence which does not suggest any formal differences between the *sardār* and the *misldār*.

According to Forster, of the numerous Sikh chiefs, some had the command of ten or twelve thousand cavalry; but this power was confined to a small number, 'the inferior officers maintaining from one to two thousand, and many not more than twenty or thirty horses'.[93] Another contemporary observer, the author of the *Haqīqat-i-Binā*, thought that everybody amongst the Sikhs was 'independent in his own place'; if any one possessed even two horses and a village he was 'not subservient to

[92] It may be pointed out that even this was not a rigid pattern. This is well illustrated by the example of Karam Singh Dulu, the chief of Chiniot, who is generally believed to be a Bhangi *sardār* : Gupta, *A History of the Sikhs*, III, 4-5, 40, 45 & 50. However, Qazi Nur Muhammad, who accompanied Ahmad Shah Abdali in his invasion of 1764-65, attributes the conquest of Chiniot to Jhanda Singh Bhangi : *Jangnāma*, 178. Aliuddin, while referring to the contest between Mahan Singh Sukarchakia and Jai Singh Kanhiya quite explicitly states that 'Karam Singh Dulu, who was an associate of Mahan Singh kept up the appearance of siding with Jai Singh': '*Ibratnāma*, 326. Another statement of Bute Shah is equally suggestive. Referring to Jhanda Singh of Sultanvind who had been patronized by Karam Singh Dulu, he says that, 'though he had become an associate of the Bhangis, Karam Singh continued to help him in all situations' : *Tārīkh* (SHR 1288), 526-27. Bute Shah also tells us of Tara Singh, supposedly a Bhangi, that 'he first served the Bhangis and then became an associate of the Kanhiyas and occasionally associated with Gujjar Singh' : ibid., 529. The 'Bhangi' *sardārs* Bhag Singh Hallowalia and Nahar Singh Chamiariwala sometimes sided with Gujjar Singh, and at others, with Mahan Singh, eventually accepting Ranjit Singh's offer of service : ibid., 529-31. Similarly, Amar Singh Bagga, who was supposed to be a Kanhiya, sided with Mahan Singh in the latter's fight against the Kanhiya chief Jai Singh : Aliuddin, '*Ibratnāma*, 327-28.

[93] *Journey* (*1782-1784*), I, 291. Elsewhere, Forster relates an incident in which he was told by a Sikh that 'he disdained an earthly superior, and acknowledged no other master but his Prophet': ibid., 286.

anyone else'.[94] Prinsep's remark that the Panjab in the late eighteenth century was 'ruled by seventy thousand sovereigns'[95] is obviously an exaggeration but it does underline the essential autonomy of the individual *sardār* within his own territories. There is absolutely no doubt that each *sardār* worth the name, irrespective of his affiliation to one group or another, exercised the powers and prerogatives of an independent ruler in his own territories. All appointments of officials, from the *nāzim* to the *patwārī*, were made by the *sardār* without reference to any other temporal ruler.[96] In this respect, the difference between Ranjit Singh in 1839 and Hakumat Singh in 1752 is a difference only of degree.

The autonomy of the individual *sardār* comes into high relief in his relations with other rulers, whether Sikh or non-Sikh. In the last quarter of the eighteenth century, when the principle of hereditary succession was accepted by all not only in the case of the so-called chiefs of *misls* but also in the case of the individual *sardār* of a *misl*, interesting combinations and alliances of *sardārs* amongst themselves and with non-Sikh chiefs become clearly noticeable. For example, Sahib Singh Bhangi, in the life-time of his father Gujjar Singh (d. 1788), aligned himself with Mahan Singh Sukarchakia (whose sister

[94] *Haqīqat-i-Binā wa 'Urūj-i-Firqa-i-Sikhān* (anon.), 46:

هر یک در جای خود مختار است و اگر کسی دو اسپ دارد
و یک دیهه در جاگیر خود گرفته محتاج مجرای سلام کسی نیست

Furthermore,

صاحب صد سوار و دو صد سوار به همین دستور است

[95] *Origin of the Sikh Power*, 29.

[96] This is clearly evident from hundreds of references to grants of land made and *sanads* given by scores of *sardārs* who appointed their own *kārdārs*, *qānūngos*, *patwārīs*, *'āmils*, and even *dīwāns* in some cases: see, for example, *Foreign/Political Proceedings*, 15 October 1852, No. 116; 14 January 1853, Nos. 222-23; 10 June 1853, No. 217.

was married to Sahib Singh) against his own brother and father.[97] Nahar Singh of Chamiari joined hands with the Bhangis and other *sardārs* as and when it suited his interests and purposes. Similarly, Bhag Singh Hallowalia, who is generally regarded as a Bhangi, joined hands sometimes with Gujjar Singh Bhangi and at others with Mahan Singh Sukarchakia.[98] Karam Singh Man acquired territories in association with the Bhangis, but his son Ram Singh came to associate himself with Mahan Singh.[99] On several occasions, Sikh *sardārs* entered into alliances with non-Sikh chiefs against similar combinations of Sikh and non-Sikh rulers.[100] The essential autonomy of the individual *sardār* emerges clearly also in his ability to treat some other chiefs as his vassals.

The most important evidence in support of the authority of the collective body of the Khālsa is believed to be supplied by the coins struck by the Sikh *sardārs* during the eighteenth century. On the basis of the legends on these coins, it has been argued by several historians that by attributing their success to the grace of their Gurus the Sikh *sardārs* merged their individual entity in the collective entity of the Sikh Panth and

[97] Ahmad Shah, *Tārīkh*, 411,

[98] Bute Shah, *Tārīkh* (SHR 1288), 529-31.

[99] Griffin & Massy, *Chiefs and Families*, I, 462-63. It is interesting to note that Ram Singh Man married his only child, Sada Kaur, to the son of Bhag Singh Hallowalia who had originally been an associate of the Bhangis.

[100] One can find many well-known examples of the Sikh *sardārs* entering into alliances with non-Sikh chiefs. The best known would be Jhanda Singh Bhangi's alignment with Raja Ranjit Dev of Jammu against a combination of the latter's son and Charhat Singh Sukarchakia and Jai Singh Kanhiya. On another occasion Mahan Singh Sukarchakia aligned with Raja Brij Raj Dev of Jammu against the combined forces of the Kanhiyas, Bhangis and the Ahluwalias. Later, he joined hands with Raja Sansar Chand of Kangra and Jassa Singh Ramgarhia against Jai Singh Kanhiya. Within a few years Jai Singh Kanhiya was an ally of both Mahan Singh and Sansar Chand. Similarly, the Chaththas of Rasulnagar were in alliance with Gujjar Singh Bhangi and fought against Mahan Singh. Raja Sultan Khan of Bhimbar too was in alliance with Sahib Singh Bhangi. Nizamuddin Khan of Qasur joined hands with Jassa Singh Ramgarhia, Gulab Singh Bhangi, Sahib Singh Bhangi and Jassa Singh Dulu at Bhasin against Ranjit Singh.

derived the sovereignty of the Panth from God. The coin struck for the first time in 1765, called Gobind Shāhī, had the following verse inscribed on it:[101]

Deg-o-tegh-o-fateh-o-nusrat be-dirang
Yāft as Nānak Gurū Gobind Singh

This was the inscription used by Banda on his seal.[102] The other inscription, used for the first time by Banda on his coin, and then by the Sikh chiefs of Amritsar, reads:[103]

Sikka zad bar har do 'ālam tegh-i-Nānak wāhib ast
Fateh-i-Gobind Singh Shāh-i-Shāhān fazl-i-sacchā sāhib ast

It may be readily conceded that in the inscriptions used on the Sikh coins in the Panjab proper, sovereignty is not derived from an individual. It does not follow, however, that sovereignty was vested in the collective entity of the Khālsa. In the case of the chiefs of Patiala and Jind, the inscription used clearly implies that they accepted the suzerainty of a temporal ruler, Ahmad Shah Abdali.[104] It can be argued indeed that the derivation of sovereignty from the Gurus and God enabled each individual to assert his independence of any temporal lord. For all practical purposes, the individual chief became a sovereign ruler not in spite of the coin but because of it.

Such has been the weight, however, of a misconceived evidence of the Gobind Shāhī and Nanak Shāhī coins that even Ranjit Singh is regarded by some historians as merely a representative of the *sarbat khālsa*. Ranjit Singh, it is said,

[101] Freely rendered: 'Bounty and power and unlimited victory are the gifts received by Guru Gobind Singh from (Guru) Nanak'.

[102] Ganda Singh, *Life of Banda Singh Bahadur*, *facsimile* facing page 153; C.J. Rodgers, 'On the Coins of the Sikhs', *Journal of the Asiatic Society of Bengal* (cited hereafter as *JASB*), Vol. L, Part 1, No. 1, 79.

[103] Rodgers, 'On the Coins of the Sikhs', *JASB*, 81. A free rendering would read thus : 'With the help of the sword of (Guru) Nanak, the coin is struck in both the worlds. The victory of Gobind Singh, the King of Kings, is due to the grace of the True Lord'.

[104] Griffin, *Minor Phulkian Families*, 285-87 n 2. The inscription on the Patiala and Jind rupee reads :

Hukm shud az qādir-i-bechūn b'Ahmad Pādshāh
Sikka zan bar sīm-o-zar az auj-i-māhī tā b'māh

A free rendering would be as follows : 'The Eternal Lord ordered Ahmad Pādshāh to strike coin in silver and gold from the Pisces to the Moon'.

did not rule in his own name; his effigy did not appear on the coins he struck; the seal of government bore no reference to him. The government likewise was not to be a personal affair, but the '*Sarkār Khālsāji*' of the people who brought it into being; 'the Court' for the same reason came to be known as the '*Durbār Khālsāji*'.[105] It may be pointed out that the term *khālsāji*, whether used with *sarkār* or *darbār*, did not refer to the Sikh people. It referred only to the individual ruler in question, whatever his title.[106] Ranjit Singh, in fact, approved of the epithet *sarkār-i-wālā* (His Exalted Majesty) for himself.[107]

[105] Khushwant Singh, *Ranjit Singh*, 47. Khushwant Singh is not alone. According to Cunningham, who has generally been followed by the later writers particularly in this respect, Ranjit Singh 'attributed every success to the favour of God, and he styled himself and the people collectively the "Khalsa", or commonwealth of Govind. . . . His own name and his own motives were kept carefully concealed, and everything was done for the sake of the Guru, for the advantage of the Khalsa, and in the name of the Lord': *A History of the Sikhs*, 152 & n 1.

Sinha asserts that 'theocratic commonwealth or the *Khalsa* of which each individual Sikh considered himself as a member, was a potent force and Ranjit Singh always showed due deference to it. . . . He might have been absolute, but he always acted in the name of the *Khalsa*. He did not assume the title of King but rather the impersonal designation of *Sarkar* to denote the source of orders. In referring to his government he always used the term *Khalsaji* or *Sarkar Khalsaji*. On his seals he had the inscription "God the helper of Ranjit" ' : *Ranjit Singh*, 137.

See also, Chopra, *Sovereign State*, 93.

[106] This is amply borne out by the contemporary documents : 'Introduction', *Pindori Documents*, 34-35. In Documents XXII, XXIII, XXIX and XXX, the term *Khālsajī* has been used explicitly for the individual *sardār*. The editors infer that 'the power and authority of the Sikh State was considered to be vested in the person of the ruler. This is as true of the autonomous Sikh principalities of the eighteenth century as of the government of Ranjit Singh and his successors' : ibid., 85. It may be noted in this connection that the terms referring to the orders of the issuing authorities and to the authorities themselves are some of the old Mughal terms : *parwāna-i-wālā, amr-i- dāwar, hukm-i-'ālī, hukm-i-aqdas, amr-i-jalīl-ul-qadr, faiyāz-i-zamān, sarkār-i-mu'alla, huzūr-i-anwar, sarkār-i-ālī, khudāwand-i-ni'mat*, for example.

[107] Amar Nath, *Zafarnāma-i-Ranjit Singh* (ed. Sita Ram Kohli), (cited hereafter as *Zafarnāma*), 16-17. Amar Nath adds that Ranjit Singh did not approve of the epithet *huzūr* for himself on the significant assumption that the latter could be used appropriately for only the

Ranjit Singh was akin to his eighteenth-century predecessors in continuing the use of those inscriptions on coins which had been first used by Banda on his seal and coin. The eighteenth-century Sikh chiefs were akin to Ranjit Singh in not having any constitutional check on the use of their power. The difference between Ranjit Singh and his father and grandfather was only of degree. Indeed, the position of all the Sikh chiefs during the period of sovereign Sikh rule is better understood in terms of the monarchical form of government.[108] To invoke democratic diets and republican confederacies which regretfully vanished because of the autocratic postures of the *de facto* Sikh *sardārs* is to misconceive their position from the very beginning.

God Almighty. Nevertheless, the epithet *huzūr* is also used for Ranjit Singh in his *parwānas* : see, for example, *Pindori Documents*, XXXV & XXXVI.

[108] In Sikh literature dealing with government and administration, and even visualising an ideal Sikh state, there is no conception of a form other than the monarchical : see, for example, Grewal, 'Prem Sumarag : An Ideal Sikh Social Order', *Guru Nanak to Ranjit Singh*, 79-83; also, 'Eighteenth Century Sikh Polity', ibid., 92-100.

3

The Vassals

From the very beginning, the Sikh rulers were familiar with the idea and practice of suzerainty which implied political control over an autonomous chief but not direct administration. Perhaps no other legacy of the Mughal times was cherished with equal ease or consistency by the Sikh rulers. In the hills, particularly, was preserved this age-old tradition throughout the period of Sikh rule.

Around 1750, in the hills of the Panjab and Kashmir, there were over forty vassal principalities, subordinate to the Mughal emperor. They fell into three groups. The eastern group between the rivers Satlej and Ravi consisted of nearly a dozen principalities.[1] Nearly the same number constituted the central group between the Ravi and the Chenab.[2] Both these groups were attached to the province of Lahore through the *faujdārs* of Kangra and Jammu. The western group between the Chenab

[1] Also known as the Kangra hill states, these were Kangra, Kulu, Chamba, Mandi, Suket, Bilaspur (Kahlur), Nurpur, Kutlehr, Guler, Jaswan, Siba and Datarpur. Of these principalities, the closest to the plains were Kangra, Nurpur, Guler, Jaswan, Siba, Datarpur and Kutlehr. The most inaccessible were Chamba and Kulu.

[2] The central group consisted of the Rajput chiefships of Jammu, Basohli, Bhaddu, Bandralta, Chenini, Bhadarwah, Kishtwar, Bhau, Riasi, Bhoti, Samba, Jasrota, Lakhanpur and Mankot. The closest to the plains were Jammu, Bhau, Riasi, Bhoti, Samba, Jasrota, Lakhanpur and Mankot, and the least accessible were Kishtwar, Bhadarwah and Chenini.

and the Indus consisted of about a score of chiefships, subservient to the governor of Kashmir.[3]

In 1752-53, when Ahmad Shah Abdali took over the Mughal provinces of Lahore and Kashmir, he came to assert his suzerainty over all the hill principalities attached to those provinces.[4] However, his control was never uniformly exercised. It was most effective in the western group. Elsewhere, it was little more than nominal. In fact, Ranjit Dev of Jammu[5] and

[3] The well-known among these were Bhimbar, Punchh, Rajauri, Akhnur, Khari Khariali, Pakhli, Dhamtaur, Gandgarh, Darband, Tarbela, Uri, Garhi and Muzaffarabad. With the exception of Akhnur, all of these were under Muslim chiefs, whether Rajput, Afghan or Gakhkhar. Akhnur and Bhimbar were close to Gujrat in the plains; Khari Khariali was close to Jehlam; and Punchh was accessible from Rawalpindi while Rajauri was the least accessible of these. Closest to the plains between the Indus and the Jehlam were Pakhli, Dhamtaur, Darband and Tarbela. Uri was closest to the valley of Kashmir and Muzaffarabad and Garhi were rather inaccessible even from the valley.

For more information, see Kirpa Ram, *Gulzār-i-Kashmir*, 13-14; Mir Ahmad, *Dastūr al-Amal-i-Kashmir*, f 187a; Charles Ellison Bates, *A Gazetteer of Kashmir*, 179, 228-29, 248, 280-83 & 393-94; J. Hutchison & J. Ph. Vogel, *History of the Panjab Hill States* (cited hereafter as *Panjab Hill States*), I, 45.

[4] *Catalogue of the Bhuri Singh Museum* at Chamba contains enough evidence on this point. A *farmān* of May-June 1762, issued by Ahmad Shah Abdali, confirms the *jāgīr* of the *pargana* of Pathiar on Raja Umed Singh of Chamba on the recommendation of Raja Ranjit Dev of Jammu: ibid., 56-59. It is significant to note that according to a *parwāna* dated 9 March 1744, Pathiar had been given to Umed Singh's predecessor, Dalel Singh, by Zakariya Khan, the Mughal governor of Lahore: ibid., 54-56. Hutchison and Vogel fail to realise that even the Mughal *faujdār* of Kangra had become subordinate to Ahmad Shah: see *Panjab Hill States*, I, 76 & 361, for example. A *farmān* of Ahmad Shah issued in September-October 1762 clearly indicates that Saif Ali Khan, formerly the Mughal governor of Kangra, was under Ahmad Shah Abdali's control. In this *farmān* Raja Umed Singh of Chamba is directed to submit the revenues of Chari to Saif Ali Khan : *Catalogue of the Bhuri Singh Museum*, 59-61. In fact, even the successors of Ahmad Shah claimed suzerain rights over the Panjab hill chiefs: ibid., 71-72, C. 17, & CC. 44-47.

[5] Ranjit Dev of Jammu co-operated with Ahmad Shah in his Kashmir campaigns of 1752 and 1762; obtained the *parganas* of Zafarwal, Sanktara and Aurangabad, besides an annual grant of rice from Kashmir. He asserted supremacy over the hill states between the

Ghamand Chand of Kangra[6] increased their territories and consolidated their power during the lifetime of Ahmad Shah.

When the Sikh *sardārs* wrested the Panjab plains from Ahmad Shah Abdali, they asserted their own suzerain claims over the hill principalities. Jassa Singh Ramgarhia collected tribute from Kangra, Nurpur, Jaswan, Siba, Basohli, Mandi, Suket, Bhadarwah and even Chamba.[7] In 1776, Jai Singh Kanhiya replaced Jassa Singh as the overlord of these hill principalities and by 1783, he succeeded in occupying even the fort of Kangra. The control of the Kanhiyas, certainly effective over Chamba, was extended to Kulu also.[8] Gujjar Singh

Chenab and the Ravi, including the principalities of Basohli, Bhadarwah and Kishtwar; and, at one time, struck his coin as a clear token of his sovereign status : Kahan Singh Balauria, *Tawārīkh-i-Rājputān-i-Mulk-i-Panjab* (cited hereafter as *Tawārīkh-i-Rājputān*), 287; Ganesh Das, *Rāj Darshinī*, ff 221b, 235b & 236a. *Cf.* Kahan Singh Balauria, *Tārīkh-i-Rājgān-i-Jammu-o-Kashmir* (cited hereafter as *Tārīkh-i-Rājgān*), 72; Gupta, *A History of the Sikhs*, I, 77, 105, 125 & 178; Ganda Singh, *Ahmad Shah Durrani*, 152, 187, 189, 284 & 285.

[6] Ghamand Chand, the Katoch chief of Kangra, actively cooperated with Ahmad Shah Abdali and received from him the title of *rāja* in 1762. With the decreasing hold of Ahmad Shah over the Panjab, he succeeded in strengthening his principality at the cost of his neighbours, and Kangra under him was restored to its ancient limits : Hutchison & Vogel, *Panjab Hill States*, I, 176; Gupta, *A History of the Sikhs*, I, 126, 145, 155 & 189; Ganda Singh, *Ahmad Shah Durrani*, 152, 267, 274 & 288.

[7] *Catalogue of the Bhuri Singh Museum*, 71, C. 33.

Forster, travelling through these hills in 1782-83, noticed the establishment of Sikh supremacy as an accomplished fact. He also makes mention of the fort of Talwara in Datarpur as specially constructed for an effective control of these hill states : *Journey (1782-1784)*, I, 198, 201, 223, 225, 226, 227, 229, 235, 248 & 291. *Cf.* Hutchison & Vogel, *Panjab Hill States*, I, 177, 209, 211, 262, 315, 317, 361 & 362; II, 392 & 609-10; Man Mohan, *History of the Mandi State*, 71.

[8] In a document containing the seal of Gurbakhsh Singh, son of Jai Singh Kanhiya, Raja Raj Singh of Chamba is making the request that one-third of Kulu may be put in his possession on the condition that he would pay the revenues to the *khālsa* as he had placed himself under *his* protection: *Catalogue of the Bhuri Singh Museum*, 69, C. 20. According to a *sanad* of Jai Singh Kanhiya, the amount payable by Chamba as tribute was fixed at Rs. 4001: Hutchison & Vogel, *Panjab Hill States*, I, 316. See also, *Gazetteer of Kangra*, 39n 2.

Bhangi and Sahib Singh Bhangi extracted *nazrāna* from Bhimbar and Khari Khariali. Ranjit Dev of Jammu was obliged to accept the overlordship of Jhanda Singh Bhangi.[9] Later on, not only the chiefs of Jammu but also some of the chiefs in the neighbourhood, like Alam Singh of Akhnur, became tributary to Mahan Singh Sukarchakia.[10]

Ranjit Singh was the first Sikh ruler to subvert a large number of hill principalities. His conflict with Sansar Chand of Kangra who cherished the idea of his own supremacy is easily understandable.[11] In 1802, Sansar Chand invaded the territories of Lakhanpur and Kathua across the Ravi and Ranjit Singh thwarted his design by assisting Budh Singh Bagga against him. In the year following, Sansar Chand was obliged to relinquish control over Bajwara.[12] Soon afterwards, he was embroiled in a protracted war with the Gurkhas and had to approach Ranjit Singh for help in 1808. By 1809, he was forced to hand over the fort of Kangra to Ranjit Singh. The treaty of 1809 was signed between two sovereign rulers.[13] But within a few years, Sansar Chand was made to accept a subordinate position. He was shorn of much of his territory and he died in 1824 as a petty vassal of Maharaja Ranjit Singh.[14]

[9] Ahmad Shah, *Tārīkh*, 407-08 & 410; Aliuddin, *'Ibratnāma*, 301-02

[10] Sohan Lal, *Umdat*, II, 23-24 & 25. *Cf.* Hutchison & Vogel, *Panjab Hill States*, II, 549. The annual tribute paid by Jammu to its Sikh suzerains, according to the authors, was 30,000 rupees.

[11] Sansar Chand, the grandson of Ghamand Chand, captured the fort of Kangra, which had remained in Mughal possession for a century and a half, and asserted his supremacy over a large number of hill principalities, including Mandi and Chamba. In the words of Amar Nath, Sansar Chand around 1800, was holding aloft the banner of 'none but I': *Zafarnāma*, 4. See also, Sohan Lal, *Umdat*, II, 22-23 & 23-24; Hutchison & Vogel, *Panjab Hill States*, I, 79, 177 & 180-82.

[12] Sohan Lal, *Umdat*, II, 52, 53 & 56.

[13] For an English translation of the treaty, see Griffin & Massy, *Chiefs and Families*, I, 73-74. It may be noted incidentally that the territories like Kotwalbah and Chauki which had belonged to Kutlehr at one time, and the former principality of Siba and some territory conquered by Sansar Chand from the rulers of Mandi in the past, are included among those which Ranjit Singh was expected to recover for Sansar Chand in return for the fort of Kangra.

[14] The traveller William Moorcroft visited the court of Sansar Chand in

Many of the dependencies of Sansar Chand in the Kangra hills were also annexed to the kingdom of Lahore. Already, in 1809, several of these had become tributary to Ranjit Singh. These included Jaswan, Nurpur, Datarpur, Kutlehr, Guler and Siba, the last two under Raja Bhup Chand. In 1813, Raja Bhup Chand was deposed and his entire territory in the submontane was annexed.[15] The neighbouring principality of Jaswan was taken over in 1815.[16] Raja Bir Singh of Nurpur who had proved to be an unwilling vassal since 1809, was obliged to come to Amritsar in 1815 and was asked to pay a heavy *nazrāna* which he could not pay. He was imprisoned, his *dera* was plundered and troops were sent to occupy his territories, including Lakhanpur which was a part of Nurpur at this time.[17] On the death of Raja Gobind Chand of Datarpur in 1818, his son Jagat Singh was not allowed to succeed to his territories and the principality was annexed.[18] Kutlehr was taken over in 1825.[19]

1820, and observed that the loss of territory and dependencies suffered by the Katoch chief had so much reduced his revenues that he had 'but 70,000 rupees a year for the expenses of himself and his family after paying his troops'. In Moorcroft's estimate, the total revenues of Sansar Chand at one time were thirty-five lakhs of rupees : *Travels in the Himalayan Provinces of Hindustan and the Panjab etc., 1819-1825* (cited hereafter as *Travels (1819-1825)*, 76 & 78-79. See also, Sohan Lal, *Umdat*, II, 297 & 308; *Gazetteer of Kangra*, 44.

[15] Sohan Lal, *Umdat*, II, 129-30 & 150-51. *Cf.* Hutchison & Vogel, *Panjab Hill States*, I, 206-07; Griffin & Massy, *Chiefs and Families*, I, 73; *Gazetteer of Kangra*, 41. Bhup Chand is also mentioned as Bhup Singh in some of these works.

According to Sohan Lal, Raja Bhup Chand was detained at Lahore and released only when he agreed to hand over the fort of Guler and his territories to the Maharaja's troops. The actual occupation was effected by Lala Narain Das.

[16] Sohan Lal, *Umdat*, II, 184. According to this account, the Raja of Jaswan was detained by the Maharaja at Lahore because some of the neighbouring *rājas* had commented on the fertility of Jaswan and the strength of its fortress. See also, Bute Shah, *Tārīkh*, V, f 240b. *Cf. Gazetteer of Kangra*, 41.

[17] Sohan Lal, *Umdat*, II, 184 & 338; also, IV, (i), 5. *Cf.* Hutchison & Vogel, *Panjab Hill States*, I, 263-64; II, 553; *Gazetteer of Kangra*, 42.

[18] Hutchison & Vogel, *Panjab Hill States*, I, 212. *Cf. Gazetteer of Kangra*, 42.

[19] Sohan Lal, *Umdat*, II, 323. See also, Hutchison & Vogel, *Panjab Hill*

Jammu in the central group, like Kangra in the eastern, experienced the pressure of Ranjit Singh's arms soon after his conquest of Lahore. By 1809, the chief of Jammu was reduced to the status of a regular vassal.[20] The smaller states like Riasi, Samba and Dalpatpur were annexed by 1812 when the Raja of Mankot was ejected by Prince Kharak Singh.[21] At the same time, Ghausa, the *dārogha* of the *topkhāna*, conquered Kathua and captured the fort of Taragarh.[22] In 1815, Raja Jit Dev of Jammu, the great-grandson of Ranjit Dev, was summoned to the court and Bhayya Ram Singh was sent to Jammu to administer those territories.[23] The principality of Jammu stood virtually annexed, thus, in 1815.

In the western group of principalities, the first to be invaded was Akhnur, though it was annexed in 1812.[24] Khari Khariali had been annexed already in 1810 and Bhimbar in 1811.[25] Then came the turn of Punchh. In 1814, at the time of the second Kashmir campaign, Raja Ruhullah Khan of Punchh cast his lot with the Afghan governor of Kashmir for which his territory was ravaged by the Lahore troops. The fort of

States, II, 489-90; *Foreign Political Proceedings*, 26 December 1846, No. 648. *Cf*. *Gazetteer of Kangra*, 42-43.

[20] Sohan Lal, *Umdat*, II, 92; Kirpa Ram, *Gulābnāma*, 128-29. The latter places the conquest of Jammu in 1808 and the former in 1809. According to Sohan Lal, Mian Mota supported Ranjit Singh against his kinsman, Raja Jit Dev of Jammu.

[21] Amar Nath, *Zafarnāma*, 70.

[22] Sohan Lal, *Umdat*, II, 129. See also, Bute Shah, *Tārīkh*, V, f. 266a.

[23] Sohan Lal, *Umdat*, II, 180.

[24] According to Sohan Lal, troops were sent against Raja Alam Singh of Akhnur in 1807 when he was obliged to pay 13,000 rupees as *nazrāna*. At the same time, territory in the neighbourhood of Akhnur was brought under the direct administration of Ranjit Singh: ibid., 68. The fort was taken over in 1812.

[25] Ibid., 100-01, 103 & 127-28. Raja Sultan Khan of Bhimbar who had agreed to pay 40,000 rupees as *nazrāna* in 1808, soon proved to be an unwilling vassal. See also, Amar Nath, *Zafarnāma*, 70.

Sultan Khan was released in 1819 and he assisted the Darbar troops in the Kashmir campaign. A part of his former territory was given to him in reward but he died a few years later : Hutchison & Vogel, *Panjab Hill States*, II, 728.

Kotli and the surrounding territory came into the possession of Ranjit Singh in 1815. Punchh itself was annexed in 1819.[26] The Hazara and Pakhli region, between the Jehlam and the Indus, was annexed in 1818 but effectively subjugated around 1825 by Hari Singh Nalwa.[27]

After Ranjit Singh's death, three more principalities were annexed to the kingdom of Lahore. These were Kulu and Mandi in the eastern group, and Rajauri in the western. Kulu was invaded by the Lahore troops in 1839; its capital, Sultanpur, was occupied and the *rāja* was made a prisoner. With the exception of Saraj, which was farmed to the Raja of Mandi for 32,000 rupees, the territories of Kulu, including Lahaul, were brought under the direct administration of Lahore, and a force was stationed in Kulu to ensure the collection of revenues.[28] In 1840, General Ventura was sent against Mandi to collect arrears of tribute. He imprisoned Raja Balbir Sen and occupied his territories and forts. The *rāja* was released in 1841 and allowed to return to Mandi, but virtually as a farmer.[29] Rajauri too was annexed in 1841.[30]

Large though was the number of principalities subverted by Ranjit Singh and his successors, the number of those retained in subordination to Lahore was much larger. Most of them were rather distant from the plains, like Chamba, Kulu, Mandi and Suket in the eastern group; Bhadarwah and Basohli in the

[26] Amar Nath, *Zafarnāma*, 82; Sohan Lal, *Umdat*, II, 265; Bute Shah, *Tārīkh*, V, ff 240a-b. See also, Hutchison & Vogel, *Panjab Hill States*, II, 553-54 & 722-23.

[27] Amar Nath, *Zafarnāma*, 135. The chiefs of Pakhli and Dhamtaur were tributary to Ranjit Singh already in 1814: *Events at the Court of Ranjit Singh, 1810-1817* (Eng. tr.), cited hereafter as *Events (1810-1817)*, 176 & 198. See also, *Gazetteer of Hazara*, 23-29.

[28] Hutchison & Vogel, *Panjab Hill States*, II, 470-72 & 482; Griffin & Massy, *Chiefs and Families*, I, 93.

[29] *Foreign/Political Proceedings*, 28 December 1846, No. 639. See also, Man Mohan, *History of the Mandi State*, 104-10; Hutchison & Vogel, *Panjab Hill States*, II, 402.

[30] Amar Nath, *Zafarnāma*, 91. See also, Sohan Lal, *Umdat*, II, 174-75, 177, 180-81, 182-83, 254-55 & 265; Hutchison & Vogel, *Panjab Hill States*, II, 690-94.

central; and Muzaffarabad in Kashmir. The existence of Rajauri, which indeed was less accessible than Bhimbar and Punchh, cannot be explained in geographical terms; it was deliberately kept up by Maharaja Ranjit Singh in appreciation for the loyalty of Raja Rahimullah Khan and the services rendered by him particularly during the Kashmir campaign. Bilaspur had territories on both sides of the river Satlej and was left intact because of the intervention of the British Indian Government on the basis of the Treaty of Amritsar.[31] The principality of Siba was revived after over twenty years due to Raja Dhian Singh's influence with the Maharaja.[32]

Payment of tribute by the vassal chiefs was regarded as the substance of their submission to the suzerain, and therefore, the essential condition of vassalage. The chiefs of Chamba, Kulu, Mandi and Suket paid regular tribute to the rulers of Lahore.[33] The chief of Bilaspur paid tribute to the Lahore Darbar for his territories on the right bank of the Satlej.[34] *Nazrāna* was also collected from the central principalities like Jammu, Basohli, Jasrota, Bhaddu and Samba, and the western principalities like Bhimbar, Punchh and Rajauri.[35] The petty

[31] In 1819, the right bank of the river Satlej was invaded by a Sikh force under Desa Singh Majithia, assisted by a contingent from Raja Sansar Chand. The forts of Pichotra, Nikalgarh and Biholi Devi were captured. The Sikhs also crossed the Satlej at Bilaspur, but the British Government then intervened and the force retired. 'It would appear, however, that from that time if not earlier, the State had to pay tribute to the Sikhs for the territory on the right bank': Hutchison & Vogel, *Panjab Hill States*, II, 507. See also, *Khālsa Darbār Records*, Bundle 21, Vol. III, 205.

[32] Raja Dhian Singh was married to a cousin of Raja Gobind Singh, the former chief of Siba: Ahmad Shah, *Tārīkh*, 487-88. See also, *Foreign/Political Proceedings*, 26 December 1846, No. 647; Kahan Singh Balauria, *Tārīkh-i-Rājgān*, 179; also, *Tawārīkh-i-Rājputān*, 445. *Cf. Gazetteer of Kangra*, 42.

[33] Sohan Lal, *Umdat*, II, 192-93, 286 & 315; Ahmad Shah, *Tārīkh*, 463.

[34] Hutchison and Vogel refer to a *sanad* dated 6 March 1815, according to which the Raja of Bilaspur undertook to pay regular tribute to the Lahore Darbar : *Panjab Hill States*, II, 507. In 1819, he agreed to pay 70,000 rupees : Sohan Lal, *Umdat*, II, 249.

[35] Ahmad Shah, *Tārīkh*, 454 & 462; Amar Nath, *Zafarnāma*, 44, 52, 58, 118 & 121; Sohan Lal, *Umdat*, II, 130, 153, 164, 352, 356, 368-69,

rulers of Muzaffarabad, Uri and the other chiefships in Kashmir paid annual tribute to the Maharaja through his governor of Kashmir.[36]

Any evasion or refusal on the part of the vassal chief to pay *nazrāna* was tantamount to contumacy and contumacy meant the certain appearance of a Sikh commander. Fateh Singh Ahluwalia was sent against the 'contumacious' chiefs of Bhimbar and Rajauri to bring them back to submission. After a successful campaign, he suggested to the Maharaja that an adequate number of troops should be stationed in that region to ensure continued obedience.[37] In 1817, Prince Kharak Singh and Diwan Moti Ram were instructed 'to punish' the '*zamīndārs*' of 'Chhib and Bhau'.[38] In 1819, Diwan Ram Dayal and Fateh Singh Ahluwalia were sent against the *zamīndārs* of Darband who were reported to have become refractory.[39] In 1821, Misar Diwan Chand and the Atariwala *sardārs* were appointed 'to punish' the Khakha and Bamba '*zamīndārs*' in Kashmir.[40] Punitive campaigns remained a familiar incidence throughout the period of Sikh rule precisely because the suzerain did not tolerate the non-payment of tribute and the vassal did not relish its payment.[41]

Campaigns for the collection of *nazrāna* were partly necessitated by the suzerain's desire to collect more even from the chiefs who had not been refractory. There are numerous

388-89 & 404; Bute Shah, *Tārīkh*, V, ff 200b & 270 a; Kahan Singh Balauria, *Tawārīkh-i-Rājputān*, 67 & 501. See also, *News of the Court of Ranjit Singh for the year 1825* (Persian Misc. 65), National Archives of India, New Delhi (cited hereafter as *News* (*1825*), 125, 127, 205 & 209.

[36] Ganeshi Lal, *Siyāhat-i-Kashmir* (Eng. tr.), 37. According to this account, the annual tribute from these chiefs amounted to a third of their revenues. The chief of Uri reportedly paid 4000 rupees a year and the chiefs of Muzaffarabad and Dopatta paid 7000 rupees each : Charles Ellison Bates, *A Gazetteer of Kashmir*, 179, 283 & 393-94.

[37] Sohan Lal, *Umdat*, II, 174-75 & 177.

[38] Ibid., 201.

[39] Ibid., 269, 272 & 275.

[40] Amar Nath, *Zafarnāma*, 151; also; 133, 137, 139 & 147. See also, Moorcroft, *Travels* (*1819-1825*), 436-37.

[41] See, for example, Kirpa Ram, *Gulzār-i-Kashmir*, 261-62; *Events* (*1810-1817*), 58, 68, 170 *et passim*; Sohan Lal, *Umdat*, II, 366, 371 & 375.

instances of increase in tribute with the passage of time. The Raja of Jammu, for example, was obliged to pay 40,000 rupees in 1810 though in the beginning he paid only 20,000.[42] Similarly, Raja Isri Sen of Mandi was asked to pay 30,000 rupees as tribute in 1810; two or three years later, the amount of annual tribute was raised to 50,000 rupees. His successor Zalim Sen (1826-39) was obliged to pay 75,000 rupees a year till 1839.[43] In the case of Suket, only 5,000 rupees were levied as tribute in 1810, but the amount gradually rose to 20,000, and once even to 30,000 rupees.[44] The Raja of Chamba paid 30,000 rupees as tribute in 1807. In 1816, the *vakīl* of the *rāja* presented himself before the Maharaja at Adinanagar with *hundīs* worth 40,000 rupees. But even this amount did not cover the whole tribute due from him and, for the remaining amount, Lala Ramanand, the *sarrāf*, and Ilaichigir, the *faqīr*, stood surety (*zāminī*).[45]

In contemporary records and chronicles, there are references to *mu'āmala* as something distinct from *nazrāna*. In the *Khālsa Darbār Records*, the amount of *mu'āmala-i-qadīm* is generally given separately from the amount of *nazrāna* due.[46] For the year 1816, for example, Diwan Amar Nath mentions 65,000 rupees as the *mu'āmala* and 30,000 rupees as the *nazrāna* due from the Raja of Mandi.[47] There is a possibility that the term

[42] Amar Nath, *Zafarnāma*, 12 & 58.

[43] *Foreign/Political Proceedings*, 26 December 1846, No. 639. According to Sohan Lal, the Raja of Mandi used to pay 70,000 rupees but in 1821 he was asked to pay one lakh : *Umdat*, II, 287-88 : also, ibid., 102-03 & 194. For the amounts fixed for Mandi, Suket, Kulu and Chamba in 1823, see ibid., 306. See also, Amar Nath, *Zafarnāma*, 141; Ahmad Shah, *Tārīkh*, 463.

[44] *Foreign/Political Proceedings*, 26 December 1846, No. 639. By 1839, General Ventura was ordered to eject the Raja of Suket, but the Raja agreed to furnish contingents for service in addition to the payment of *nazrāna*. *Cf. Gazetteer of Suket State*, 31-32. The annexation of Suket, Mandi and Kulu, according to the Gazetteer, was considered necessary because of the design of conquering central Tibet.

[45] Sohan Lal, *Umdat*, II, 69, 129, 193 & 277.

[46] *Khālsa Darbār Records*, Bundle 3, Vol. IV, 109 & 189.

[47] *Zafarnāma*, 98 & 158. Sohan Lal also makes a similar distinction and refers to the *mu'āmala* of the past and present to be submitted by the Raja of Mandi in 1837 : *Umdat*, III (Eng. tr.), 338, 439 & 449.

mu'āmala here refers to arrears. It must be added, however, that Kahan Singh Balauria refers to two *pattas*, one of 1814 and the other of 1845, which indicate that persons serving the Lahore Darbar were sometimes granted revenue-free lands by the other vassal chiefs apparently on orders from the Lahore Darbar.[48] There is an equal possibility therefore, that the term *mu'āmala* refers to the amount of revenue taken by the suzerain from a vassal in addition to the stipulated annual tribute.[49]

The vassal chiefs generally bound themselves to place a number of troops at the disposal of the suzerain. Numerous instances of contingents actually supplied by them to Maharaja Ranjit Singh and his successors are found in contemporary chronicles. The Rajas of Basohli, Jasrota and Nurpur came to Amritsar in 1807, to place their troops at the Maharaja's service.[50] The chiefs of the Jammu area were ordered to support Diwan Mohkam Chand with their contingents in his campaign against Raja Sultan Khan of Bhimbar in 1810. When Mohkam Chand was sent against the Raja of Kulu in 1812, he was supported by the contingents supplied by Raja Sansar Chand and other hill chiefs. The rulers of both the eastern and western groups of principalities supplied contingents

[48] *Tawārīkh-i-Rājputān*, 139 & 144. See also, Sohan Lal, *Umdat*, III (Eng. tr.), 401, 446 & 449; Ram Sukh Rao, *Srī Fateh Singh Partāp Prabhākar*, ff 241b, 324b & 341b.

[49] The position may be further clarified with reference to the Mughal times. It has been observed recently that the Mughal rulers attempted 'to change the character of the tribute payable by the chiefs into land revenue' approximating it to the actual production: Nurul Hasan, 'The Position of the Zamindars in the Mughal Empire', *Indian Economic and Social History Review* (cited hereafter as *IESHR*), I, No. 4, 111. In fact, the revenues from the territories of many vassal chiefs under the Mughals were paid annually to whomsoever they were assigned in *jāgīr*. When not assigned to a person, such revenues went to the Imperial Treasury, for they were treated as assigned to the *khālisa*. This *jama* 'was required to be paid in addition to *nazrāna* or *peshkash*: Irfan Habib, *Agrarian System of Mughal India* (cited hereafter as *Agrarian System*), 184, 185 & n 10.

Cf. Cunningham, *A History of the Sikhs*, 383, Appendix XXXVIII. Cunningham, writing in the early 1840s, and not caring to make any distinction between *nazrāna* and *mu'āmala*, gives the impression that *all* the resources of the tributary chiefs were at the disposal of the Lahore Darbar.

[50] Sohan Lal, *Umdat*, II, 79.

for the Kashmir campaigns of 1814 and 1819.[51] In fact, there are many such examples for the decade from 1809 to 1819.[52] This particular condition of vassalage was fulfilled by the chiefs of the small and large principalities alike.[53]

In their mutual relations and in their relations with other sovereign powers, the vassal chiefs were subject to the control of the suzerain who could, and sometimes did, resort to effective intervention. Raja Dayal Chand of Chenini represented to Maharaja Ranjit Singh that Raja Suchet Singh had forcibly occupied Chenini and that Jamwal brothers had divided it among themselves. The Maharaja issued a *farmān* for its restoration to him and Raja Dhian Singh actually restored his share from Chenini to Raja Dayal Chand.[54] In 1816-17, the Raja of Kulu had to pay 80,000 rupees as fine for having entertained Shah Shuja of Kabul against the wishes of the Maharaja.[55] Raja Gulab Singh was allowed to conquer Ladakh for which he paid tribute to the Lahore Darbar.[56]

It was a common practice of the Maharaja and his successors to take hostages from the vassal chiefs.[57] In 1822,

[51] Sohan Lal, *Umdat*, II, 248, 254, 255 & 262; Amar Nath, *Zafarnāma*, 58, 69-70 & 80; Bute Shah, *Tārīkh*, V, f 209 b.

[52] *Events (1810-1817)*,71, 84, 86, 88, 89, 103, 105, 131, 135, 147, 152, 154, for example. These instances cover, among others, the chiefs of Kangra, Nurpur, Guler, Jaswan, Jammu, Basohli, Punchh, Bhimbar and Rajauri.

[53] The chief of the petty principality of Siba who was paying only 1,500 rupees as tribute and the Raja of Mandi who was paying over 15,000 were both required to furnish contingents, 'to render feudal service to the paramount power': E. Lake to F. Currie, *Foreign/Political Proceedings*, 26 December 1846, No. 639.

[54] Hutchison & Vogel, *Panjab Hill States*, II, 583. *Cf.* Kahan Singh Balauria, *Tawārīkh-i-Rājputān*, 380.

[55] Hutchison & Vogel, *Panjab Hill States*, II, 469.

[56] In 1838, the Maharaja was reported to have received 30,000 rupees in Ladakh currency as 'a tribute from the Governor of Ladakh': C.M. Wade to W.H. Macnaughten, *Foreign/Political Consultation*, 8 August 1838, Nos. 28-29. See also, Sohan Lal, *Umdat*, III (Eng. tr.), 282 & 431.

[57] For example, the son of Raja Zabardast Khan of Punchh was kept in Lahore as a hostage: Ahmad Shah, *Tārīkh*, 478. The son of Raja Agar Ḵhan of Rajauri too was detained at the court: Sohan Lal, *Umdat*, II, 258-59.

when the Jamwal brothers were given *rājgī*, it was formally stipulated that Hira Singh and the family of Raja Dhian Singh were to reside permanently in Lahore.[58] With reference to the ruling *rājas* of Baramula and Muzaffarabad who were tributaries of Ranjit Singh, the traveller Hugel observed in 1835, that 'one of every family was datained as a hostage in Kashmir'.[59] The vassal chief himself could at any time be called upon to appear personally before the suzerain. Moorcroft noted rather regretfully that Raja Sansar Chand had to go to Lahore every year to pay respects to the Maharaja.[60] Sansar Chand was hardly an exception.[61]

Succession to the *gaddī* of a vassal principality was controlled in theory by the suzerain, and in practice, the successor had to accept conditions of vassalage before he got due recognition. Thus, on Raja Sansar Chand's death, his son Anirudh Chand paid one lakh of rupees and received the *qashqa-i-mulkdārī* and the *khil'at* of *rājgī* from Maharaja Ranjit Singh.[62] In the case of Kulu, the brother and son of the

[58] *Chattar Singh Collection*, M/304, Punjab State Archives, Patiala. It is very clearly laid down in this Document that 'the family and the retainers of Mian Dhian Singh along with his son Hira Singh shall permanently reside in the capital of Lahore' : J.S. Grewal & Indu Banga, 'Ranjit Singh, the Suzerain', *Proceedings Punjab History Conference (1970)*, 79.

[59] *Travels in Kashmir and the Panjab*, 116.

[60] *Travels (1819-1825)*, 78. See also, Sohan Lal, *Umdat*, II, 307.

[61] Anirudh Chand, the son and successor of Sansar Chand, paid personal visits to the Lahore Darbar : Sohan Lal, *Umdat*, II, 323 & 358-59. Ranbir Chand, grandson of Sansar Chand, too visited the court a number of times : ibid., III (Eng. tr.), 258 & 395. Raja of Basohli was expressly ordered to present himself on Dussehra with a horse and a golden saddle as *nazr* : ibid., 175. For some other instances, see *Events (1810-1817)*, 106, 108, 109, 113, 119, 123 *et passim*. These cover the principalities like Nurpur, Bhimbar, Rajauri, Akhnur and Punchh as well as Kangra. See also, Ram Sukh Rao, *Srī Fateh Singh Partāp Prabhākar*, f 341 b.

At any rate, representatives (*vakīls*) of the vassal chiefs were expected to reside near the court : see, for example, *Events (1810-1817)*, 9, 40, 51, 55, 106, 172, 176 & 189; Sohan Lal, *Umdat*, III (Eng. tr.), 22, 140, 158, 162, 175, 259, 341, 395, 407, 408 & 422.

[62] Amar Nath, *Zafarnāma*, 161 & 165. See also, Ahmad Shah, *Tārīkh*, 487. *Cf.* Griffin & Massy, *Chiefs and Families*, I, 78; Hutchison & Vogel, *Panjab Hill States*, I, 193.

deceased *rāja* were both claimants to the *gaddī*; the Maharaja ordered that the one who paid the stipulated *nazrāna* first should be acknowledged as the legitimate successor.[63] That succession depended on the pleasure of the sovereign is particularly evident from the cases of Datarpur and Basohli. On the death of Raja Gobind Chand of Datarpur in 1818, his son Jagat Singh was not allowed to succeed on any terms at all.[64] However, on the death of Raja Mahinder Pal of Basohli in 1813, his minor son Bhupinder Pal was allowed on the old terms to succeed his father.[65] But on Bhupinder Pal's death in 1835, his infant son Kalyan Pal was deposed and the *rājgī* of Basohli was conferred upon Hira Singh.[66]

Ranjit Singh created new *rājas* of his own. Jodhbir Chand, the son of Raja Sansar Chand by a Gaddan wife, whose sisters were taken in marriage by Ranjit Singh, was given the title of *rāja* with the territory of Nadaun yielding nearly a lakh of rupees.[67] Similarly, Fateh Chand, the younger brother of Raja Sansar Chand, was made a *rāja* and given Rajgir in *jāgīr* when

[63] Bute Shah, *Tārīkh*, V, f 245 a.

In the case of Mandi, Zalim Sen paid to the Maharaja a lakh of rupees as the price of his succession to the *gaddī* in 1826. And in 1839, in the absence of a legitimate male heir, he approached the Maharaja for a formal recognition of his nominee, Balbir Singh. The request was granted and Balbir Singh succeeded Zalim Sen as Raja Balbir Sen (1839-1851): Man Mohan, *History of the Mandi State*, 94-95 & 98.

[64] *Foreign/Political Proceedings*, 26 December 1846, No. 648. *Cf. Gazetteer of Kangra*, 42.

[65] Sohan Lal, *Umdat*, II, 147; Bute Shah, *Tārīkh*, V, f 217a.

[66] Kahan Singh Balauria, *Tārīkh-i-Rājgān*, 108; Sohan Lal, *Umdat*, III (Eng. tr.), 284. It may be pointed out that the *gaddī* of Basohli was briefly restored to Kalyan Pal (ibid., 311) only to be reconfirmed in its conferment upon Raja Hira Singh in 1837: see 55 n 77 & 56 n 80, below. *Cf.* Hutchison & Vogel, 'History of Basohli State', *JPHS*, IV, No. 2, 96.

[67] *Foreign/Political Proceedings*, 26 December 1846, No. 639. According to this report, Jodhbir Chand gave a sister in marriage to Sardar Basawa Singh Sandhanwalia also. The *jāgīr* of Jodhbir Chand had dwindled to 30,000 rupees by 1845. *Cf.* Griffin & Massy, *Chiefs and Families*, I, 78-79 ; Kahan Singh Balauria, *Tawārīkh-i-Rājpūtān*, 432; Sohan Lal, *Umdat*, II, 395.

he agreed to give his grand-daughter in marriage to Hira Singh.[68] Zorawar Singh, the younger brother of Raja Charhat Singh of Chamba, was made the *rāja* of Bhadarwah.[69] Maharaja Sher Singh 'selected Thakar Singh, a first cousin, once removed, of Ajit Singh, made him Raja, and gave him Waziri Rupi in jagir'.[70]

The famous Jamwal brothers obviously did not constitute an exception in being created *rājas* by Maharaja Ranjit Singh. At any rate, Mian Kishora Singh and his sons Gulab Singh, Dhian Singh and Suchet Singh were first given Jammu, Bhoti, Bandralta, Chenini and Kishtwar in 1820 by way of *jāgīr* in lieu of service.[71] They were also permitted to extend their territories.[72] One of the conditions imposed upon them was to

[68] Hutchison & Vogel, *Panjab Hill States*, I, 194. According to Sohan Lal, Fateh Chand's son also was given *rājgī* by Ranjit Singh in 1829: *Umdat*, II, 390. For Fateh Chand's services to the Lahore Darbar, see ibid., 373-74. See also, Kahan Singh Balauria, *Tawārīkh-i-Rājpūtān*, 431-32.

[69] Hutchison & Vogel, *Panjab Hill States*, I, 325; *Catalogue of the Bhuri Singh Museum*, 74, C. 69.

After Ranjit Singh's death, Raja Sri Singh, son of Raja Charhat Singh, was ordered by the Lahore Darbar to give Bhadarwah to Zorawar Singh's son.

[70] J.B. Lyall, *SR Kangra*, 117: 'It is said that they offered to hand over the whole country to him at a heavy tribute; but Thakar Singh was a dull and timid kind of man, and refused the responsibility'. According to another report, Thakar Singh was given a *jāgīr* of 12,000 rupees a year while the Kulu territories were actually taken over by the Lahore Darbar: *Foreign/Political Proceedings*, 26 December 1846, No. 648.

[71] A copy of the *sanad* granted to Mian Kishora Singh and his sons Gulab Singh, Dhian Singh and Suchet Singh, can be seen in Document M/503, *Chattar Singh Collection*, PSA, Patiala. For its transcription, and transliteration see J.S. Grewal & Indu Banga, 'Ranjit Singh, the Suzerain', *Proceedings Punjab History Conference* (*1970*), 72-75.

[72] Document M/503 of the *Chattar Singh Collection* presents an extremely interesting piece of evidence on this point. The text of the *sanad* is dated 15 Maghar, Sammat 1877 (A.D. 1820), which contains the following addition: 'Whenever there is any increase in territory through the grace of Sat Gurūjī, it shall be reported to His Majesty'. It was with reference to this clause that Gulab Singh ousted the ruling chiefs of the principalities granted to him and his brothers, and even added territories to those originally bestowed in 1820. It may

extirpate Mian Dido who had been a source of constant trouble in the Jammu area for several years.[73] Two years later, after the extirpation of the rebel Dido, Gulab Singh, Dhian-Singh and Suchet Singh were given the *rājgī* of Jammu and the neighbouring principalities. Among other things, they bound themselves to serve in Kashmir and in other near or distant tracts in accordance with the orders of the Maharaja.[74]

be pointed out here that the conferment of a territory did not necessarily put the recipient in possession of the grant. Raja Dhian Singh, for example, had earlier been given a *jāgīr* in Ramgarh in lieu of service of 200 men. Those in occupation of the fort of Ramgarh refused to surrender the fort. Misar Diwan Chand had to help Dhian Singh in taking possession of Ramgarh : Kirpa Ram, *Gulābnāma*, 153-54. See also, Ram Sukh Rao, *Srī Fateh Singh Partāp Prabhākar* f 383a.

[73] Mian Dido was a descendant of Raja Dhrub Dev of Jammu. Unlike the other descendants and successors of Dhrub Dev and Ranjit Dev, Dido decided to oppose Ranjit Singh in his attempt at bringing the territories of Jammu under his direct control. Several expeditions had to be sent against him : Sohan Lal, *Umdat*, II, 201; Kahan Singh Balauria, *Tārīkh-i-Rājgān*, 279-82; Kirpa Ram, *Gulābnāma*, 194-204. Document M/503 of the *Chattar Singh Collection*, dated 15 Maghar, Sammat 1877 (A.D. 1820) leaves no doubt that in the latter half of 1820, Dido was still abroad and effective and his extirpation was one of the important conditions on which the *jāgīr* of Jammu had been granted to Mian Kishora Singh and his sons. See also, Amar Nath, *Zafarnāma*, 141; Sohan Lal, *Umdat*, II, 280-83.

[74] Document M/504 of the *Chattar Singh Collection* is a *sanad* granted to Gulab Singh, Dhian Singh and Suchet Singh, dated 3 Hār, Sammat 1879 (A.D. 1822). It demonstrates, in the first place, that the *rājgī* of Jammu was conferred collectively on all the three brothers (their father having died by then). It repeats some of the conditions of the grant of *jāgīr* in 1820. But no tribute is mentioned, not even the token tribute which we find in the *sanad* of 1820. It does not necessarily follow that the *rājgī* of Jammu did not imply payment of tribute. In fact, the payment of *nazrāna* and *mu'āmala* was one of the pre-conditions for the grant of *rājgī*: Sohan Lal, *Umdat*, II, 298.

According to Kirpa Ram, however, the *rājgī* of Jammu was first offered to Dhian Singh and when he declined it in favour of his elder brother Gulab Singh, it was given to the latter in 1822. Kirpa Ram also gives out that Suchet Singh was given the title of *rāja* later, with the *jāgīr* of Ramnagar, and Dhian Singh was not given the title of *rāja* at all : *Gulābnāma*, 209, 210, 211 & 212-14.

It is interesting to note here that, according to Diwan Amar Nath, it was Dhian Singh who was placed on the *masnad* of Jammu in 1822, and then he presented Gulab Singh and Suchet Singh to the

The influence, prestige and the resources of the new *rājas* went on increasing till the end of Ranjit Singh's reign. 'In the court of the Maharaja', it was observed by a contemporary, 'there are three men of obscure origin, . . . who are raised to the highest pitch of favour—namely, Raja Gulab Singh, Raja Dhian Singh and Suchet Singh. The Maharaja consults them upon all occasions; no favours can be procured but by their recommendation, and all suitors at first endeavour to gain these three men over to their side by presents and sometimes by flattery'.[75] In 1827, Dhian Singh had been given the title of *rāja-i- rājgān, rāja-i-kalān bahādur* and the *rāj* of the country of 'Bhimbar and Chhibal'.[76] In 1837, his son Hira Singh was given the title of *rāja* and the principalities of Jasrota and Basohli.[77] Emily Eden thought of Dhian Singh in 1838 as 'the ruler of one-third of the Punjab',[78] At the time of Ranjit

Maharaja who conferred the title of *rāja* on them also. The '*nizāmat*' of Jammu, with the territories up to Kishtwar, was given to them: *Zafarnāma*, 152.

[75] Mohan Lal, *Journal of a Tour through the Panjab, etc.*, 12.

[76] Document M/507, dated 7 Hār, 1884 (A.D. 1827), *Chattar Singh Collection*, refers explicitly to the grant of title and the territory (*rāj-o-khitāb*) to Raja Dhian Singh. For text and translation, see J.S. Grewal & Indu Banga, 'Ranjit Singh, the Suzerain', *Proceedings Punjab History Conference (1970)*, 80-81. No other *rāja* is known to have received such a title from Ranjit Singh. 'This would make Dhian Singh the premier vassal of Ranjit Singh': ibid., 82. *Cf.* Amar Nath, *Zafarnāma*, 185; Sohan Lal, *Umdat*, II, 343.

According to contemporary accounts, the ceremony of the grant of *rāj-o-khitāb* was performed with great state. The courtiers and *jāgīrdārs* were directed to present *nazrs* to Dhian Singh, 'while a proclamation was issued, that if anyone, in future called him Mian he should be fined 1000 rupees, and that if not a public servant, he should lose his nose and ears': Shahamat Ali, *Sikhs and Afghans*, 96.

[77] Document M/511, *Chattar Singh Collection. Cf.* Kirpa Ram, *Gulābnāma*, 364; Kahan Singh Balauria, *Tārīkh-i-Rājgān*, 107.

The '*ilāqa* of Jasrota had formerly been in the *jāgīr of* Raja Suchet Singh. Its conferment upon Hira Singh led to contention and wrangling between the Jamwal brothers. It may be added that Mian Sohan Singh, the adopted son of Raja Suchet Singh, was given the *rājgī* of the latter's territories after his death in 1844: Sohan Lal, *Umdat*, IV, (iii), 52.

[78] *Up the Country*, II, 21.

For some early references to Gulab Singh's eminence in the kingdom of Lahore, see Charles Hugel, *Travels in Kashmir and the Panjab*,

Singh's death, the Jamwal brothers controlled nearly all the former principalities between the Ravi and the Jehlam.

Like the Jamwal brothers, all vassal chiefs were left with a large measure of autonomy within their territories. The administrative arrangement and the fiscal pattern of the principality were determined by the chief himself and not by the suzerain. For example, Sohan Lal refers to the administration of the principality of Basohli by Raja Suchet Singh as *bandobast-i-kohistān-i-mut'aliqa-i-khud.*[79] Basohli had remained tributary to Ranjit Singh for about twenty-five years before it was bestowed upon Hira Singh. Till that time the *ahlkārs* of Basohli had been appointed by its chiefs to look after the administration of revenue and *jāgīrs* in accordance with its traditional modes. When Hira Singh took over Basohli, he appointed his own *ahlkārs* and presumably made his own arrangements for the assessment and collection of revenue.[80] Evidently, the vassal chief was fully autonomous in the internal administration of his territory. In matters of transit through his principality however, he felt the pressure of the suzerain. He was expected to provide all possible assistance to the royal troops and other persons authorized by the suzerain to pass through his territories.[81] Merchandise and other goods exempted from duty by the suzerain could pass free of duty through the territory of the vassal who was held responsible for a safe transit.[82] The vassals of the Sikh rulers were by no means confined to the hills. Some of the big and small chiefs of the Panjab plains in the late eighteenth century were obliged to pay tribute to their Sikh overlords on a temporary or regular basis. The Chaththas of Rasulnagar, for instance, had paid tribute to Mahan Singh Sukarchakia before their territory was annexed in

89-90; also, 288; G.T. Vigne, *A Personal Narrative of a Visit, etc.*, 253; Victor Jacquemont, *Letters From India*, II, 1.

[79] *Umdat*, II, 327.

[80] Kahan Singh Balauria, *Tārīkh-i-Rājgān*, 108. The author reproduces a royal *parwāna* and a *parwāna* from Raja Hira Singh to this effect.

[81] See, for example, Sohan Lal, *Umdat*, III (Eng. tr.), 494, 547 & 552.

[82] In 1833, for instance, Ranjit Singh ordered the *kārdārs* and officials of all the vassals and *jāgīrdārs* concerned not to collect duty on grain and other merchandise sent to Kashmir which was suffering from a famine : ibid., 177.

1783.[83] Mahan Singh received tribute also from several Sikh chiefs of the upper Bari Doab.[84] Even the minor Sikh rulers were familiar with the idea and the practice.[85] Ranjit Singh obviously was not the first Sikh ruler to assert suzerain claims over other Sikh chiefs but he made the most effective use of this legacy. In fact, in the plains his general policy was to claim suzerainty over autonomous chiefs as a prelude to the annexation of their territories. The situation was so fluid that it is not easy to perceive detailed similarity of suzerain-vassal relationship in the hills and the plains. Nor were all the conditions of vassalage imposed uniformly. Nevertheless payment of tribute, which was the essence of vassalage, appears to have existed in all situations involving both Sikh and non-Sikh chiefs.

Nearly all the non-Sikh chiefs to have been reduced to vassalage were on the fringes of the core dominions.[86] The chiefs of Khushab, Sahiwal and Pind Dadan Khan, were allowed to remain tributary for a few years before they were ejected from their territories.[87] Some other chiefs of the upper Sindh Sagar Doab, who eventually lost their territories, were first forced to pay *nazrāna*.[88] Ahmad Khan, the Sial chief of Jhang, was made tributary in 1803 and his territory was finally annexed in 1816.[89] The chief of Mankera also had paid an ever-increasing tribute to Ranjit Singh for over a decade before Mankera

[83] Sohan Lal, *Umdat*, II, 19 & 34.

[84] Ibid., 16.

[85] For example, when Jodh Singh Kalsia conquered the fort of Chandigarh, which was in the territories of the chief of Sirmur, he gave it to his tributary (*bājguzār*), Raja Gopal Singh of Mani Majra: Nagina Ram Parmar, *Ravi Parkāsh*, II, 562. For a list of the *bājguzārs* of the Kalsia chiefs, see ibid., 597-99.

[86] Nawab Nizamuddin Khan, and later, his brother, Qutubuddin Khan, of Qasur were the only important exceptions.

[87] Sohan Lal, *Umdat*, II, 97; Ahmad Shah, *Tārīkh*, 460 & 462. See also, Sinha, *Ranjit Singh*, 16.

[88] Amar Nath, *Zafarnāma*, 45; *Gazetteer of Hazara*, 126 & 127.

[89] Jhang appears to have been annexed to the kingdom of Lahore sometimes between April and December 1816: *Events (1810-1817)*, 246 & 258. According to Prinsep, however, Ahmad Khan Sial was dispossessed of his territories sometimes during the middle of 1815: *Origin of the Sikh Power*, 88. See also, Sinha, *Ranjit Singh*, 16; Chopra, *Sovereign State*, 10 n 3.

was annexed in 1821.[90] Before Ranjit Singh subverted the trans-Indus territories between 1831 and 1836, the chiefs of Dera Ghazi Khan, Dera Ismail Khan and Tank and Bannu had also been paying tribute to him.[91]

Ranjit Singh's attitude towards Multan and Bahawalpur becomes meaningful in the context of suzerain-vassal relationship. According to Faqir Azizuddin, the well-known courtier of Ranjit Singh, in the beginning, the chief of Multan used to be reluctant to pay tribute and troops had to be despatched against him; but then the whole matter gradually became 'well settled'.[92] Nawab Muzaffar Khan of Multan was obliged to pay *nazrāna* for the first time in 1803.[93] In 1809, his *vakīls* were kept in Lahore to ensure the regular payment of *nazrāna*.[94] In 1810, the amount of annual tribute was fixed at two lakhs, an amount which the '*nāzim*' of Multan was believed to have paid to the rulers of Kabul.[95] Henceforth, a part of the tribute often fell into arrears in spite of the pressure put on the *vakīls*, and troops had occasionally to be sent against Muzaffar Khan.[96] These arrears had piled up when Multan was annexed in 1818.[97]

By 1818, the chiefs of Bahawalpur had paid *nazrāna* to the Maharaja for over a decade.[98] In the 1820s, Nawab Sadiq

[90] Sohan Lal, *Umdat*, II, 99, 189, 190, 198, 200, 201, 202, 205, 211, 239, 254 & 287; Amar Nath, *Zafarnāma*, 100, 120 & 134; Bute Shah, *Tārīkh*, V, ff 246b & 247a. See also, *Events (1810-1817)*, 76, 89, 197, 216, 249, 251 & 280; Sinha, *Ranjit Singh*, 60.

It may be added that the deposed chief of Mankera was installed as a vassal in Dera Ismail Khan before Dera Ismail Khan was also taken over by the Maharaja.

[91] Dera Ghazi Khan was annexed in 1831, Peshawar in 1834 and Tank, Bannu and Dera Ismail Khan between 1834 and 1836: Sohan Lal, *Umdat*, III (Eng. tr.), 44, 52, 76, 188-89, 289, 300 & 349. *Cf.* Sinha, *Ranjit Singh*, 106-07.

[92] Sohan Lal, *Umdat*, II, 284.

[93] Ibid., 55; Sinha, *Ranjit Singh*, 15.

[94] Sohan Lal, *Umdat*, II, 102. See also, Bute Shah, *Tārīkh*, V, f 195a; *Events (1810-1817)*, 11, 37, 64, 136, 144, 173, 184, 244, 246, 248, 257, for example.

[95] Sohan Lal, *Umdat*, II, 115.

[96] Ibid., 186-87. See also, Amar Nath, *Zafarnāma*, 99.

[97] Sohan Lal, *Umdat*, II, 189 & 202-03; Amar Nath, *Zafarnāma*, 101. *Cf.* Sinha, *Ranjit Singh*, 56-57.

[98] Sohan Lal mentions 1807 as the year of the submission of Nawab

Khan and Nawab Rahim Yar Khan paid nearly five lakhs of rupees a year to the Maharaja.[99] The whole of this amount cannot, however, be treated as *nazrāna* because after its conquest in 1820, Ranjit Singh had placed Dera Ghazi Khan under the Nawab of Bahawalpur.[100] When Dera Ghazi Khan came to be administered directly in 1831, the amount paid by the Nawab of Bahawalpur as *nazrāna* was reduced.[101] Like the chiefs of Bilaspur in the Panjab hills, the chiefs of Bahawalpur paid tribute to Ranjit Singh for only the territories on the right bank of the Satlej.[102] It may now be added that Ranjit Singh's insistence on getting '*muā'mala*' from Kashmir, several years before its actual annexation, is not without significance in the context of his assertion of suzerain claims in numerous other situations.[103]

Muhammad Bahawal Khan to Ranjit Singh : *Umdat*, II, 65. For some transactions between Maharaja Ranjit Singh and the Nawab of Bahawalpur before 1818, see *Events (1810-1817)*, 187, 194, 240, 242, 243, 267 & 280.

[99] Nawab Sadiq Khan, the son and successor of Muhammad Bahawal Khan, was asked to pay 1 lakh and 50 thousand rupees as the first four-monthly instalment in 1820 : Sohan Lal, *Umdat*, II, 274. A year later, an additional lakh of rupees was collected from the Nawab : ibid., 295. Bute Shah also states that the Nawab of Bahawalpur used to pay 4 lakhs to the Maharaja and the amount was increased to 5 lakhs : *Tārīkh*, V, f 268a. Fryer mentions five lakhs, four of which were paid as revenue and one lakh as *nazrāna* : *SR Dera Ghazi Khan*, 37. See also, Prinsep, *Origin of the Sikh Power*, 104.

[100] Dera Ghazi Khan was held by Nawab Samad Khan on behalf of the rulers of Kabul. In 1817, he was asked by Ranjit Singh to pay one lakh of rupees. He refused to pay this amount on the plea that he was 'a mere leaseholder' of Dera Ghazi Khan which belonged to Wazir Fateh Khan Barakzai : *Events (1810-1817)*, 265-66. Dera Ghazi Khan was occupied by the troops of Bahawalpur with the support of Ranjit Singh : Sohan Lal, *Umdat*, II, 276.

[101] Sohan Lal, *Umdat*, III, (i), 51; 75; (v), 104-05. See also, *News (1825)*, 61.

[102] See 46, n 31.

[103] See, for example, *Events (1810-1817)*, 21, 61-62, 85, 226 & 247-48; Sohan Lal, *Umdat*, II, 181; Amar Nath, *Zafarnāma*, 80. *Cf.* Prinsep, *Origin of the Sikh Power*, 75; Chopra, *Sovereign State*, 14; Sinha, *Ranjit Singh*, 46. For a discussion of the point, see the author's *Agrarian System of the Sikhs (1759-1849)*, Ph.D. Thesis, Guru Nanak University, Amritsar, 1974, 95-97.

In the plains, the Sikh chiefs too were obliged to acknowledge Ranjit Singh's suzerain claims. Across the Satlej, in 1806, he bestowed a sword and a *khil'at* of 21 pieces upon Raja Sahib Singh of Patiala who had offered a *nazrāna* of 70,000 rupees.[104] Some of the other chiefs to acknowledge Ranjit Singh's suzerainty by offering *nazrāna* and receiving a *khil'at* in return were Jaswant Singh of Nabha, Bhag Singh of Jind, Lal Singh of Kaithal, Gurdit Singh of Ladwa, Karam Singh of Shahabad, Rani Daya Kaur of Ambala, Bhagwan Singh of Buria, Jodh Singh of Kalsia, Hari Singh of Ropar, Gopal Singh of Mani Majra and Ranjit Singh of Manuali.[105] They all paid tribute in 1807 also.[106] By 1808, the Maharaja was virtually the overlord of this region.

However, the Sikh vassals of Ranjit Singh were not confined to the Satlej-Jamna Divide. In 1805, he took *nazrāna* from Budh Singh Faizullahpuria and allowed him to remain in possession of Jalandhar; at this time, *nazrāna* was paid also by Tara Singh Dallewalia.[107] Bhag Singh Bagga in the upper Bari Doab submitted to Ranjit Singh and, after Bhag Singh's death, his son was allowed to succeed to the chiefship as a vassal.[108] The Nakai chiefs in the Dipalpur region had started paying tribute in 1802.[109] Nidhan Singh of Daska submitted to the Maharaja in 1807 and paid 30,000 rupees as *nazrāna*.[110] The descendants of some of the once most powerful *sardārs* were reduced by Ranjit Singh to the status of vassals. In 1807, he insisted that Sahib Singh Bhangi should offer presents to him and receive a *khil'at* in return.[111] Jodh Singh

[104] Amar Nath, *Zafarnāma*, 39-40; Raja Ram Tota, *Iqbālnāma -i- Ranjit Singh* (cited hereafter as *Iqbālnāma*), ff 21b & 22a.

[105] Amar Nath, *Zafarnāma*, 41-42. For these and the list of 'minor' chiefs, dependant on Ranjit Singh and subject to his authority, see Griffin, *Minor Phulkian Families*, 617, Appendix D, & 618, Appendix E.

[106] See, for example, Raja Ram Tota, *Iqbālnāma*, f 22b.

[107] Sohan Lal, *Umdat*, II, 61.

[108] Ibid., 55-56.

[109] Amar Nath, *Zafarnāma*, 22. See also, Sohan Lal, *Umdat*, II, 55; Aliuddin, *'Ibratnāma*, 341; Munshi Bakhtawar Lal, *Tārīkh-i-Montgomery*, 11.

[110] Sohan Lal , *Umdat*, II, 68.

[111] Ibid., 69; Amar Nath, *Zafarnāma*, 44.

Ramgarhia remained a vassal of the Maharaja for nearly a decade.[112] Even Sada Kaur paid 20,000 rupees as *nazrāna* when she was given Wadhni and Pattoke, across the Satlej, in 1808.[113] In fact, no Sikh chief of any importance seems to have escaped Ranjit Singh's suzerain claims.

Towards the end of Ranjit Singh's reign, the Ahluwalia chiefs stood in nearly the same relationship to him as the Jamwals or the chiefs of Rajauri. In 1802, Ranjit Singh had entered into a treaty with Fateh Singh Ahluwalia as another sovereign chief.[114] In 1806, however, when Jagraon across the Satlej was given to Fateh Singh he was asked to pay 40,000 rupees as *nazrāna*.[115] The *Umdat-ut-Tawārīkh* contains numerous references to orders given to Fateh Singh for compliance. In fact, he maintained contingents for service and received *jāgīrs* from Ranjit Singh.[116] When the Ahluwalia chief died in 1836, his son was given a *khil'at* by the Maharaja and he paid a *nazrāna* of 4,25,000 rupees before succeeding to his possessions.[117]

[112] Amar Nath, *Zafarnāma*, 48.

[113] Sohan Lal, *Umdat*, II, 177-78; Amar Nath, *Zafarnāma*, 88.
An important aspect of the tussle between Sada Kaur and her overmighty son-in-law was that he refused to treat her as a sovereign ruler and she refused to be treated as an appendage.

[114] Sohan Lal, *Umdat*, II, 50-51.

[115] Amar Nath, *Zafarnāma*, 41.

[116] See, for example, *Events (1810-1817)*, 38, 91 & 224; *Foreign/Political Consultation*, 29 December 1849, No. 49 A(38); Raja Ram Tota, *Iqbālnāma*, ff 204 a-b; Griffin, 'History of the Kapurthala State', *Minor Phulkian Families*, (481-82). During Fateh Singh's stay across the Satlej in 1826, his territories in the Jalandhar Doab were taken over and given on *ijāra* by the Maharaja: ibid., 490. For detail of these territories, see Diwan Ramjas, *Tārīkh-i-Riyāsat-i-Kapurthala*, 166. Fateh Singh had to submit the accounts of his *kārdārs* regarding the 'collection of the amounts of *ijāra*' and the *mu'āmala* to the *daftar-i-mu'alla* at Lahore: Sohan Lal, *Umdat*, III (Eng. tr.), 30, 46, 179, 216, 284, for example. It may also be pointed out that Fateh Singh's chronicler, Ram Sukh Rao, also confirms the impression that his patron had eventually become subservient to Maharaja Ranjit Singh : *Fateh Singh Partāp Prabhākar*, ff 326b-327a, 338a *et passim*.

[117] Amar Nath, *Zafarnāma*, 120. See also, Sohan Lal, *Umdat*, III (Eng. tr.), 311, 312 & 313-14. For some light on Nihal Singh Ahluwalia's subordinate position *vis-a-vis* the Lahore Darbar, see ibid., 241, 354' 359, 375, 377, 394, 501-02, 566 & 582. See also, 'Statement Exhibiting

In retrospect, we can see that the strength of a traditional mode of politico-administrative relationship and the weakness of the Sikh rulers in terms of resources made the superimposition of power upon autonomous areas a matter almost of necessity. Suzerainty implied superior claims but limited control and vassalage enabled the subordinate chief to enjoy the substance of power within his principality. Pockets of more or less autonomous administration remained in existence for short or long terms in subordination to the superior political power of the Sikh chiefs. The tradition of autonomy in some areas was so strong that Ranjit Singh resuscitated old principalities under new vassals. Furthermore, his general policy towards the Sikh and Muslim chiefs of the plains was very much similar to his policy towards the hill chiefs, both Hindu and Muslim. However, subject largely to the political geography of the region in which a principality was situated and its distance from the centre of gravity, all the conditions of vassalage were not uniformly imposed on all the vassals. Consequently, their status varied widely in relation to the suzerain.

Altogether, the vassal chiefs formed an important section of the ruling class of the period. Some of them were also among the foremost *jāgīrdārs* of Ranjit Singh and his successors. Their share in the revenues of the empire was as considerable as their role in its administration.

the Strength and Disposition of the Sikh Army', *Foreign/Secret Consultation*, 27 April 1844, No. 180.

4

Revenue Administration: Units and Functionaries

Contemporary records and chronicles contain numerous references to units and functionaries of revenue administration during the Sikh times. The terms most frequently used for the administrative units are *sūba*, *pargana*, *ta'alluqa*, *zila'*, *'ilāqa*, *tappa*, *tope*, *chakla*, *mauza'* and *deh*. The terms generally used for the functionaries are *sūbadār*, *nāzim*, *hākim*, *'āmil*, *kārdār*, *tahsīldār*, *qānūngo*, *chaudharī*, *muqaddam* and *patwārī*.

However, all these units and functionaries did not exist throughout the Sikh period or the Sikh dominions. Also, each of these terms did not necessarily refer to a distinct unit or office. The *sūba*, for instance, came into meaningful currency only in the nineteenth century, particularly after the conquest of Multan and Kashmir by Ranjit Singh. The unit called *tope* or *chakla* did not exist in all parts of the Sikh dominions. The terms *mauza'* and *deh* were synonymous, connoting 'village', and *'ilāqa* was used in its literal, loose sense of 'area'. The *pargana*, the *ta'alluqa* and the *zila'* generally referred to one and the same unit. The terms *sūbadār* and *nāzim* referred to the same functionary and *hākim* was used interchangeably with *sūbadār* and *nāzim* on the one hand and with *'āmil* and *kārdār* on the other. The term *tahsīldār*, used very rarely, was practically a substitute for the *kārdār*. Consequently, we have to consider only five units: the *sūba*, the *ta'alluqa*, the *tappa*, the *tope* and the *mauza'*. And among the functionaries we have to consider the *nāzim*, the *kārdār*, the *qānūngo*, the *chaudharī*, the *muqaddam* and the *patwārī*.

Ganesh Das states that Diwan Singh was appointed to the *sūbadārī* of Multan after its conquest by the Bhangi Sardars Jhanda Singh and Ganda Singh.[1] The use of the term *sūbadārī* for Diwan Singh's office is not without significance. It is used in connection with an area covered by a former *sūba* of the Mughal empire. By analogy it could be used for the Mughal *sūba* of Lahore also. But the *sūba* of Lahore was occupied by a large number of *sardārs* and none of them ruled over a territory in any sense comparable to the Mughal *sūba* of Lahore or any other *sūba* of the Mughal empire in terms of revenue and extent. The occupation of Multan proved to be temporary and, throughout the late eighteenth century, there was no scope in any single principality for an administrative unit resembling the *sūba*. The primary divisions of sovereign principalities bore greater resemblance to an average *pargana* of the Mughal times.

Such indeed was the weight of this legacy that the Mughal *sūba* of Lahore was never revived as a single administrative unit even under Ranjit Singh, though the entire territory was under his control. Contemporary references to the *sūba* of Lahore during the Sikh times, which have misled modern historians to believe in the existence of the *sūba* under Ranjit Singh, mean nothing more than the area formerly covered by it.[2] This area was actually divided into a number of primary divisions like Kangra, Jalandhar Doab, the Majha, Wazirabad, Jhang, Hazara and Pind Dadan Khan.[3] Similarly, notwithstanding the belief of the historians in the existence of the *sūba* of Peshawar, the trans-Indus territories were divided into several primary units: Peshawar, Kohat, Bannu (with Tank), Dera Ismail Khan, and Dera Ghazi Khan.[4]

[1] *Chār Bāgh*, 132.

[2] See, for example, Sita Ram Kohli, 'Land Revenue Administration under Maharajah Ranjit Singh', *Journal of the Panjab Hisotrical Society*, VII, No. 1 (cited hereafter as 'Land Revenue Administration', *JPHS*), 75; Chopra, *Sovereign State*, 84.

[3] Diwan Dina Nath is reported to have mentioned 'seven great districts' in the dominions of Ranjit Singh: Kashmir, Multan, Peshawar, Kangra, Jalandhar Doab, Wazirabad and Pind Dadan Khan: John Lawrence to H.M. Elliot, *Foreign/Secret Consultation*, 30 October 1847, No. 95.

[4] For references to the *sūba* of Peshawar as one of the four *sūbas* see, for example, Chopra, *Sovereign State*, 84; Sinha, *Ranjit Singh*, 140;

The formation of administrative units in the Sikh dominions was broadly connected with the process of territorial occupation. The core areas of the Mughal *sūba* of Multan were conquered by Ranjit Singh at one time, and therefore, the Sikh *sūba* of Multan was constituted from the very beginning, and its resemblance with its Mughal counterpart in terms of area and revenues increased with the subsequent addition of territories.[5] The only Mughal province to be conquered entirely at one time was the province of Kashmir and it was treated as a regular province of the kingdom of Lahore from the time of its conquest in 1819 to that of its conferment upon Gulab Singh by the British in 1846. Thus, on the whole, the kingdom of Ranjit Singh and his successors was divided into nearly a dozen primary units, the number and extent varying with time. Only two of these resembled the *sūbas* of the Mughal empire. The remaining, about ten units, were much smaller, each comparable to an average *sarkār* of the Mughal times.[6] The customary division of the kingdom of

B.J. Hasrat, *Life and Times of Ranjit Singh*, 293. Kohli, however, is reluctant to treat Peshawar as a *sūba* and the term used by him for the frontier territory across the Indus is *'ilāqa-i-Peshawar*: 'Land Revenue Administration', *JPHS*, 76.

For some detail of these and other primary units, see the author's *Agrarian System of the Sikhs (1759-1849)*, Ph.D. Thesis, Guru Nanak University, Amritsar 1974, 139-41.

[5] By 1831, as the *sūbadār* of Multan, Diwan Sawan Mal was holding, besides Multan, the territories of Shujabad, Muzaffargarh, Dera Ghazi Khan, Mankera, Leiah, Jhang, Chiniot, Sayyidwala, etc., 'up to Sukhanwala which was only 10 *kos* from Lahore': Munshi Hukm Chand, *Tārīkh-i-Zila'-i- Multan* (cited hereafter as *Tārīkh-i-Multan*), 470.

[6] The absence of the *sarkār* as a unit in the Sikh times is easily understandable. Under the Mughals, the province of Lahore was never divided into *sarkārs* as distinct from the *doābs*. Also, for all practical purposes, the Afghan province of Kashmir in the late eighteenth century, does not appear to have been divided into *sarkārs*. In the late eighteenth century, the parts of the Delhi province between the rivers Satlej and Jamna were divided into a large number of principalities and there was no occasion for the reconstitution of a *sarkār*. In the Panjab proper, it was more natural to think in terms of *doābs* rather than any new units larger than the *parganas*. Where such larger units were brought into existence they were treated as provinces. Even under Ranjit Singh, with the absence of *sarkār* as an administrative unit from the provinces of Lahore and Kashmir, there was no reason for dividing the province of Multan into

Lahore into the four *sūbas* of Lahore, Multan, Kashmir and Peshawar projects not merely an over-simplification but a historical inaccuracy.

In contemporary records and chronicles, there are frequent references to both *ta'alluqa* and *pargana* as an administrative unit. In a *Dastūr al-'Amal* which was written under the patronage of a Sikh *nāzim* of Kashmir, 36 *parganas* are enumerated, a large majority being the same as the *mahāl* in the *Ā'īn-i-Akbarī*.[7] Ahmad Shah uses the term *pargana* not only with reference to Kashmir, but also for the Sikh dominions and he uses it synonymously with *mahal*.[8] Similarly, Ganesh Das uses the term *pargana* for the administrative units into which each of the five *doābs* of the Panjab was divided.[9] Bute Shah on the other hand, uses *ta'alluqa* for the administrative unit next to the province.[10] In the *Khālsa Darbār Records*, there are long lists of *ta'alluqas* as well as *parganas*. Preference for the one over the other of these terms, or an indifferent use of either, is clearly reflected in the earliest settlement reports of the nineteenth century.[11] Even the orders issued by the Sikh rulers contain both the terms. For example, the orders of Hakumat Singh, Sada Kaur and Tara Singh refer to the *pargana* of Kahnuwan,

sarkārs. As a territorial unit, the *sarkār* did not fit into the general administrative set up.

For an anachronistic use of the term *sarkār*, see Munshi Bakhtawar Lal, *Tārīkh-i-Montgomery*, 19. The author talks of the *sarkār* of Dipalpur at a time when the region was occupied by several chiefs known as the Nakais.

[7] Mir Ahmad, *Dastūr al-'Amal-i-Kashmir*, ff 26a-57b. See also, Abul Fazl, *Ā'īn-i-Akbarī*, II (Eng. tr.), 367-70. *Cf*. Kirpa Ram, *Gulzār-i-Kashmir*, 14; Sinha, *Ranjit Singh*, 152.

[8] *Tārīkh*, 86-87, 142, 146, 147, 162, 288, 293, for example.

[9] *Chār Bāgh*, 161, 162, 170, 172, 221, 295, 296, 298, 299, 300, 301, 304-05, for example.

[10] *Tārīkh* (SHR 1288), 495-500.

[11] For example, the term *pargana* is used in the summary settlement reports of the region across the Satlej and the lower Rachna Doab, while the term *ta'alluqa* is used in the reports of other areas: 'SSR Cis-Satlej', *Foreign/Political Consultation*, 31 December 1847, No. 1830; 'SSR Lower Rachna Doab', *Foreign/Secret Consultation*, 28 April 1848, No. 64; 'SSR Upper Bari, Upper Rachna, Chaj and Lower and Upper Sindh Sagar Doabs', ibid., Nos. 61, 63, 65 & 66, respectively.

Pathankot, Bianpur and Batala,[12] while the orders of Prince Kharak Singh, Diwan Moti Ram and Maharaja Ranjit Singh refer to the *ta'alluqas* of Talibpur, Manawar, Awankh and Gharo-Batala.[13]

An essential clue to a correct understanding of the administrative unit next to the province lies in the terms used for one and the same area during the Sikh period. Sada Kaur, for instance, used both *ta'alluqa* and *pargana* for Bianpur in two different orders.[14] Edward Lake uses the term *ta'alluqa* for Kahnuwan, Batala and Pathankot for each of which the term *pargana* is used in contemporary *parwānas*.[15] Abbott in the Jalandhar Doab uses *ta'alluqa* for those very areas for which Temple and Montgomery use *pargana*.[16] The evidence of the *Khālsa Darbār Records*, on the whole, supports the view that the *ta'alluqa* had become a synonym of the *pargana*.[17] More often than not, the terms *pargana* and *ta'alluqa* were used for the unit next to the province.

[12] *Pindori Documents*, XIX, XXIX, XXXI, XXXIV & XLIV.

[13] Ibid., XXXVIII, XLI & XLII.

[14] Ibid., XXXII & XXXIV.

[15] 'SSR Upper Bari Doab', *Foreign/Secret Consultation*, 28 April 1848, No. 61, para 1. See also, *Pindori Documents*, XIX, XXIX, XXXI & XLIV.

[16] S.A. Abbott, 'Memorandum of the First Eight Years, of British Rule in the District of Hooshearpore', *Selections from the Public Correspondence of the Punjab Administration* (cited hereafter as *Selections PCPA*), Vol. III, No. 4, 291 & 297; J.A.L. Montgomery, *SR Hoshiarpur*, 125-30.

[17] In fact, the three terms, *pargana*, *ta'alluqa* and *zila'* are used rather indifferently in the *Khālsa Darbār Records*. The point may be clarified with reference to Wazirabad. At one place, the title given is 'the *parganas* and *ta'olluqas* of Wazirabad': Bundle 34, Vol. III, 221-23. At several other places 'the *ta'alluqa* of Wazirabad' is considered with its subdivisions generally called *zila'* but sometimes also called *ta'alluqa*: Bundle 23, Vol. III, 55; Bundle 2, Vol. VI, 63-65, 67-69, 71-79, 81-87, 89-91 & 93-95. Consequently, at one place we have *zila'* Nathuwal of the *ta'alluqa* of Wazirabad and at another, *ta'alluqa* of Nathuwal of the *ta'alluqa* of Wazirabad : Bundle 23, Vol. III, 67 & 71, respectively. It may be interesting to note that for Hallowal, as a subdivision of Wazirabad, both *pargana* and *ta'alluqa* are used at one place and there also appears a term like *pargana-i-ta'alluqa-i-Qila-i-Kotla* : ibid., 119. See also, Bundle 5, Vol. I, 562. It may be pointed out that occasionally the term *ta'alluqa* is used interchangeably with *zila'*. Its equation with *pargana*, however, is much more common.

The size of an average *ta'alluqa* or *pargana* of the Sikh times was much smaller than the size of an average *pargana* of the Mughal times. For instance, the district of Gujranwala in the early British times covered 26 *ta'alluqas* of the Sikh times,[18] but only three or four *parganas* of the Mughal times.[19] The breaking-up of the Mughal *parganas* was an obvious consequence of the piecemeal occupation of territory by a large number of *sardārs* in the third quarter of the eighteenth century.[20] Baden Powell observed that the Mughal *pargana* was remembered only in some parts of the Panjab; elsewhere, it had become 'confused' with the Sikh *ta'alluqa* or *'ilāqa.*[21] Even when the term *pargana* was kept up in the Panjab during the Sikh times, it did not necessarily refer to an older unit of area. In Kashmir, on the other hand, the change introduced was marginal,

[18] In Gujranwala, the lowest number of villages in a *ta'alluqa* is given as 5 and the highest 205. On the average, however, there were 30 to 40 villages in a *ta'alluqa*. In these *ta'alluqas* appear not only the old *pargana* names like Sodhran, Eminabad, Wazirabad, Shaikhupura, but also the new ones like Nangal Duna Singh, Qila Didar Singh, Qila Mian Singh, Qila Bathawala, Akalgarh and Gujranwala itself. For detail, see Statement of 'Original Usurpation and Distribution of Territories by the Sikh Confederacy', *SR Gujranwala (1866-1867)*, 9-11.

[19] See, for example, Ganesh Das, *Chār Bāgh*, 249-50, 255 & 272.

According to the *qānūngoī* records of Aurangzeb's reign, the *pargana* of Zafarwal had 328 villages whereas in the *Khālsa Darbār Records* Zafarwal is listed as one of the nine subdivisions of the *'pargana-i-ta'alluqa-i-*Hallowal': *Gazetteer of Sialkot*, 15; *Khālsa Darbār Records, Bundle* 28, Vol. III, 119, respectively.

[20] There are numerous instances of old administrative units being parcelled among several participants in a conjoint conquest, the most typical being the conquest and subsequent partition of the Mughal *sarkār* of Sarhind between hundreds of small and big *sardārs*. For a graphic description, see chapter II, 18 n 32. Ibbetson's description may also be generally applicable at least in our present context: 'Every few villages that were held in separate jagir were often called a pargana, though, the individual villages might be miles apart. . . . In fact, there were two concurrent systems of parganas, one based upon locality, and the other upon the assignment of the land revenue': *SR Karnal*, 40. The latter obviously was the *ta'alluqa* or the 'possession' of an individual *sardār*.

[21] Baden Powell, *Land Systems of British India*, II, 730.

if at all there was any.[22] The number of *ta'alluqas* or *pargana* in the areas covered by the Sikh dominions on the whole was much larger than the number of *parganas* during the Mughal times.[23] But there is no justification for treating the *ta'alluqa* as a subdivision of the *pargana*.[24]

The subdivision of the *pargana* or *ta'alluqa* was in fact the *tappa*.[25] Ahmad Shah refers to some *tappa* headquarters in the Kangra hills and also across the river Satlej.[26] There are several other references to *tappas* in the hills and also across the Satlej.[27] According to Ganesh Das, the *pargana* of Pharwala had four *tappas* and Dangli had eight; Rohtas had four *tappas*; Gujrat and Shahjahanpur had eight each; Herat and Bahlolpur had seven each; Shaikhupura had eight *tappas*; and Batala had four.[28] According to some early settlement reports, Chhachh

[22] The Sikhs are said to have created four new *parganas* in Kashmir: Charles Ellison Bates, *A Gazetteer of Kashmir*, 4.

[23] The preponderance of the term *ta'alluqa* in the *Khālsa Darbār Records* appears to have been the reason for its uniform use in his *Catalogue* by Kohli to the exclusion of the term *pargana* altogether: see, *Catalogue of Khalsa Darbar Records*, II, 13-14, 21-22, 27-28, 34-35, 42, 47-48 *et passim*.

[24] For the treatment of the *ta'alluqa* as a subdivision of the *pargana*, see, for example, Kohli, 'Land Revenve Administration', *JPHS*, 76. Chopra, *Sovereign State*, 84. Chopra equates *pargana* with a district and *ta'alluqa* with a *tahsīl* of the British times. More recently, Hasrat also expresses the same view: *Life and Times of Ranjit Singh*, 293 & 302.

[25] Irfan Habib does not mention *tappa* as a fiscal unit in the Mughal times but he does notice the use of the word *tappa* in a *farmān* of Jahangir: *Agrarian System*, 291 n 107.

According to B.R. Grover, however, *tappa* as a fiscal unit existed even in pre-Mughal times and during Akbar's reign it was made a uniform feature of revenue administration: 'Raqba-Bandi Documents of Akbar's Reign', *Proceedings Indian Historical Records Commission*, XXXVI, Part 2, 59-60 & nn 21-23. See also, Noman Ahmad Siddiqi, *Land Revenue Administration Under the Mughals, 1700-1750* (cited hereafter as *Land Revenue Administration*), 31 n 53, 42, 82, & 159 n 22.

[26] *Tārīkh*, 148, 152 & 153.

[27] For example, *Foreign/Political Consultation*, 31 December 1847, Nos. 2470-75; 'SSR Cis-Satlej', ibid., 31 December 1847, No. 1830, para 11, respectively.

[28] *Chār Bāgh*, 162, 163, 168, 170, 172, 256. 257, 272 & 298.

and Pothuhar in the Sindh Sagar Doab were divided, respectively into four and eight *tappas*.[29] According to another report, Peshawar was divided into five and Bannu into twenty *tappas*.[30] In some parts of the Sikh dominions, the term *zila*ʻ was also used for the subdivision of a *ta*ʻ*alluqa*. For example, the *ta*ʻ*alluqa* of Wazirabad in the *Khālsa Darbār Records* has nine *zila*ʻ*s* and we may be sure that *zila*ʻ in this context refers to the *tappa* subdivision of the *ta*ʻ*alluqa*.[31] The number of villages in a *tappa* varied from two to a few dozens though occasionally a *tappa* could consist of a single village.[32].

In some parts of the Sikh dominions, *tappas* were further divided into *topes* or *chaklas*. Just as the number of *tappas* in a *pargana* varied from *pargana* to *pargana*, so did the number of *topes* or *chaklas* in a *tappa* vary from *tappa* to *tappa*. In the *tappa* of Akya in the *pargana* of Gujrat, for instance, there were five *topes*; in Bala there were three; in Kandu there were six; and in Handu there were three. In the *tappa* of Jiv Waraich in the *pargana* of Herat, there were eighteen *topes* and in the *tappa* of Helan only eight. The *tappa-i*-Akbari in the *pargana* of Eminabad had five *topes*; Waraich and Cheema had eight; Khanpur Chautra had six; and the *tappa-i*-Alamgiri had two *topes*. The number of villages in a *tope* varied from place to place. In a few cases, a single village constituted a *tope*.[33]

Though a well or a hamlet was treated as the basic fiscal

[29] 'SSR Upper Sindh Sagar Doab', *Foreign/Secret Consultation*, 28 April 1848, No. 66.

[30] *Foreign/Secret Consultation*, 18 November 1843, No. 26; 'Diary of H.B. Edwardes', *Punjab Government Records* (*1847-1849*), V, 224, respectively. Shahamat Ali also mentions several *tappas* in the trans-Indus area : *Sikhs and Afghans*, 277.

[31] Bundle 2, Vol. VI, 63-65, 83-87, 89-91, 93-95; also, Bundle 23, Vol. III, 1. In this respect Wazirabad was not an exception : see, for example, for the *ta*ʻ*alluqa* of Hallowal, ibid., 103, 107 & 119.

[32] In the '*pargana*' of Gujrat, for instance, one of its *tappas*, named Alamgiri had only one village, and another *tappa* named Kandu had six *topes*, each consisting of a number of villages : Ganesh Das, *Chār Bāgh*, 170 & 171. See also, *Khālsa Darbār Records*, Bundle 2, Vol. VI, 67-69, 71-87, 89-91, 93-95.

[33] J.S. Grewal & Indu Banga (tr. & ed.), *Early Nineteenth-Century Panjab*, 18.

unit at places,[34] the smallest unit of revenue administration was the village (*mauza'* or *deh*). Its boundaries were usually marked and entered in revenue records. The majority of villages in the Sikh dominions consisted of three main parts : habitational, agricultural and wasteland or pasture.

Turning to the functionaries connected with revenue administration, the person appointed to look after a province, the primary unit, was generally called *nāzim*. He was directly responsible to the ruler and held office in accordance with the pleasure of his master. There was no fixed tenure of his office and no regular pattern appears to emerge from the actual appointment of *nāzims* made by Ranjit Singh and his successors. In the Kangra hills, Sardar Desa Sigh Majithia and his son acted as *nāzims* for over thirty years.[35] In the Jalandhar Doab, Diwan Mohkam Chand was succeeded by several *nāzims* from 1814 to 1845.[36] Long tenures of office were ordinarily not allowed to the *nāzims*. Under Ranjit Singh and his successors, eleven *nāzims* were appointed to Kashmir between 1819 and 1845.[37] Of all these, Mihan Singh enjoyed the longest term of about seven years till his death in 1841. Diwan Chand

[34] Barkley, 'Character of Land Tenures', *Report on the Administration of the Punjab (1872-1873)*, 13. See also, chapter V, 93 n 22 & 96 n 38.

[35] 'Statistical Notes on the Punjab', *Foreign/Secret Consultation*, 26 December 1846, Nos. 1325-27; *Gazetteer of Kangra*, 218.

[36] Besides Mohkam Chand's own son Moti Ram, these *nāzims*, among others, included Avitabile, Faqir Nuruddin, Misar Rup Lal and Shaikh Ghulam Muhiyuddin : Ganesh Das, *Chār Bāgh*, 381; Amar Nath, *Zafarnāma*, 45 & 47; Griffin & Massy, *Chiefs and Families*, I, 160 & 161.

[37] The Sikh *nāzims* of Kashmir were Misra Diwan Chand, Diwan Moti Ram, Sardar Hari Singh Nalwa, Diwan Moti Ram (second term), Chuni Lal, Diwan Kirpa Ram (son of Moti Ram), Bhamman Singh, Prince Sher Singh, Mihan Singh, Shaikh Ghulam Muhiyuddin and his son Imamuddin.

For detail, see Kirpa Ram, *Gulzār-i-Kashmir*, 251-63; Mir Ahmad, *Dastūr al- 'Amal-i-Kashmir*, ff 3b & 4a; *Tārīkh-i-Kashmir* (anon.), ff 202a-b, 204 a & 206a-b; Ganeshi Lal, *Siyāhat-i-Kashmir*, 22 & 26; Kirpa Ram, *Gulābnāma*, 326; *News (1825)*, 15; Sohan Lal, *Umdat*, II, 221, 261-62, 290, 377 & 380; III, (i), 111 & (ii), 201; IV, (ii), 28-29; Amar Nath, *Zafarnāma*, 117, 141, 162-63, 176 & 226-27.

and Bhamman Singh held office for less than a year. The average tenure of the *nāzims* of Kashmir was from two to three years. Of the several *nāzims* of Multan, Sawan Mal enjoyed the longest tenure—about fifteen years.[38]

The *nāzim* was allowed to wield considerable power in the territory under his jurisdiction.[39] His primary duty was to maintain peace and order in his territory and to submit regular instalments of revenue to the royal treasury.[40] The opinion that so long as the *nāzim* sent enough money to Lahore his methods were not questioned or even looked into,[41] might have been true of the 1840s, but Ranjit Singh was generally

[38] Sukh Dayal, Sham Singh Peshawria, Jawahar Mal and Hazari Badan Singh had been the governors of Multan before Sawan Mal who was succeeded by his son Mul Raj. After Hazari Badan Singh and before the appointment of Sawan Mal, several *nāzims* including Tulsidhar, Dhian Singh, Babu Baj Singh and Kharak Singh, remained in office, each for a month or two: Munshi Hukm Chand, *Tārīkh-i-Multan*, 470. See also, Sohan Lal, *Umdat*, II, 263; *News* (*1825*), 23-24, 49 & 277.

Sawan Mal appears to have been the *nāzim* of Multan from 1830 to 1844. Sohan Lal refers to him as the *nāzim* of Multan for the first time in 1830: *Umdat*, II, 407. Earlier he is mentioned among the *kārdārs* of Multan: ibid., 349, 355, 378 & 382. In fact, Sawan Mal got his first independent charge in this region as the *ijāradār* of Shujabad after having worked with Hazari Badan Singh for three years, and remained in this position for another two years when Multan also was given to him: Munshi Hukm Chand, *Tārīkh-i-Multan*, 470. It may be interesting to note that from the *News of the Court of Ranjit Singh* it is clear that Hazari Badan Singh became the *nāzim* of Multan in the early part of 1825: *News* (*1825*), 49. *Cf.* Chopra, *Sovereign State*, 87.

[39] For example, with reference to the *nāzims* of Kangra, a British settlement officer observed that all fiscal, military and miscellaneous charges relating to receipts and disbursements fell under their authority: G.C. Barnes, *SR Kangra*, quoted in J.M. Douie, *Punjab Settlement Manual*, 20. Probably, the *nāzims* of outlying provinces, like Avitabile in Peshawar and Hari Singh Nalwa in Hazara, enjoyed still greater powers.

[40] According to John Lawrence, the *nāzim* was required to punctually send the revenues collected from the territory under his charge: 'Statistical Notes', *Foreign/Secret Consultation*, 26 December 1846, Nos. 1325-27.

[41] This opinion was generally held by the early British administrators of the Panjab. For a typical example, see Douie, *Punjab Settlement Manual*, 19.

very vigilant in exercising strict control over his *nāzims*. Jawahar Mal was removed from the *nizāmat* of Multan because he wantonly killed an innocent person.[42] Sham Singh Peshawaria was removed because he proved to be oppressive.[43] Chuni Lal, the *nāzim* of Kashmir in 1825, was ordered to make prompt payment of the *rasūm* due to Jamadar Khushal Singh when the latter made a complaint.[44] Ranjit Singh's instruction to his *nāzims* to regard the subject people as a 'trust from God' became all the more significant for his alacrity in action.[45]

The *nāzims* who enjoyed long terms of office were also some of the best: Desa Singh Majithia in Kangra, Lehna Singh Majithia in Kangra and the Majha, Misar Rup Lal in the Jalandhar Doab, Mihan Singh in Kashmir and Diwan Sawan Mal in Multan. Kirpa Ram praises Mihan Singh for remitting the *muhalatāna* of two annas in a rupee and two *traks* in a *kharwār* which had been imposed in the days of Sukh Jiwan, the first Afghan governor of Kashmir.[46] Several other measures of public welfare are attributed to Mihan Singh.[47] Misar Rup Lal was regarded as 'an able and humane

[42] *News (1825)*, 23-24.

It may be added that Ranjit Singh's intelligence service was extremely efficient and he was keen to know from all sorts of sources what was happening in the different parts of his kingdom.

[43] Amar Nath, *Zafarnāma*, 134.

[44] *News (1825)*, 67-68.

[45] For example, in 1833, the year of famine in Kashmir, Ranjit Singh wrote a sarcastic letter to Kanwar Sher Singh, who was the *nāzim* of Kashmir at this time, in order to make him realize that he had been neglecting his duties: Sohan Lal, *Umdat*, III, (ii), 180. Soon afterwards, Sher Singh was removed from the *nizāmat* and Mihan Singh was appointed in his place with very strict injunctions to restore Kashmir to its former prosperity : ibid., 201; Amar Nath, *Zafarnāma*, 226-27.

For some other examples of Ranjit Singh's keenness to investigate into reports and complaints against the functionaries of the state, see Sohan Lal, *Umdat*, III, (i), 9, 12-13 & 129; (ii), 133, 134; 139, 145, 179, 180 & 268; *Events (1810-1817)*, 38, 86, 87, 254 & 271.

[46] *Gulzār-i-Kashmir*, 256-57.

Traks and *kharwārs* were the units of weight used in Kashmir. One *trak* was equal to about 4½ Lahore seers (a seer being equal to about 21 *chhatāks*) and 16 *traks* made one *kharwār* ('ass load'): 'Diary of R.G. Taylor', *Punjab Government Records (1847-1849)*, VI, 31.

[47] 'Mihan Singh decided cases justly and quickly, and won a great

ruler' who had keen interest in the prosperity of the Jalandhar Doab and whose assessment was 'light and equitable'.[48] Diwan Sawan Mal 'handled the revenue affairs of Multan with commendable ability, brought the country under cultivation, made the people contented and happy and submitted larger revenues to the royal treasury than any of the former functionaries'.[49] Lehna Singh Majithia enjoyed a good reputation in the hills as 'a mild and lenient governor'.[50] Avitabile was praised for his 'good system of police and revenue', and for his 'wise and vigorous management'.[51] His tenure, however, was not long. But he was not the only 'good' *nāzim* to get a short term of office.[52]

reputation in Kashmir.' In his time, 'agricultural advances were made free of interest, proper weights were introduced, and the fraudulent middlemen were punished': Walter Roper Lawrence, *Valley of Kashmir*, 200. See also, Kirpa Ram, *Gulzār-i-Kashmir*, 255-57; Amar Nath, *Zafarnāma*, 226-27; Sohan Lal, *Umdat*, III, (ii), 201. The monumental *Dastur al-'Amal-i-Kashmir* compiled under Mihan Singh's patronage is a testimony to his interest in even the remotest hamlets in Kashmir.

[48] Griffin & Massy, *Chiefs and Families*, I, 356. See also, 'Memorandum of the First Eight Years, of British Rule in the District of Hooshearpore', *Selections PCPA*, Vol. III, No. 4, 292.

[49] Ganesh Das, *Chār Bāgh*, 381. According to Munshi Hukm Chand, Diwan Sawan Mal 'was a wise administrator and the people of Multan mention his name with great respect'. He was regular in attending to the affairs of his office and used to sit there daily for several hours. Besides administering justice personally, he paid very careful attention to revenue papers : *Tārīkh-i-Multan*, 470 & 471. Douie describes Sawan Mal as 'an oriental ruler of the best type' who did much to restore the prosperity of the country which had been desolated by 'a century of anarchy': *Punjab Settlement Manual*, 20. According to the settlement officer of Multan, Diwan Sawan Mal was 'one of the very few men in India, who had been able to combine the exaction of a very full revenue with the complete contentment of the people from whom it is exacted' : E.D. Maclagan, *SR Multan*, 6. For a near contemporary report on Sawan Mal's administration, see *General Report upon the Administration of the Punjab Proper (1849-50 & 1850-51)*, 89-90.

[50] *Gazetteer of Kangra*, 218.

[51] Shahamat Ali, *Sikhs and Afghans*, 57 ; 'Diary of R.G. Taylor'. *Punjab Government Records (1847-1849)*, VI, 2, respectively. See also, Genesh Das, *Chār Bāgh*, 250.

[52] General Ventura in Dera Ghazi Khan and Amar Singh Majithia in

The *nāzims* were sometimes allowed to administer their territories through a deputy or a *mukhtār-i-kār*. Ghulam Muhiyuddin is believed to have acted as the governor of Kashmir on behalf of Prince Sher Singh.[53] Kirpa Ram acted as the *nāzim* of the Jalandhar Doab on behalf of his father Diwan Moti Ram.[54] Mahan Singh acted as the deputy of Sardar Hari Singh Nalwa in Hazara.[55] In 1845, Sardar Chatar Singh Atariwala appointed Chaudhari Shahbaz Khan as his *mukhtār-i-kār* in the Rajauri region.[56] The *parwānas* of Sardar Chatar Singh and his son Sher Singh addressed to Chaudhari Shahbaz Khan provide interesting insights into the functions performed by the *mukhtār-i-kār*.[57] He was authorized to scrutinize *parwānas* relating to *jāgīrs* and to release them after verification. He was expected to collect revenues, with the help of additional troops if necessary. The

Hazara present two more examples of 'good' administrators who did not enjoy long terms of office : see F.W.R. Fryer, *SR Dera Ghazi Khan*, 37; Muhammad Azim Beg, *Tārīkh-i-Hazara*, II, 691, respectively.

[53] Kirpa Ram, *Gulābnāma*, 314 ; *Tārīkh-i-Kashmir* (anon.), f 205b. Wasakha Singh, who was the '*sāhib-i-kār*' of Prince Sher Singh before the coming of Ghulam Muhiyuddin, had been arrested and charged with misleading the prince and mismanaging the affairs of Kashmir: Muhammaduddin Fauq, *Muqammal Tārīkh Kashmir*, III, 32.

[54] S.M. Latif, *History of the Panjab*, 432. This arrangement was only a repetition of an earlier situation in which Moti Ram himself had deputised in the Jalandhar Doab for his father Mohkam Chand who was conducting the Kashmir compaign in 1812.

[55] Muhammad Azim Beg, *Tārīkh-i-Hazara*, II, 699.

[56] *Parwānajāt-i Atārīwāla*, I, 7 & 8.

It may be pointed out that the *zamīndārs* were ordered by the Lahore Darbar to submit revenues to the *mukhtār-i-kār* and the commandants were ordered to obey him and to open the forts to his *thānadārs* and his troops: ibid., 7, 9, 11 & 13.

[57] Ibid., 57, 63, 67, 71, 91, 97, 119, 121, 129 & 135.

In 1847, Sardar Sher Singh Atariwala acted in place of his father Sardar Chatar Singh and Chaudhari Shahbaz Khan continued to be the *mukhtār-i-kār*. He is asked to supply grain to the troops (ibid., II, 67 & 101), to send the troops of the *jāgīrdārs* (ibid., 67), and to give the salt *mandīs* of Pind Dadan Khan in *ijāra* regularly (ibid., 11).

Various other duties were performed by the *mukhtār-i-kār*. He was paid by the *nāzim* in cash as well as in *jāgīr* : ibid., 35.

collected revenues were to be sent by the *mukhtār-i-kār* either directly to the state treasury or to someone authorized by the *nāzim* to receive them. The *mukhtār-i-kār* was expected to deal with the vassal chiefs of the area under his jurisdiction on behalf of the *nāzim*.

Every *nāzim* was assisted by a number of officials called *kārdārs*. The term *kārdār* was used for officials employed by the princes and the *jāgīrdārs* as well.[58] It was used by the contemporaries also for the administrators of towns and even *katras*;[59] for the managers of salt markets;[60] and for the officials of customs.[61] Nevertheless, it was used most frequently for persons appointed to look after the administration of *ta'alluqas* or *parganas*,[62] and it was, thus, interchangeable with the term *'āmil*.[63]

The *kārdār* was generally appointed by the ruler and normally had to submit a formal deed of acceptance before he was appointed.[64] There was no fixed tenure of the *kārdār*. What was expected from him is indicated by an order of Maharaja Ranjit Singh issued to Chaudhari Kanhiya who was appointed to the *kārdārī* of the *ta'alluqa* of Bhimbar with effect from the *kharīf* crop of 1837. His first task was to take accounts of the *kharīf* crop of 1836 and the *rabī'* crop of 1837 from the former *kārdār* of that *ta'alluqa* and to keep with him sums thus realized. He was asked to collect the revenues of the *kharīf* crop of 1837 and to assess the revenues for the *rabī'*

[58] See, for example, Munshi Bakhtawar Lal, *Tārīkh-i-Montgomery*, 19, 21, 23 & 35; Griffin & Massy, *Chiefs and Families*, II, 121, 182 & 311, respectively.

[59] See, for example, Amar Nath, *Zafarnāma*, 140; Ahmad Shah, *Tārīkh*, 481; Griffin & Massy, *Punjab Chiefs*, I, 292.

[60] See, for example, Sohan Lal, *Umdat*, II, 394 & 401.

[61] *Foreign/Political Consultation*, 21 May 1852, No. 142.

[62] For examples of the use of the term *kārdār* by Sohan Lal for the administrators of Adinanagar, Pathankot, Nurpur, Jandiala and Gujrat, see *Umdat*, II, 306; V, 22 & 125.

[63] See, for instance, *Pindori Documents*, XVIII, XXI, XXV, XXIX, XXXV, XXXVIII, XLII & XLIV.

[64] Sayyid Mehar Shah, the *kārdār* of Bhera, for example, was confirmed in office only after he had sent his *razā-nāma*: Sohan Lal, *Umdat*, V, 37.

crop of 1838. He was instructed to keep in view the increase in revenues and in agriculture and to be upright and sympathetic in dealing with the people, keeping their well-being at heart. He was also instructed not to decide any important suits without getting the Maharaja's approval.[65]

Instructions issued to *kārdārs* by Diwan Sawan Mal clarify the duties which every *kārdār* in Multan was expected to perform.[66] He was to let cultivation and the revenues increase, to see that canals were cleared and excavated in time, to appraise or divide crops, and to assess the revenue in consultation with the village headmen. He was instructed to send a list of the current prices signed by the village headmen and the '*zamīndārs*' on the first of Hār every year. And in the month of Bhādon every year, he was expected to go to Multan in order to settle his accounts. He was asked to send the revenues punctually in six instalments, three each for the *kharīf* and the *rabī*'. He was expected to protect the people of the *ta'alluqa* against thieves and other criminals. The culprits were to be put under detention by the *kārdārs* and orders of imprisonment and fine were to be given in due course by the *nāzim*. The *kārdār* was instructed to pay the soldiers personally and in accordance with the fixed scales.[67]

[65] The transcription of this order is given by Kohli in the 'Land Revenue Administration', *JPHS*, 87. *Cf.* G.C. Barnes, *SR Kangra*, quoted in Douie, *Punjab Settlement Manual*, 20: 'His daily routine of duty was to provide for the proper cultivation of the land, to encourage the flagging husbandman, and replace if possible the deserter. His energies were entirely directed towards extending the agricultural resources of the district, and the problem of his life was to maintain cultivation at the highest possible level, and at the same time to keep the cultivator at the lowest point of depression'.

[66] Munshi Hukm Chand, *Tārīkh-i-Multan*, 471-72. See also, *SR Muzaffargarh*, 52. Though the first work was published later, there is every possibility that Edward O'Brien, the settlement officer of Muzaffargarh, had relied for this information upon Munshi Hukm Chand who had been the Extra Assistant Commissioner of Multan.

[67] The soldiers of the *kārdār* were divided into the 'war' and 'revenue' departments and their pay scales varied accordingly. The *kārdār* was also allowed a small establishment consisting of a treasurer and a writer. For some detail, see *SR Muzaffargarh*, 53; Munshi Hukm Chand, *Tārīkh- M ltan*, 472.

The *kārdār* was thus primarily a fiscal officer and his most important duty was to collect revenue. He used to keep a proper record of the collections made and the expenditure incurred. All orders relating to payment of cash or alienation of revenues in favour of individuals were preserved by the *kārdār* and receipts, or acknowledgments, of the payments made by him were also maintained.[68] In the case of orders of revenue-free grants in which places were left unspecified, the *kārdār* used his discretion to specify a suitable area.[69] He was sometimes asked to remit stipulated amounts to commandants and *thānadārs* for disbursement among the troops.[70] The accounts of the *kārdār* were regularly audited. A defaulting *kārdār* was liable to fine, imprisonment, confiscation of property, transfer or dismissal, depending upon the seriousness of the case.[71]

[68] For alienation of revenues through the *kārdārs*, see *Foreign/Political Consultation*, 16 April 1852, No. 99 (through the *kārdār* of Dera Ismail Khan); ibid., 7 May 1852, Nos. 40-43 (through the *kārdār* of Shahdara); *Foreign/Political Proceedings*, 30 April 1852, Nos. 99-102 (through the *kārdār* of Khangarh); ibid., 14 November 1851, No. 55 (through the *kārdār* of Ramnagar); ibid., 18 June 1852, Nos. 181-85 (through the *kārdārs* of Shaikhupura, Ramnagar and Gujranwala); ibid., 7 January 1853, Nos. 238-42 (through the *kārdār* of Rawalpindi); ibid., 24 June 1854, Nos. 204-05 (through the *kārdār* of Dipalpur.

There are numerous references in the *Umdat-ut-Tawārīkh* to individuals receiving cash from *kārdārs* in accordance with the orders of the Maharaja, while the *kārdārs* are asked to keep the receipts so that their accounts may accordingly be credited. For the preservation of such *parwānas* by the *kārdārs* in their records see, for example, *Foreign/Political Consultation*, 29 December 1849, No. 49A(31).

[69] In the *ta'alluqa* of Qadian for example, the *kārdār* gave 1000 rupees in cash for the *rabī'* of 1847 but promised to give a village worth 2000 rupees a year, the amount of the *jāgīr* of Sardar Bhur Singh. Before the *kharīf* crop, however, the grantee obtained *jāgīr* worth 3000 rupees. The *kārdār* gave him the village of Thikri worth 3100 rupees. Sardar Bhur Singh submitted the additional 100 rupees to the treasury: ibid., 29 December 1849, No. 49 A(31). See also, *Foreign/Political Proceedings*, 15 October 1852, No. 122; ibid., 10 June 1853, No. 217.

[70] See, for example, *News (1825)*, 50-51; *Events (1810-1817)*, 206.

[71] See, for example, Sohan Lal, *Umdat*, II, 403 ; IV, (i), 62; (iii), 23; V, 23, 38 *et passim.* See also, Munshi Hukm Chand, *Tārīkh-i-Multan*, 4 72; *Events (1810-1817)*, 38, 83, 89, 162, 170 & 221.

No *kārdār* as a rule was allowed to serve at one place for a long time. Serveral cases of the transfer of *kārdārs* are given in the *Khālsa Darbār Records*.[72] Occasionally, a *kārdār* was transferred on a complaint from the *zamīndārs*. The *'āmil* of Jhang was ordered in 1825 to repair to the court because of such a complaint.[73] Much more frequently, however, the *kārdārs* were transferred from one place to another as a matter of policy. Five persons served as *kārdārs* in Dipalpur between 1806 and 1827.[74] Similarly, in the *ta'alluqa* of Malka Hans, four persons served as *kārdārs* between 1813 and 1821.[75] Conversely, a single person served as a *kārdār* in several different places at different times.[76] Ganesh Das provides a very interesting list of the administrators of Gujrat and, on the basis of this information, the average stay of the *kārdār* in the kingdom of Lahore comes to nearly two and a half years.[77]

The salary of the *kārdār* was broadly in proportion to the annual net value of the area under his charge.[78] Gauhar Mal,

To mention a typical situation, in 1832, the accounts of Ram Chand, the *kārdār* of Amritsar, were checked and it was found that he had paid only Rs. 86,000 to the government from a total assessment of 101,000 rupees. Jamadar Khushal Singh was ordered to realize the balance of 15,000 rupees from Ram Chand: Sohan Lal, *Umdat*, III, (ii), 145.

[72] See, for example, Bundle 4, Vol. IV, 1, 8 & 19.

[73] *News* (*1825*), 325.

[74] Munshi Bakhtawar Lal, *Tārīkh-i-Montgomery*, 30-40.

[75] Ibid., 45-46.

[76] This was Kanhiya Lal, a grandson of Diwan Moti Ram: Griffin & Massy, *Chiefs and Families*, II, 164.

[77] *Chār Bāgh*, 200-03. See also, Douie, *Punjab Settlement Manual*, 20.

[78] This is evident from the figures given by John Lawrence. His report contains, among other things, the name of the *kārdār*, the annual collection from the area and the salary of the *kārdār*: 'Statistical Notes on the Punjab', *Foreign/Secret Consultation*, 26 December 1846, Nos. 1325-27.

Notwithstanding John Lawrence's view to the contrary, an average 'collectorship' formed a reasonably good unit, neither too small, nor too large. In fact, the number of such collectorships was more than half of the sixty *ta'alluqas* listed by John Lawrence himself. Moreover, nearly 15 *kārdārs* out of 35 were holding single *ta'alluqas* like Dipalpur, Satghara, Hujra, Fatehgarh, Narot, Sherpur, Saurian, Shaikhupura, Chhachh and Rawalpindi. At one time, the 'province' of Jhang alone had 40 *kārdārs*: A. Cocks, 'SSR Lower Rachna Doab',

who was getting 2,400 rupees a year at one time, was holding ten *ta'alluqas*.[79] Ganda Mal, who was getting 360 rupees a year, was holding only nine villages.[80] Though the salary of the *kārdār* ranged from 150 to 2500 rupees, the majority of the *kārdārs* received something between 500 and 1,000 rupees a year.[81] It may be added that some of the *kārdārs* were paid through *jāgīrs* which were resumed on their transfer, presumably because they were given fresh *jāgīrs* in the *ta'alluqas* to which they were sent.[82]

Mere pay was not the only inducement for a person to accept the *kārdār's* office. There were certain recognized perquisites which could amount sometimes to the equivalent of the fixed salary.[83] The *kārdārs* were allowed to receive subsistence allowance on a fixed scale when they went on government duty.[84] The *kārdārs* in Kashmir generally received one *trak* on every *kharwār* of grain collected.[85] There was a standing custom in the Panjab by which the '*zamīndārs*' gratuitously provided the *kārdārs* with wood, and their horses and cattle with fodder. At certain seasons of the year, the *kārdārs*

Foreign/Secret Consultation, 28 April 1848, No. 64, para 5. There were 17 *kārdārs* in Kangra under Sardar Lehna Singh Majithia. G.C. Barnes, the well-known settlement officer of Kangra, appears to be right in stating the general position that a *kārdār* was appointed over every '*pargana*': quoted in Douie, *Punjab Settlement Manual*, 20.

79 'Diary of J. Nicholson', *Punjab Government Records (1847-1849)*, VI, 357-58.

80 'Diary of L. Bowring', ibid., 421.

81 See, for example, 'Statistical Notes on the Punjab', *Foreign/Secret Consultation*, 26 December 1846, Nos. 1325-27.

82 *Khālsa Darbār Records*, Bundle 4, Vol. IV, 1, 8, 19, for example.

83 Barnes, *SR Kangra*, quoted in Douie, *Punjab Settlement Manual*, 20.

84 The following scales of the daily subsistence allowance are given in the settlement report for the *kārdārs* under Diwan Sawan Mal :

floor	3 seers
ghī	$\frac{1}{4}$ seer
dāl	$\frac{1}{4}$ seer
gram for horse	3 seers
spices	1 anna

SR Muzaffargarh, 53.

85 'Diary of P.S. Melvill', *Punjab Government Records (1847-1849)*, VI, 204, 206 & 217. See also, Mir Ahmad, *Dastūr al-'Amal-i-Kashmir*, Part 2, f 59a.

used to get the green blades of corn and other crops from the cultivators.[86] They were also expected to get *nazrāna* which they had to pay into government treasury. The *rasūm* of the government in some areas amounted to 4.5 per cent of the revenue, while the *kārdārs* received 4 rupees per village, per annum.[87] In their own turn, the *kārdārs* paid *nazrs* and *rasūm* to the ruler in accordance with his orders.

Unlike the *kārdār*, the *qānūngo* performed his functions in the *ta'alluqa* more or less permanently. During the Mughal times, originally there used to be one *qānūngo* for a *pargana*, but in the reign of Aurangzeb, the number of *qānūngos* had considerably increased and more than one *qānūngo* could be appointed in a *pargana*.[88] Many of the old families of *qānūngos* continued to hold that office during the Sikh times. Ganesh Das, for example, mentions old families of *khatrīs*, including his own, which held the office of the *qānūngo* in Rohtas, Bahlolpur, Takht-Hazara, Gujrat, Herat, Sialkot, Pathankot, Batala and Kalanaur.[89] Also, more than one *qānūngo* was in many cases appointed to a *pargana* or a *ta'alluqa*. The Bedi and Mehta *khatrīs*, for example, were the *qānūngos* of Haibatpur Patti, and the *qānūngoī* of Jalandhar belonged to Sehgals and Thapars.[90] In Wazirabad, a *brāhman* named Jai Singh was appointed as a *qānūngo* by Jodh Singh, while the Sahni *khatrīs*

[86] 'SSR Upper Rachna Doab', *Foreign/Secret Consultation*, 28 April 1848, No. 63, para 12.

[87] 'SSR Upper Sindh Sagar Doab', ibid., No. 66. See also, *SR Muzaffargarh*, 53; Munshi Hukm Chand, *Tārīkh-i-Multan*, 656; Munshi Gopal Das, *Tārīkh-i-Peshawar*, II, 387. See also, *Khālsa Darbār Records*, Bundle 3, Vol. IV, 31, 53 & 55.

[88] For the position of the *qānūngo* during the Mughal times, see Irfan Habib, *Agrarian System*, 127, 131 n 10, 186, 203-04 & n 35, 235, 252, 262 287-91; Noman Ahmad Siddiqi, *Land Revenue Administration*, 88-90. See also, B N. Goswamy & J.S. Grewal, *Mughals and the Jogis of Jakhbar*, 90 n 16; also, *Pindori Documents*, 91 n 6.

[89] *Chār-Bāgh*, 163, 168, 175, 209, 211, 221, 295-96 & 298.

It is possible that the office of the *qānūngo* was not maintained in the tribal areas in the upper Sindh Sagar Doab particularly where the tribal chiefs and other locally influential men undertook to collect the share of the government : see, for example, 'Diary of J. Nicholson', *Punjab Government Records (1847-1849)*, VI, 314.

[90] Ganesh Das, *Chār Bāgh*, 301-03.

continued to hold *qānūngoī* as of old.[91] In the *News of the Court of Ranjit Singh* there are references to *qānūngos* in the plural in a single *ta'alluqa* or a town.[92] In the contemporary documents there is ample evidence that three or four *qānūngos* held office at one and the same time in the '*pargana*' of Batala.[93] The number of Muslim *qānūngos* had increased during the reign of Aurangzeb. It is difficult to estimate their proportion in the Sikh times, but their existence is beyond any doubt.[94]

The *qānūngo* was indispensable for the revenue administration at the *pargana* or the *ta'alluqa* level. He was the chief source of reliable information relating to area statistics, local revenue rates, revenue receipts, and practices of the *ta'alluqa* or the *pargana*. As a survival from the Mughal times, his office provided probably the strongest link between the old and the new.[95] In the Mughal times, the *qānūngo* was generally paid 2 per cent of the collections made from the area under his jurisdiction. In the Sikh times, he was paid either a certain percentage of the produce or cash at 30 rupees a month.[96] In the *Khālsa Darbār Records*, there are references also to grants of revenue-free land made to *qānūngos*.[97] An order of Maharaja

[91] Ganesh Das, *Chār Bāgh*, 250. The *qānūngoī* of Zafarwal was held by an old *brāhman* family : ibid., 219.

[92] *News (1825)*, 1 & 104.

[93] See, for example, J.S. Grewal, *In the By-Lanes of History*, Documents, I, V, XXIV & XXXIII.

[94] For example, Ganesh Das refers to Ismatullah as one of the *qānūngos* of Gujrat in the time of Gujjar Singh Bhangi: *Chār Bāgh* 176. Murad Ali Kakezai is mentioned as the *qānūngo* of Pasrur in the *Khālsa Darbār Records* : Bundle 5, Vol. XIII, 275. The Documents of the *Bhandārī Collection*, PSA, Patiala, show the existence of several Muslim *qānūngos* in Batala during the Sikh times.

For the continuance of the office of *qānūngo* in Kashmir under the Sikhs see, for example, Mir Ahmad, *Dastūr al-'Amal-i-Kashmir*, Part 2, f 59a.

[95] For a discussion of the functions of the *qānūngo* in the Mughal times, see Irfan Habib, *Agrarian System*, 287-91.

[96] Kohli, 'Land Revenue Administration', *JPHS*, 88.

[97] See, for example, Bundle 5, Vol. XIII, 79, 113, 127 & 247, respectively for Jawahar Mal, the *qānūngo* of Shadiwal, who got 35 *ghumāons*; sons of Ratan Chand, the *qānūngo* of Wainki who got 'wells'; Devi Sahai and Dhanpat Rai, the *qānūngos* of Sanktara, who got 78 *ghumāons*.

Ranjit Singh refers to the customary dues of *qānūngoī* and also to sawāī and one seer per maund of the produce.[98]

Like the *qānūngo*, the *chaudharī* and the *muqaddam* occupied an extremely important position in the machinery of revenue collection. According to one *Dastūr al-'Amal*, whereas in the Mughal times, *chaudharāī* had been generally hereditary, in the Sikh times, preference was given to competent nephews over incompetent sons of a deceased *chaudharī*.[99] Each *pargana* or *ta'alluqa* was divided into a number of *tappas* and in each *tappa* a *chaudharī* was appointed for the purpose of revenue collection.[100] The hereditary heads of *tappas* in the Bannu region were called *maliks* and the term generally used for them in the Peshawar area was *arbāb*.[101] The *muqaddam* on the other hand, was generally appointed for a single village.[102] In fact,

[98] Griffin & Massy, *Chiefs and Families* (*1940*), I, 136. The *rasūm-i-qānūngoī* in Kashmir consisted of about 16 *manwatta* of grain from every *kharwār* : Mir Ahmad, *Dastūr al-'Amal-i-Kashmir*, Part 2, f 57a. See also, 'Diary of P.S. Melvill', *Punjab Government Records* (*1847-1849*), VI, 217.

It may be added that a *manwattā*, according to this officer, was equal to three-fourths of a *kharwār*. According to another account, however, a *manwattā* was equal to about 1½ Lahore seers: Ganeshi Lal, *Siyāhat-i-Kashmir*, 38.

[99] Ghulam Muhammad, *Dastūr al-'Amal*, f 15a.

For the position of the *chaudharī* during the Mughal period, see Irfan Habib, *Agrarian System*, 126-27, 131 n 10, 174, 231, 232, 235, 242, 246 n 23, 252, 254, 255, 259 n 8, 289-90, 291, 292, 293, 294 & 297; Noman Ahmad Siddiqi, *Land Revenue Administration*, 90-91. See also, B.R. Grover, 'Nature of *Dehai-i-Taaluqa* (Zamindari Villages), and the Evolution of the *Taaluqdari* system during the Mughal Age', *IESHR*, II, No. 2, 171-72.

[100] Munshi Bakhtawar Lal, *Tārīkh-i-Montgomery*, 1-2.

[101] See, for example, 'Diary of H.B. Edwardes', *Punjab Government Records* (*1847-1849*), V, 224-25; 'Diary of R.G. Taylor', ibid., (*1846-1849*), IV, 415 & 434 ; Munshi Gopal Das, *Tārīkh-i-Peshawar*, II, 386-89.

[102] It appears that the offices of the *chaudharī* and the *muqaddam* were not necessarily exclusive. Ganesh Das refers to Chaudhari Shah Baz, Chaudhari Wali Dad and Chaudhari Sikandar, each as the *muqaddam* of a village in the Chaj Doab : *Chār Bāgh*, 163, 205 & 208. Another contemporary appears to assume that the terms *chaudharī* and *panch* referred to the same position : William Murray, 'Reports on the Protected Sikh and Hill States (1824)', *Punjab Government Records* (*1807-1857*), I, 234. In any case, the *chaudharī* of a *tappa* could also be the *muqaddam* of his own village.

more than one *muqaddam* (or *lambardār* or *panch*) could be found at places in a single village for each of its major subdivisions generally known as *tarafs* and *pattīs*.[103]

Murray's description of the panch in the Ambala region appears to possess wider validity, though not his assumption that every village had only one *panch* :

> Each village forms a distinct community within itself, and has its *Punch* or *Chowdree* who holds lands in *inam* and being the hereditary head of the place all affairs are referred to him for his advice and decision; he looks jealously to the preservation of the boundaries, settles the sum each *Asamee* has to pay, and may be considered the mutual agent of the cultivator and the Government. In fact the maintenance of good order, the promotion of cultivation and the suppression of crime rests with the *Punch* upon whose virtue, or vice the fair name of the village must stand or fall in the estimation of the neighbours.[104]

Chaudharīs and *muqaddams* were generally given revenue-free lands for the purpose of extending cultivation either directly or through the '*zamīndārs*' of the village. Such grants of revenue-free land were given not only in the time of Ranjit Singh but also earlier by other Sikh rulers.[105] There are frequent references in the early British records to *in'āms* 'formerly held' by *panchas* and *lambardārs*.[106] This is amply confirmed in the *Khālsa Darbār Records*. The *chaudharīs* of Merowal, for example, held revenue-free lands in four villages, and one of these grants had been originally given by the chief

[103] See, for example, *SR Karnal*, 93-94; *SR Lahore*, 66.

[104] 'Reports on the Protected Sikh and Hill States (1824)', *Punjab Government Records (1807-1857)*, I, 234-35.

[105] For example, in '*pargana*' Gurdaspur the Kanhiya Sardars Jai Singh, Gurbakhsh Singh, Fateh Singh and Hakumat Singh, and Nidhan Singh Randhawa had made grants of revenue-free land to *chaudharīs* and *muqaddams* before Ranjit Singh took over : 'Statement of Inam Zamindaris in Purgannah Gurdaspur', *Foreign/Political Consultation*, 5 September 1856, Nos. 109-15.

[106] For example, 'SSR Cis-Satlej', *Foreign/Political Consultation*, 31 December 1847, No. 1829, para 14; No. 1830, para 17; No. 1832, para 5.

named Dal Singh to Jafar Khan of Merowal in 1780.[107] Ranjit Singh confirmed several such grants, for example to Chaudhari Khuda Yar in Jalalpur, Chaudhari Tek Chand Hundal in Hallowal, Chaudhari Qadir Bakhsh Kahlon in Zafarwal, Chaudhari Shadi Khan in Malikpur, Chaudhari Suba Khan in Qila Suba Singh, Chaudhari Ghulam Qadir in Wazirabad and Chaudhari Fattu in Zafarwal.[108] The *in'āms* given to *chaudharīs* and *muqaddams* were not supposed to be collected in excess of the government demand; they were deducted from the revenue so that the claim was upon the government and not upon the peasant proprietors.[109]

Chaudharīs and *muqaddams* generally received certain percentage of the revenues collected. There are references in the *Khālsa Darbār Records* to *pachotra*, or 5 per cent commission, received by the *chaudharīs* and others.[110] A British settlement officer mentions the commission of 50 per cent at places.[111] This may refer to those situations in which the *chaudharīs* and *muqaddams* received *chahāram* or one-fourth from the Sikh rulers. In Hasan Abdal, on the conquest of that area, the Sikhs found that each headman had become virtually the master of his village due to the weakness of the Afghan rule and, in many cases, the Sikhs gave up one-fourth of the government share of the proceeds in order to get the remainder.[112] The

[107] *Khālsa Darbār Records*, Bundle 5, Vol. XIV, 127-36.

[108] Ibid., Vol. XIII, 59, 187, 209, 211, 217 & 219; Vol. XIV, 191; also, Vol. XIII, 231, 243, 287 & 291.

[109] *Foreign/Political Consultation*, 20 August 1852, Nos. 135-36.

[110] *Khālsa Darbār Records*, Bundle 5, Vol. III, 63-64; Bundle 4, Vol. V, 201-02; Bundle 3, Vol. I, 317. The terms used are *wajah-i-in'ām-wā-pachotra*, *in'ām-i-pachotra-i-zamīndārān*, and *in'ām-i-pachotra-wā-mālikāna*, respectively.

[111] G. Campbell to C.F. Mackeson, 'SSR Cis-Satlej', *Foreign/Political Consultation*, 31 December 1847, No. 1832, para 53.

Cf. Satish Chadra, 'Some Aspects of Indian Village Society in Northern India during the 18th century', *Indian Historical Review*, I, No. 1, 57 n 1. According to Satish Chandra, the percentage of *in'ām* allowed to the *zamīndārs* varied from region to region, from 5 to 25 per cent. See also, Irfan Habib, *Agrarian System*, 139-40; Noman Ahmad Siddiqi, *Land Revenue Administration*, 82 .

[112] 'Report on the Inam Zamindaris in the Rawalpindi District', *Foreign/Political Consultation*, 9 January 1857, Nos. 229-30.

headman of Pindi Gheb 'long enjoyed $\frac{1}{4}$ of the revenues on account of his local influence'.[113] This would mean a 'commission' of 25 per cent. In fact there were 'several hundred' of these 'Chaharum Khors', literally, the eaters of *chahāram*, in the Pindi Gheb area alone.[114] The early Birtish settlement officers raised or lowered the rates prevalent in some areas to the uniform rate of 5 per cent which, in any case, was the norm during the Sikh times as well.[115] In some cases, however, the *chaudharīs* and the *muqaddams* used to receive much more indeed. An order of Jai Singh Kanhiya shows that a *chaudharī* named Mian Khan used to enjoy not only 5 per cent commisson and 2 seers per maund and one hundred rupees in cash, but also revenue-free land measuring 160 *ghumāons*.[116]

As old as the *chaudharī* and the *muqaddam* was the *patwārī* whose primary duty was to maintain revenue records for every village under his jurisdiction.[117] During the Sikh times, there was hardly a village which had a *patwārī* entirely for itself. In the Majha, for example, clusters of three to six or eight villages were formed into *tappas* and a single *patwārī*

113 *Foreign/Political Proceedings*, 7 January 1853, No. 228.
The reference here probably is to Malik Alla Yar, the 'principal of the *zamindars* of Pindi Gheb' who received one-fourth of the share of the government from the *tappa* of Sil which comprised nearly half of the Gheba area: 'Diary of J. Nicholson', *Punjab Government Records (1847-1849)*, VI, 312.

114 Loc. cit.

115 *Foreign/Political Consultation*, 31 December 1847, No. 1829, para 14.
It may be pointed out that those who suffered diminution in their commission were generally dissatisfied with the new arrangements which minimized their former importance and advantages.

116 'Statement of Inam Zamindaris in Purgannah Gurdaspur', ibid., 5 September 1856, Nos. 109-15.

117 It is generally believed, probably on the basis of Abul Fazl's reference to the '*patwārī* of each village' that in the Mughal times every village had a *patwārī* to record its expenditure and income: *Ā'īn-i-Akbari*, II, 49. What Abul Fazl implies, however, is that there was no village without a *patwārī*, which leaves the possibility of one *patwārī* keeping the records of more than one village. For the position of the *patwārī* during the Mughal period, see Irfan Habib, *Agrarian System*, 134-35; Noman Ahmad Siddiqi, *Land Revenue Administration*, 19-20.

looked after the records of each of these *tappas*.[118] In Gujranwala, on the average, nearly five villages were covered by a single *patwārī*.[119] According to a contemporary report, 'the patwari keeps the records and attends the Kunneea or appraiser of the fields, noting down the asamee's name and making out the dues from each to government in his Khet Khusrah or field book, which serves as a check to the Tehseeldar's Khusrah and Jammabundee accounts'.[120] The customary remuneration of the *patwārī* ranged from 1 per cent to 2 per cent of the collection made from the villages under his jurisdiction.[121]

In retrospect, it is easy to see that the framework of revenue administration did not undergo any substantial change during the period of Sikh rule. The units of revenue administration remained the same. The province, the *pargana*, the *tappa* and the village are as much in evidence during the Sikh times as in the Mughal. The administrators also were the same. The *nāzim* or the *sūbadār*, the *kārdār* as the counterpart of the Mughal *'āmil*, the *qānūngo*, the *chaudharī*, the *muqaddam* and the *patwārī* provided the machinery of administration now as before. However, the number of primary divisions, and consequently the number of *nazīms*, the number of '*parganas*' and consequently the number of *kārdārs*, increased during the Sikh times. Obviously, the size of these units and the importance of those who administered them decreased. These changes did introduce a difference, but a difference only of degree. It is the continuum, essentially, that is more important than change during this period of a political revolution.

[118] *SR Lahore*, 69. See also, *SR Gujranwala*. There is no need to assume that the word *tappa* was used everywhere for such a group of villages. More probably, a *patwārī* looked after a *tope* during the Sikh times.

[119] *SR Gujranwala*, 49.

[120] William Murray, *Punjab Government Records* (*1807-1857*), I, 235.
For any verification, therefore, not only the papers of the *qānūngo* but also the records of the *patwārī* had to be consulted.

[121] *Cf.* Ghulam Muhammad, *Dastūr al-'Amal*, f 14b. According to this author, a quarter seer in a maund was received by the *patwārī* at some places, and half a seer at others. Where paid in cash, the *haqq-i-khidmat-i-patwārī* was ½ anna in at rupee. According to this statement, the *patwārī's* commission ranged from over ½ to over 3 per cent.

5

Land Revenue

'In revenue matters', according to a contemporary *Dastūr al-'Amal*, 'the Sikh *sardār* looked to his own interest and the inclination of the cultivators'. It goes on to mention *ghalla-bakhshī*, *kankūt* and *zabtī* as the methods of assessment and collection practised in the Sikh dominions at different times and places.[1] In retrospect, we know that, besides *batāī* or *ghalla-bakhshī*, *kankūt* and *zabtī*, and a mixture of two or more of these, assessment during the Sikh times was made also on ploughs and wells. Similar diversity existed in the rate and mode of payment.

Of all the methods of assessment *batāī*, or crop-sharing, was the most important because it was the most prevalent.[2] The

[1] Ghulam Muhammad, *Dastūr al-'Amal*, f 14a.

[2] *Batāī* was prevalent in most of the Jalandhar Doab and the region across the Satlej ; in the Chaj, the Rachna and the Bari Doabs including the Dipalpur and Multan regions; it was in vogue also in the valleys of Kangra and Kashmir : see *SR Ludhiana*, 170; *SR Karnal*, 105; 'SSR Jullundur Doab', *Foreign/Political Proceedings*, 31 December 1847, No. 2443, para 30; 'SSR Chaj, Rachna and Bari Doabs', *Foreign/Secret Consultation*, 28 April 1848, Nos. 61 & 63-65; Munshi Bakhtawar Lal, *Tārīkh-i-Montgomery*, 10-11; Munshi Hukm Chand, *Tārīkh-i-Multan*, 656.

For the prevalence of *batāī* in Kashmir, see 'Diwan Kishan Lal's Account of Kashmir' (Eng. tr.) : *Foreign/Secret Consultation*, 31 March 1848, No. 68. In fact, crop-sharing was the mode of assessment and collection in Kashmir even for the 'cash crops' like tobacco, saffron and cotton and the other '*ujnass-i-keemutee*' : 'Diary of P.S. Melvill', *Punjab Government Records* (*1847-1849*), VI, 191, 197, 217, for example. This was prevalent also in the territories under Diwan Sawan Mal: *Gazetteer of Multan*, 124; *SR Montgomery*, 130. The term used in the Montgomery area was *wandāī*.

phrase '*batāī lutāī*' or *batāī* is plunder represents the viewpoint of the rulers who regarded it as cumbersome and expensive.[3] The government was likely to lose some of its share through misappropriation of a part of the produce by the cultivator. However, *batāī* as the method of assessment was popular with the cultivator because of its equity. He paid a share from the actual produce and had the satisfaction of not being cheated by either the vagaries of weather or the rise or fall of prices.[4]

Kankūt, or appraising the standing crop, was only a little less popular than *batāī* and at places it was more prominent.[5] It brought certain definite advantages to the government without being unfair to the cultivator. It was the actual crop which was estimated and assessed. The cultivator could know from his experience whether or not any proposed appraisal was close to the expected yield. The government, on its part, did not have to watch the heaps of the grain.[6] The *khasra-i-zabt-i-kankūt* was

[3] The system of *batāī* was found 'cumbersome and expensive' by the rulers for a variety of reasons. Chances of misappropriation of a part of the produce by the cultivator or others could not be eliminated till the actual division took place and quite an establishment was required to watch the different heaps of grain on the field. Also, the share of the government had to be either stored in granaries or sold at the current prices.

[4] In fact, no mode offered 'such a show of justice as the Government and its subject dividing the gifts of nature on the spot': William Murray, 'Reports on the Protected Sikh and Hill States (1824)', *Punjab Government Records (1807-1857)*, I, 237. To the majority of the Sikh rulers, who had known the peasant's preference for *batāī*, it could appeal because of its simplicity as well.

[5] *Kankūt* as a method of assessment was prominent all over the upper Sindh Sagar Doab, particularly in Attock and Rawalpindi: *Gazetteer of Rawalpindi*, 109, 110, 111, & 112; 'SSR Upper Sindh Sagar Doab', *Foreign/Secret Consultation*, 28 April 1848, No. 66. In the Chaj and Rachna Doabs as a whole *kankūt* was an important method of assessment: 'SSR Chaj and Rachna Doabs', ibid., Nos. 63-65; *Gazetteer of Sialkot*, 93. In the Dipalpur area, this system was generally followed till Diwan Sawan Mal's time and was prevalent in parts of Multan too: Munshi Bakhtawar Lal, *Tārīkh-i-Montgomery*, 10-11; *SR Montgomery*, 139-40; Munshi Hukm Chand, *Tārīkh-i-Multan*, 656, respectively. It was popular also in the Jalandhar Doab and the region across the Satlej: see, for example, *SR Hoshiarpur*, 126; *SR Karnal*, 105; *SR Ludhiana*, 170.

[6] The description of *kankūt* given by the settlement officers of Montgomery is worth reproducing:

The *kārdār* or sub-farmers appointed accountants (mutsaddi) according

carefully prepared, containing information on the name of the cultivator, description of the crop, dimensions and area of the field and the estimated yield. In the *jama'bandī*, or the rent roll, the total estimated yield and the shares of the state and the cultivator for each crop and the value of the state's share were entered.[7] According to one contemporary estimate, *batāī* and *kankūt* accounted for four-fifths of the land-revenue collected from the territories of the Lahore Darbar in 1847.[8]

However, even in those areas where *batāī* and *kankūt* were prominent, *zabt* remained in existence as a method of assessment. It involved fixed cash rates for unit areas of crops on the basis of periodic measurement.[9] The Sikh chiefs applied this method

to the estimated area under cultivation. Each mutsaddi was accompanied by two measurers who calculated the area of each field by pacing up two sides. These men were known as *kāchhū-kadmī* or *kadam kash.* The mutsaddi prepared a field register in which the fields lying together of each tenant or cultivator were entered as one holding; the produce was then estimated and the amount of grain entered. The calculation of the produce involved a good deal of haggling, and the amount entered was usually the result of a compromise.

C.A. Rao & W.E. Purser, *SR Montgomery*, 139-40. For further detail, see *Gazetteer of Sialkot*, 94.

[7] The village records of Wazirabad under General Avitabile, showing the instalments of revenue paid and other detail, were praised by the early British administrators : 'Diary of R.G. Taylor', *Punjab Government Records (1847-1849)*, VI; 7; also, 21. In Multan, Diwan Sawan Mal instructed the *kārdārs* to ensure that the records of *batāī*, and presumably of *kankūt* also, were kept by three persons : the *muharrir*, the *dabīr* and the *panch* : Munshi Hukm Chand, *Tārīkh-i-Multan*, 472.

[8] Henry Lawrence to H.M. Elliot, *Foreign/Secret Consultation*, 30 October 1847, No. 110. *Cf.* Kohli, 'Land Revenue Administration', *JPHS*, 76-79; Chopra, *Sovereign State*, 78-79.

[9] Except for Kashmir, the units of area generally used for the purpose of measurement were *kanāl*, *bighā* and *ghumāon*. The basic unit of length was *karam* or *karū* (equal to 3 *hāths* or length of hand from the elbow to the tip of the middle finger or about 18 inches and a square *karam* was known as *biswānsī*; 20 *biswānsī* made 1 *biswā* and 20 *biswās* or four *kanāls* made 1 *bigha*. For the *ghumāon*, the smallest unit of area was *sarsaī* or 1 square *karam*. 9 *sarsaīs* made 1 *marla*, 20 *marlas* made a *kanāl* and 8 *kanāls* or 2 *bighas* made 1 *ghumāon* which was nearly equal to 1 English acre : see, for example, Baden Powell, *Land Systems of British*

to superior or perishable crops like cotton, indigo, sugarcane, tobacco, poppy, safflower, chillies, oilseeds, pulses and vegetables. This was 'equally true of the ruler of the Punjab and the pettiest Sikh Chieftains to the south of the Sutlej'.[10] At places, *zabtī* rates were applied also to the excess of staple crops.[11] Mixed assessment prevailed in some places, *batāī* being adopted for the *rabī'*, *kankūt* for the *kharīf* and *zabt* for the 'cash crops'.[12] A slight variation of this arrangement was known as *chukā*.[13]

Whatever the method, there was a large variation in the rates of assessment prevalent in different parts of the Sikh dominions. This variation was caused generally by the condition of the soil, the mode of irrigation and the expense of cultivation. The rate of *batāī* and *kankūt* varied from one-third to one-half for the unirrigated and from one-fourth to one-sixth for the irrigated lands in much of the former Mughal province of Lahore and the territories across the Satlej.[14] In Kashmir,

India, II, 558-59. See also, 'Diary of R.G. Taylor', *Punjab Government Records (1847-1849)*, VI,14-15.

In Kashmir, however, measurement of land was reckoned according, to the 'quantity of seed sown', a '*kharwār*' of land meaning the extent of ground that one *kharwār* of seed would sow : Mir Ahmad, *Dastūr al-'Amal-i-Kashmir*, f 133b. See also, Ganeshi Lal, *Siyāhat-i-Kashmir*, 137. For *kharwār*, see chapter IV, 73 n 46.

[10] Douie, *Punjab Settlement Manual*, 19.

[11] See, for example, *SR Muzaffargarh*, 85; *SR Montgomery*, 140; *Gazetteer of Multan*, 124.

[12] See, for example, 'Reports on the Protected Sikh and Hill States (1824)', *Punjab Government Records (1807-1857)*, I, 236; 'SSR Cis-Satlej', *Foreign/Political Consultation*, 31 December 1847, No. 1829, para 9; No. 1830, para 19; No. 1832, paras 32 and 39.

[13] *Chukā* is clearly defined as 'a settlement of money for the khureef and grain for the Rubbee crop', and that 'the cultivator must pay the whole amount whatever may happen to his crops': 'Diary of R.G. Taylor', *Punjab Government Records (1847-1849)*, VI, 10; also, 3; 'SSR Cis-Satlej', *Foreign/Political Consultation*, 31 December 1847, No. 1829, para 9; *SR Kangra*, 228; *SR Ludhiana*, 170; *SR Karnal*, 105. *Cf.* Hardit Singh Dhillon, 'Taxation System', *Maharaja Ranjit Singh*, 126.

[14] See, for example, 'SSR Chaj, Rachna and Bari Doabs', *Foreign/Secret Consultation*, 28 April 1848, Nos. 61 & 63-65; *Gazetteer of Lahore*, 129; 'SSR Jullundur Doab', *Foreign/Political Proceedings*, 31 December

one-half of the produce was taken in the case of saffron and rice; for wheat, barley and *mūng*, the rates were probably higher.[15] In Muzaffargarh, the rate varied from one-sixth to one-half; in Dera Ghazi Khan, though the usual rate was one-fourth, at places it was as low as one-seventh.[16] The rate of *batāī* and *kankūt* ranged from one-sixth to one-fourth in Multan, Dera Ismail Khan, Bannu and Tank.[17] Indeed, in the territories beyond the Indus 'except the peculiarly rich lands round Peshawar, the government share never exceeded one-third and usually averaged one-fourth to one-fifth and fell even lower down to one-eighth of the crop'.[18]

Rates in the *zabt* system varied not simply for different crops but also for the same crop in different parts of the dominions of Ranjit Singh and his successors. Cotton, for instance, was assessed at one to three rupees per *bigha* in the upper Sindh Sagar Doab, at 1¾ to 2¾ rupees in Jhang and at 1¼ to 3½ rupees per *bigha* in Multan.[19] Similarly, tobacco was assessed at about 2½ to 3¾ rupees a *bigha* in the Jalandhar Doab, at four rupees in Multan, from four to five rupees in Muzaffargarh and at eight rupees a *bigha* in Jhang.[20] The

1847, No. 2443, para 31; 'SSR Cis-Satlej', *Foreign/Political Consultation*, 31 December 1847, No. 1832, para 9; *SR Thanesar*, 32; *SR Karnal*, 10 & 105; *SR Hissar*, 13. At places in the former Mughal province of Lahore, the rates were as low as one-fifth or even one- sixth : see, for example, *SR Jullundur*, 35; Diwan Ram Jas, *Tawārikh-i-Riyāsat-i-Kapurthala*, I, 293.

[15] Ganeshi Lal, *Siyāhat-i-Kashmir*, 37-38. In the region around Bhimbar, however, the rate varied from one-half to one-fourth or even one-fifth : 'Diary of R.G. Taylor', *Punjab Government Records (1847-1849)*, VI, 24 & 26.

[16] *SR Muzaffargarh*, 85; *SR Dera Ghazi Khan*, 80.

[17] *General Report upon the Administration of the Punjab Proper (1849-50 & 1850-51)*, (cited hereafter as *GRAPP (1849-1851)*, 87-91.

[18] Ibid., 82.

[19] Respectively, 'SSR Upper Sindh Sagar Doab', *Foreign/Secret Consultation*, 28 April 1848, No. 66; *SR Jhang*, 114; Munshi Hukm Chand, *Tārīkh-i-Multan*, 656.

[20] Respectively, 'SSR Jullundur Doab', *Foreign/Political Proceedings*, 31 December 1847, No. 2443, para 61; Munshi Hukm Chand, *Tārīkh-i-Multan*, 656; *SR Muzaffargarh*, 85; *SR Jhang*, 114.

rate of assessment on sugarcane likewise ranged from 2½ to 8 rupees per *bigha*.[21]

The rates of assessment on wells varied widely.[22] In Mianwali the dominant rate was *sat-panj-bāra*.[23] In the lower Rachna Doab, however, the rates varied from 20 to 150 rupees per well.[24] Large variation in the rates of assessment on wells was often due to the fact that a single well could be used by several cultivators paying a fixed amount per yoke 'without any reference to the area of land'.[25] The rate of assessment on a yoke of bullocks employed to work a plough also varied widely. For instance, in the upper Rachna Doab, the rates ranged from 5 to 30 rupees per plough.[26] The variations can be explained largely in terms of the differences of soil, facilities of irrigation and even the breed of cattle used.

[21] For example, it was 8 rupees per *bigha* in Wazirabad and 2½ to 5 rupees a *bigha* in the Jalandhar Doab : 'Diary of R.G. Taylor', *Punjab Government Records (1847-1849)*, VI, 10; 'SSR Jullundur Doab', *Foreign/Political Proceedings*, 31 December 1847, No. 2443, para 61, respectively.

[22] Diwan Sawan Mal, for example, levied a fixed cash assessment on wells according to their quality and the circumstances of each locality : Munshi Hukm Chand, *Tārīkh-i-Multan*, 656. When the lessee cultivated more than the usual area attached to one well, the fixed sum was set aside and the whole or part of the crop was bataied : *SR Muzaffargarh*, 84-85. There were nearly 14,000 well estates in Dera Ghazi Khan alone : *SR Dera Ghazi Khan*, 75-76. In fact, individual wells were leased out for a fixed sum in the Bari, Rachna and the Chaj Doabs as well : 'SSR Chaj, Rachna and Bari Doabs', *Foreign/Secret Consultation*, 28 April 1848, Nos. 61 & 63-65. *SR Montgomery*, 140 & 142; *SR Lahore*, 3; 'Diary of J. Nicholson', *Punjab Government Records (1847-1849)*, VI, 304.

[23] *SR Mianwali*, 5. Accordihg to this rate, seven rupees per well were paid for the *rabī'* crop and five rupees for the *kharīf*. See also, Munshi Hukm Chand, *Tārīkh-i- Multan*, 474 & 656.

[24] 'SSR Lower Rachna and Lower Bari Doabs', *Foreign/Secret Consultation*, 28 April 1848, No. 64, paras 9 & 29; ibid., 30 October 1847, Nos. 129-30, para 3.

[25] 'Thus where the land was good and the Persian Wheel was kept going day and night, and required 6 *jogs*, wells paid 90 rupees a year': 'Diary of J. Nicholson', *Punjab Government Records (1847-1849)*, VI, 303.

[26] 'SSR Lower Rachna and Lower Bari Doabs, *Foreign/Secret Consultation*, 28 April 1848, No. 64, paras 9 & 27. In the lower Rachna Doab alone there were about 35,000 ploughs on which fixed but varying ates were charged : ibid., para 3.

On the whole, the rates of assessment in the trans-Indus territories were the lowest. The revenue system pressed lightly on the people of these territories 'owing to the distance from control, the less patient character of population, the insecurity of property, and the scarcity of population'.[27] Due to the scarcity of population and deficiency of rainfall, the rates in the province of Multan were lower than those in the territories formerly covered by the province of Lahore.[28] In the territories between the rivers Satlej and Jamna also, the rates of assessment were on the whole lower.[29] The highest rates prevailed in Kashmir.[30]

In the dominions of the Sikh rulers, collection of revenue was made in both cash and kind.[31] In all those areas where the system of assessment per well or per plough was prevalent, collections were normally made in cash. Similarly, for the superior crops, the cultivators had to pay mostly in cash. Payment in cash for perishable products may also be assumed to have been the norm. The prevalence of *batāī* and *kankūt*, however, would imply the right of the cultivator to pay in kind. The tenacity of the proprietors to cling to grain payments was noticed by the early British settlement officers.[32] The *kārdār* had the choice, therefore, to make the collection in kind or to sell the share of the government to whomsoever he could. There

[27] *GRAPP (1849-1851)*, 81.

[28] Douie, *Punjab Settlement Manual*, 19.

[29] See, for example, 'SSR Cis-Satlej', *Foreign/Political Consultation*, 31 December 1847, No. 1832, para 32; *SR Ludhiana*, 171; *SR Ambala*, 18; *SR Karnal*, 105.

[30] Ganeshi Lal, *Siyāhat-i-Kashmir*, 37-38.

[31] It may be interesting to know that the payment of revenues in kind did not always mean grain payment. The Pathans of Bannu, for example, voluntarily paid in guns and swords, in part payment of revenue, a course which had always been left optional to them : 'Diary of R.G. Taylor', *Punjab Government Records (1847-1849)*, VI, 163.

[32] For example, in the Jalandhar Doab before 1832, and in Kangra, collections were almost universally made in kind, and the people could not be induced to pay the revenues in cash : *Gazetteer of Hoshiarpur*, 130 & 131; 'SSR Jullundur Doab', *Foreign/Political Proceedings*, 31 December 1847, No. 2443, paras 30 & 33. For other areas, see, for example, *Gazetteer of Lahore*, 129; *Gazetteer of Gujrat*, 99; *SR Ludhiana*, 171; *SR Ambala*, 18; *SR Sirsa*, 461; *SR Karnal*, 105.

was a tendency among the *kārdārs* to dispose it off immediately by obliging the cultivators to purchase it.[33] However, grain was stored occasionally to get better prices later and more often to meet the future needs of the government. Commutation of *batāī* and *kankūt* into cash was not uncommon.[34] Occasionally, as in Kashmir and Multan, collection for the same crop was made partly in cash and partly in kind.[35] Revenue in cash was collected in instalments.[36]

[33] In December 1815, the *kārdār* of Sialkot, for example, sought permission to sell 50,000 maunds of grain which he had collected. He was ordered not to sell it for it was needed elsewhere: *Events (1810-1817)*; 257. Likewise, Prince Sher Singh, who held the *ta'alluqa* of Mukerian in *jāgīr*, always collected in kind, and his troops and retainers were fed from the store-houses and granaries of the fort of Mukerian: *Gazetteer of Hoshiarpur*, 131.

[34] The term used for this arrangement in Multan was *naqdī-jinsī*: *Gazetteer of Multan*, 123. According to a standing order of Diwan Sawan Mal, the *kārdār* was to send the schedule of rates (*nirkh-nāma*) of all grains (*ajnās*) duly signed by the *panches* and the *zamīndārs* every season: Munshi Hukm Chand, *Tārīkh-i-Multan*, 471. The rate fixed by the government was generally higher than the market rate, by one rupee a maund in the case of Gujrat, for example: 'Diary of R.G. Taylor', *Punjab Government Records (1847-1849)*, VI, 7. In Kashmir, the government usually sent a person into each *pargana* for the purpose of fixing the price of rice, the generally prevalent rate being Re. 1-6-0 per *kharwār*. However, only a certain percentage of the share of the government which varied from locality to locality was ordinarily commuted into cash: 'Diary of P.S. Melvill', ibid., 203, 206, 213, 215 & 217. See also, Ganeshi Lal, *Siyāhat-i-Kashmir*, 38.

[35] See, for example, Ganeshi Lal, *Siyāhat-i-Kashmir*, 37. In Multan, a *patta* was given for a well, fixing its assessment varying from 12 to 20 rupees in accordance with the area and nature of the crop sown. For example, it would be generally 25 *bighas* of wheat for the *rabī'*, 5 *bighas* of cotton and 15 *bighas* of *jawār* for the *kharīf*. All extra cultivation was charged according to a certain rate per *bigha*: *Gazetteer of Multan*, 124.

[36] According to the instructions issued to the *kārdārs* of Multan by Diwan Sawan Mal, they were expected to send the revenues punctually in six instalments, three each for the *kharīf* and the *rabī'*:

kharīf	—first instalment	:	15 Maghar
,,	—second instalment	:	15 Poh
,,	—third instalment	:	15 Māgh
rabī'	—first instalment	:	15 Jeth
,,	—second instalment	:	15 Hār
,,	—third instalment	:	15 Sāwan

From the methods of assessment prevalent in the Sikh dominions, it may be expected *a priori* that assessment was made both directly on the individual and indirectly on a group of cultivators. *Zabtī* rates were expected to be applied to the fields of each cultivator and *batāī* by its very definition implied actual division of the produce, involving co-sharing with the cultivators. *Kankūt* too presupposed the individual cultivator as the assessee. In actual practice, in numerous cases, collections were made from the actual cultivator as 'each man's burden was the utmost he could bear'.[37] However, individual holdings did not necessarily coincide with wells or ploughs. One single well could cover more than one cultivator [38] and a single cultivator could have more than one plough.[39] Furthermore, actual assessment on an individual holding did

Munshi Hukm Chand, *Tārīkh-i-Multan*, 471. The dates for the payment of instalments for the other territories of the Lahore Darbar appear to be the first rather than the middle of the month as is the case in Multan : *Khālsa Darbār Records*, Bundle 38, Vol. III, 193-94.

[37] W.E. Purser, *SR Jullundur*, 151. Purser further says that 'joint responsibility was not enforced', and 'if any cultivator failed the kardar made arrangements to get his land cultivated by someone else'. Also, in the villages where lands were held in plough-shares, each *asāmī* paid 'his own rent much on the principle of a Ryotwari Settlement': Prinsep, *Origin of the Sikh Power*, 168.

[38] Sometimes, several cultivators used a single well, paying a fixed amount per yoke. Besides, the usual area attached to wells paying a fixed amount of revenue ranged from forty to fifty *bighas* and could cover more than one cultivator : see, for example, *SR Muzaffargarh*, 84-85. According to Henry Lawrence, this area was about 25 acres : *Adventures of an Officer in the Service of Ranjeet Singh*, I, 241 n 1. See also, *SR Lahore*, 42. About twenty *ghumāons* was the maximum area watered by a good well around Lahore.

[39] A plough of land was a 'very variable quantity', the expression being often used to denote a fixed share in a village. However, at some places one 'plough' covered 50 *bighas* of land, at another 100 *bighas* and at still others even 200 *bighas*. The seed sown per plough likewise varied from 10 to 18 and even 25 maunds : Ghulam Muhammad, *Dastūr al-'Amal*, f 15b.

For some other estimates of the approximate area covered by the unit called plough ranging from 10 to 20 or 30 *ghumāons*, see respectively, *Gazetteer af Rawalpindi*, 65; *Gazetteer of Jullundur*, 27; *Gazetteer of Ferozepur*, 56. *Cf.* Hardit Singh Dhillon, 'Taxation System', *Maharaja Ranjit Singh*, 127.

not preclude the possibility of an intermediary collecting the revenue.[40]

Indeed, the practice of farming out a whole village or a group of villages was fairly common in the Sikh dominions. In Kashmir, the upper Kangra valley and the Jalandhar Doab, for instance, the common unit of assessment was the village.[41] The majority of villages in the Panjab were parcelled out into *tarafs* or *pattīs* among *panches*, each of whom was 'answerable for the Sirkar's or Ruler's share'.[42] When a *pattī* or a village was assessed as a whole, the *panch* or the *muqaddam* was expected to work out the internal distribution of the revenue due to the government in consultation with the cultivators.[43]

Ijāra or farming of land revenue, finds frequent mention in contemporary records, chronicles, *akhbārāt* and settlement reports.[44] Only by a careful assessment of the evidence do we

In parts of the Chaj Doab, revenue was levied on the number of ploughs employed by each man: *SR Shahpur*, 103. This practice was known in the Sindh Sagar Doab also: 'Diary of L. Bowring,' *Punjab Government Records (1847-1849)*, VI, 378.

[40] In Dera Ghazi Khan, for example, wells were grouped together for revenue purposes: *SR Dera Ghazi Khan*, 75-76. According to a contemporary estimate, only for one-seventh of the lands under cultivation in the kingdom of Lahore in 1847 did the individuals pay revenue directly to the government: Henry Lawrence to H.M. Elliot, *Foreign/Secret Consultation*, 30 October 1847, No. 110.

[41] Respectively, 'Diary of P.S. Melvill', *Punjab Government Records (1847-1849)*, VI, 205 & 216; *Gazetteer of Kangra*, 220; 'SSR Jullundur Doab', *Foreign/Political Proceedings*, 31 December 1847, No. 2443, para 30; *SR Hoshiarpur*, 126.

[42] Prinsep, *Origin of the Sikh Power*, 168.

[43] See, for example, *SR Lahore*, 90. See also, Muhammad Azim Beg, *Tārīkh-i-Hazara*, II, 717. Mulraj, the *nāzim* of Hazara fixed the lease of every village in his jurisdiction. The *jāgīrdārs* also found it convenient to assess the village rather than the individual cultivator: see, for example, 'Diary of R.G. Taylor', *Punjab Government Records (1847-1849)*, VI, 14.

[44] The term *ijāra* in Sikh times was used for the arrangement by which a certain source of income was placed in the charge of a person on the condition that he would pay a certain stipulated

get a clear picture of the system of *ijāra* in the Sikh dominions.[45] At different levels, the practice was known almost everywhere during the whole period of Sikh rule.[46] However,

sum to the state in return. For instance, Lala Sukh Dayal got the *ijāra* of the *sā'ir*, that is, taxes other than the land revenue, for 13 lakhs of rupees : Amar Nath, *Zafarnāma*, 80. The *sā'irāt* of Kashmir were given in *ijāra* in 1822 : Sohan Lal, *Umdat*, II, 261-62. In 1819, Jawahar Mal was given the *ijāra* of *shāl-dāgh* for 10 lakhs of rupees : Amar Nath, *Zafarnāma*, 132-33; *News (1825)*, 99. The great seal (*muhar-i-kalān*) of the Maharaja remained in *ijāra* for a long time with Lala Devi Das for 1,80,000 rupees till 1818 when it was given to Lala Devi Sahai for 2,25,000 rupees : Sohan Lal, *Umdat*, II, 228. Similarly, the salt mines, customs and even justice were given in *ijāra*: see, for example, *Events (1810-1817)*, 198 & 228; Kahan Singh Balauria, *Tārīkh-i-Rājgān*, 110; Mohan Lal, *Journal of a Tour through the Punjab, etc.*, 23.

[45] A superficial understanding of the evidence led to wrong assumptions on the part of early British administrators. John Lawrence, for example, asked Diwan Dina Nath why 'so many estates were farmed out' in spite of the records of the revenues of nearly the entire dominions in his office : *Foreign/Secret Consultation*, 30 October 1847, No. 95. Obviously, for John Lawrence, farming or the system of *ijāra* and the maintenance of revenue records were incompatible, in fact, almost mutually exclusive. Similarly, Henry Lawrence appears to assume that *ijāra* and *batāī* and *kankūt* were mutually exclusive : ibid., 110. Furthermore, according to Griffin, the revenue system of Ranjit Singh was an organized system of pillage, for 'the country was farmed to contractors who were bound to pay a certain sum into the State treasury, and were permitted to collect as much more as possible for themselves' : *Rajas of the Punjab*, ix. See also, Douie, *Punjab Settlement Manual*, 19.

[46] Occasional under-leasing of a few villages here and there appears to have been prevalent throughout the period of Sikh rule, particularly in the newly conquered areas. On the conquest of a new territory, the amount of *ijāra* was fixed either on a rough estimate of the revenues or on the basis of revenue-records, if available. This arrangement was likely to be temporary, the amount of *ijāra* to be revised later on. On the annexation of Peshawar, for example, Prince Naunihal Singh was offered its *ijāra* for 12 lakhs of rupees. But later, on the collection of detailed information 'on the revenue of every village', it was reduced to about 8 lakhs of rupees : Sohan Lal, *Umdat*, III, (ii), 228 & (iv), 445. In comparatively difficult tracts, villages were farmed to the locally influential middlemen whom the conqueror wished to conciliate: see, for example, *Gazetteer of Rawalpindi*, 110, 111 & 112; *Gazetteer of Sialkot*, 93; *SR Shahpur*, 56; *Gazetteer of Kangra*, 220; *Gazetteer of Jhang*, 142.

in a given area, *ijāra* could alternate with direct collection.[47] The proportion of revenue collected through *ijāra* appears to have been considerable. In 1847, even in the Panjab plains between the Beas and the Indus, one-fifth of the total revenue was collected through *ijāradārs*.[48] The *ijāradār* always undertook to pay a certain stipulated sum to the government before he was authorized to collect revenues due to the government from a given area, whether a single village or a whole province, a group of villages or a group of *ta'alluqas*.[49]

Only in exceptional situations was the *ijāradār* allowed to treat the cultivators as he liked :

> Where the country was too poor, the people too warlike, and the collections, too uncertain for the Government officials to engage in detail for the revenue, whole districts were farmed out to contractors who were authoritatively empowered to make their own terms with the people, only making good a fixed tribute to the Government.[50]

Ordinarily, however, the *ijāradār* was allowed to collect

[47] See, for example, *Gazetteer of Rawalpindi*, 110 & 111; *Gazetteer of Sialkot*, 94; *SR Gujranwala (1889-1894)*, 10; *Gazetteer of Gujrat*, 70. Munshi Gopal Das, *Tārīkh-i-Peshawar*, II, 389.

[48] According to the figures furnished by Diwan Dina Nath in 1847, the revenues collected through all kinds of *ijāra* were only a little less than one-third in the kingdom of Lahore, without Kashmir, Multan, Kangra and the Jalandhar Doab : *GRAPP (1849-1851)*, 83.

[49] *Ijāra* of the revenues of the entire province of Kashmir, for example, was held by its *nāzims*, Diwan Chuni Lal and Diwan Kirpa Ram : Amar Nath, *Zafarnāma*, 162-63 & 176. Dera Ghazi Khan and some *ta'alluqas* of Multan were at one time given to Nawab Sadiq Khan of Bahawalpur : ibid., 135. The '*ilāqa*' of Shujabad was the first independent charge of Diwan Sawan Mal as *ijāradār*: Munshi Hukm Chand, *Tārīkh-i-Multan*, 471. At places, a group of few villages or even *tappas* were given in *ijāra* : see, for example, Munshi Gopal Das, *Tarīkh-i-Peshawar*, II, 386-89. The *ijāra* of single villages when 'the headman of each village was furnished with a patent (patta)' is particularly associated with Misar Rup Lal's administration of the Jalandhar Doab : J.A.L. Montgomery, *SR Hoshiarpur*, 127. It may also be mentioned that a single well or a group of wells too were given in *ijāra*, particularly in the lower Sindh Sagar, lower Rachna and lower Bari Doabs : see 96 n 38 & 97 n 40.

[50] *GRAPP (1849-1851)*, 82.

revenues according to the rates of assessment fixed by the government, though he could adopt any method of assessment acceptable to the cultivators.[51] He was not allowed to interfere with any concessions given by the government to any grantees.[52]

The Sikh *ijāradār* was no mere contractor. The amount of *ijāra* was generally close to the revenues due to the government, the margin enabling the *ijāradār* to meet the expense of collection and to save something as a profit.[53] The *mushakhasa* or the assessed amount was generally based on records of collections made in the past.[54] The amount of *ijāra* increased

[51] The *ijāradār* was expected not to exceed the rates of assessment prevalent in his charge. Henry Lawrence states the norm in very clear terms : the share of the government on the average being two-fifths of the produce, the *ijāradar* was expected to realize the amount of *ijāra*, including his own profits 'without collecting more than two-fifths of the produce: *Adventures of an Officer in the Service of Ranjeet Singh*, I, 50-51. However, for realizing revenues from the cultivators, he could resort to 'kankut, batai, chikota or lump payments, in kind or cash, changing one mode for another' as he found it to his advantage: M.F.O'Dwyer, *SR Gujranwala (1889-1894)*, 10. But as it may be expected *a priori*, *batāi* or *kankūt* or any other method of assessment and collection could exist under the *ijāra* system. *Cf*. Kohli, 'Land Revenue Administration', *JPHS*, 76-79; Chopra, *Sovereign State*, 78-79.

[52] For instance, Abdus Samad Khan was given Leiah and Mankera in *ijāra* for 3,52,000 rupees, excluding the lands granted in *dharmarth* : Sohan Lal, *Umdat*, II, 394. In fact, the *ijāra* documents relating to a *ta'alluqa* or a smaller area generally mentioned the *dharmarth* grantees by name: see, for example, *Khālsa Darbār Records*, Bundle 3, Vol. II, 185.

[53] Sohan Lal occasionally equates the amount of *ijāra* with land-revenue or *mu'āmala* : see, for example, *Umdat*, II, 355 & 356. To cite a typical instance, in the case of Hajipur, Diwan Bhawani Das submitted in 1825 that the annual *jama'* in the papers of the *kārdārs* amounted to 33,000 rupees. The Maharaja expressed his surprise at this fall in revenues from 60,000 rupees. In spite of the *kārdār's* request for fixing the *ijāra* at 33,000 rupees the Maharaja fixed it at 45,000 : *News (1825)*, 135-36.

[54] An essential clue to the nature of *ijāra* during the Sikh times is to be found in the term *mushakhasa* or fixation of the revenue payable in advance. We may be sure that the *mushakhasa* was generally

with the increase in revenues from a given area.[55] The *ijāradār* was expected to submit a detailed statement of produce and collection; he was expected to keep the cultivators content and to extend cultivation. He gave an appropriate deed of acceptance to the government, like the following given by Raja Gulab Singh in 1835 :

> I, Raja Gulab Singh, an old servant of the exalted *sarkār*, do at this time, commit to writing and solemnly affirm that whereas the *ta'alluqas* detailed below have been bestowed upon this humble servant for the net amount of seven lakhs and three thousand Nanak Shāhī rupees of the Amritsar mint with effect from the *kharīf* crop of Sammat 1892 (A.D. 1835), this humble servant shall render the

based on verification of the expected revenues for a given territory. For example, General Ventura and Diwan Sawan Mal were ordered to prepare 'correct' reports on the revenues respectively of Dera Ghazi Khan and Jhang before these territories were given in *ijāra*: Sohan Lal, *Umdat*, III, (i), 23 & (ii), 233. See also, *Khālsa Darbār Records*, Bundle 23, Vol. III, 115; *News (1825)*, 43; 'Diary of L. Bowring', *Punjab Government Records (1847-1849)*, IV, 406, 408-09; 'Dairy of A. Cocks', ibid., 444.

In fact, the correct information of the past collections was the foundation on which the successful working of the *mushakhasa* system was based. John Lawrence testifies to the 'close approximation to accuracy' in the revenue returns furnished by the *kārdārs* in 1846 : *Foreign/Secret Consultation*, 26 December 1846, Nos. 1325-27. *Cf.* Kohli, 'Land Revenue Administration', *JPHS*, 78.

[55] If the amount of *ijāra* for a particular territory increased with the passage of time it was largely because of the extension of cultivation and good management. For instance, Diwan Sawan Mal held the *ijāra* of Shujabad and after two years the revenues of this *'ilāqa* increased by fifty per cent, and consequently, the Maharaja gave him Multan also in *ijāra* : Munshi Hukm Chand, *Tārīkh-i-Multan*, 471. This is not to suggest, however, that the amount of *ijāra* necessarily increased with time. In the case of Qila Sobha Singh and Zafarwal in 1827, for example, the Maharaja reduced the amount of *ijāra* from 1,07,000 rupees to 97,000 on a request made by Sardar Jawala Singh, the *ijāradār* : Sohan Lal, *Umdat*, II, 356. As the *ijāradār* was required to report on 'any increase or decrease in the revenues' and also to extend cultivation, it is understandable that the amount of *mushakhasa* occasionally decreased but generally increased with the passage of time.

services assigned to him with honesty, loyalty and diligence. The collected revenues shall be sent to His Majesty.... No produce from the land, not even a *dām's* worth, shall be kept concealed. Whatever the increase or decrease in the revenues of the territory bestowed upon me shall be submitted to His Majesty. I shall keep the people content and the country under cultivation.[56]

The majority of the *ijāradārs* were connected with government and administration in one way or another : Diwan Devi Das, Bhayya Ram Singh, Faqir Nuruddin, Prince Naunihal Singh, Raja Bhupinder Pal of Basohli, Raja Dhian Singh, Raja Fazl Dad Khan, Diwan Sawan Mal, Sham Singh Peshawaria, Sardar Desa Singh Majithia, Sardar Jawand Singh Maukal, for instance.[57] Far from giving lands in *ijāra* to speculators, Ranjit Singh chose his *ijāradārs* rather carefully.[58] His objective

[56] For a transcription of the original deed, see Kohli, 'Land Revenue Administration', *JPHS*, 82. For some other references to the written undertaking for *ijāra* to be given by Prince Naunihal Singh, Sardar Hari Singh Nalwa, General Ventura, and by the *zamīndārs* of the *ta'alluqa* of Fateh Ke, see Sohan Lal, *Umdat* III (i), 104 & 131; (ii), 202 & 228.

[57] See, for example, ibid., II, 202, 205, 263 & 380; III, (i), 4, 28, 44 & 76; (ii), 162, 182 & 228; V, 38. See also, Amar Nath, *Zafarnāma*, 135, 162-63, 168, 176 & 190; Aliuddin, *'Ibratnāma*, 373 & 374-75; *News (1825)*, 209.

Of the *ijāradārs* otherwise unconnected with the administration of Ranjit Singh, Ramanand, the *sāhukār* of Amritsar, presents the most conspicuous example. He had served Ranjit Singh from the time of the occupation of Amritsar and he was allowed to hold some of the *khālisa* land in *ijāra* till his death in the early 1820s : Amar Nath, *Zafarnāma*, 140 & 159. See also, *Events (1810-1817)*, 280. According to an entry dated 10 June 1822 (the only one of this year in this Collection), Ramanand was to submit accounts regarding the revenues from the territory of Sada Kaur.

[58] Ranjit Singh generally preferred to give *ijāra* to men who were connected with administration and if even then it did not work to his satisfaction, he was quick to change the *ijāradār*. The appointment of Bir Dhar Pandit who had acted as the Diwan of Kashmir under the Afghans, as the *ijāradār* of Kashmir, and his subsequent removal, is a case in point : Ahmad Shah, *Tārikh*, 123 & 478. See also, Sohan Lal, *Umdat*, II, 277. Ranjit Singh was generally not guided by any personal considerations and looked to the suitability of the persons who were

was to maximize the revenues without much extra expense.[59]

Ranjit Singh listened to the complaints of the *zamīndārs* against the *ijāradārs* and of the *ijāradārs* against the *zamīndārs*.[60] The defaulting *ijāradārs* were sometimes punished. They were never allowed to withhold any sums from the *mushakhasa*.[61] In 1818, Bhayya Ram Singh was subjected to investigation (*bāz-khwāst*) because as the *ijāradār* of the newly annexed Ramgarhia territories, he had failed to submit the *mushakhasa* in full.[62] Henry Lawrence observed that if the *ijāradār* failed in realizing the sum specified by the government :

> He is imprisoned with more or less severity, degraded, cast off, or forgiven, and allowed another chance in another quarter, with the balance written against his name, according to his interest at court, the opinion of his ability, or the cause of the defalcation.[63]

given lands in *ijāra*. For example, the offer of 3 lakhs of rupees a month made by Raja Gulab Singh and Raja Dhian Singh in 1838 for some of the territories of Diwan Sawan Mal was not accepted by the Maharaja. However, Diwan Sawan Mal was asked to pay 3 lakhs of rupees a month and he did that : Munshi Hukm Chand, *Tārīkh-i-Multan*, 471. Diwan Dhanpat Rai's request for the *ijāra* of the *ta'alluqa* of Eminabad was also refused by the Maharaja : *News (1825)*, 535. On the other hand, the Maharaja was keen to give some territory in *ijāra* to Pir Bakhsh Khan and when he refused, he was thrown into prison : ibid., 257.

[59] Fixation of the *mushakhasa* on the basis of the past collections, and the *ijāradār* making his own arrangements for the assessment and collection of revenues, was certainly economical from the viewpoint of the rulers who could be more sure of getting its revenues at a somewhat less expense. The *ijāradār* was also to extend cultivation and report all increase in revenues. Moreover, giving *ijāra* to the locally influential men, particularly in the outlying and difficult areas, had the additional political advantage of conciliating a turbulent people.

[60] See, for example, *News (1825)*, 385; Sohan Lal, *Umdat* III, (ii), 139.

[61] See, for example, 'Diary of G. Lawrence', *Punjab Government Records (1846-1849)*, IV, 329. The *ijāradārs* of a hundred villages in Peshawar, yielding 2,50,000 rupees, had been held for a default of 30,000 rupee s.

[62] Sohan Lal, *Umdat*, II, 242. After much discussion of the matter Ram Singh was to pay 10,000 rupees out of 40,000 due from him, while the rest was tobe recovered from his associates (*rafīqān*).

[63] *Adventures of an Officer in the Service of Ranjeet Singh*, I, 51. It may

An average *ijāradār* would naturally be anxious to collect the sum payable to the government irrespective of the well-being of the cultivator.[64]

It was observed by a contemporary that many respectable persons in the dominions of Maharaja Ranjit Singh and Maharaja Karam Singh of Patiala were ruined because of the farming system. They took lands in *ijāra*, defaulted and were disgraced. Nevertheless, 'where the heads of villages proposed to take their lands on a short lease' much advantage was expected; the peasant forwarded the cultivation 'for his individual benefit', and the government could receive 'a fair revenue direct from the zumeendar, with amelioration to its subject, and just equivalent to itself'.[65] In 1847, in the territories of Lahore, the heads of villages collected a little over two-thirds of the revenues collected through *ijāradārs*.[66]

Land under regular cultivation was not the only source of

be pointed out that among other things, the stability of market prices of grain and other agricultural produce was a necessary condition for the successful working of the *mushakhasa* system.

[64] However, the interest of the Maharaja in the well-being of his subjects, his alacrity to take action and his extremely efficient system of intelligence generally curbed this natural tendency. Apart from the celebrated names like Diwan Sawan Mal and Misar Rup Lal, there were *ijāradārs* at the lower levels also who were known for their good management and concern for the people. Diwan Hukma Singh, the *mustajjir* of Lahore, for instance, was regarded 'a well-wisher of the people': Sohan Lal, *Umdat*, II, 196. Pir Bakhsh Qureshi, the *ijāradār* of Mangowal in the Chaj Doab, was 'popular with the zemindars': L. Bowring, 'SSR Chaj Doab', *Foreign/Secret Consultation*, 28 April 1848, No. 65. The *kārdār* of Chhachh had adopted the *mushakhasa* system in 1833, 'apparently with general success': J. Nicholson, 'SSR Upper Sindh Sagar Doab', ibid., No. 66.

[65] William Murray, 'Reports on the Protected Sikh and Hill States (1824)', *Punjab Government Records (1807-1857)*, I, 237-38.

[66] These figures were furnished to the Board of Administration by Diwan Dina Nath, 'Chancellor of the Lahore Exchequer': *GRAPP (1849-1851)*, 83.

revenue in the Sikh dominions. The most important sources of revenue in this respect were mango orchards in the Jalandhar Doab, date trees in the province of Multan, and *singhāra* or water chestnut in Kashmir. Some of the *ta'alluqas* in Hoshiarpur were particularly famous for the abundance of orchards and a considerable amount of revenue was collected by the Sikh rulers 'from this separate source'.[67] The amount of revenue from date trees increased in Multan particularly under Diwan Sawan Mal.[68] From the *mahal-i-singhāra* in Kashmir, consisting of

[67] *Foreign/Political Consultation*, 31 December 1847, No. 2378, para 1. Such orchards initially had come down from the Mughal times but the Sikh rulers also encouraged the laying out of orchards and 'there seems to have been a general passion among all who had saved money to plant gardens in or about their native villages': ibid., paras 2 & 4. In fact, Ganesh Das gives long lists of gardens laid out by influential persons in the Panjab. It may be interesting to note that in and outside the city of Lahore alone there were more than forty gardens associated with well-known personages at the court of Ranjit Singh : *Chār Bāgh*, 277-78. Kashmir too did not lose its traditional fame for orchards : Mir Ahmad, *Dastūr al-'Amal-i-Kashmir*, ff 83b-84a.

A certain proportion of land used for orchards was made revenue-free. Sometimes orchards belonging to the rulers were given in *jāgīr* : see, for example, Grewal, *In the By-Lanes of History*, Document XXXVI. See also, 'Statement of the Principal Jagirdars of the Lahore Durbar', *Foreign/Political Consultation*, 29 December 1849, No. 49 A.

[68] Date trees were in abundance particularly in the '*parganas*' of Tulamba, Sarai Sidhu, Lodhran, Mailsi and Shujabad in Multan : Munshi Hukm Chand, *Tārīkh-i-Multan*, 698. In *mauza'* Fatehpur alone there were more than a lakh of date trees : ibid., 694.

The proprietors of land were generally the owners of the trees, but not in all the villages. When the Sikh rulers asked the proprietors to take the contract and the latter refused, outsiders were brought in as contractors and some of them eventually became *māliks* of the trees. Diwan Sawan Mal used to auction trees to contractors and if they happened to be outsiders, the proprietors were given one-eighth to one-fourth of the income : ibid., 697.

Date trees were a source of income to the government in other areas also. Of all the trees in Muzaffargarh, the 'largest revenue was derived from the date trees': Edward O'Brien, *SR Muzaffargarh*, 88. They brought revenue also in the lower Chaj Doab, around Sahiwal and Shahpur : 'Diary of L. Bowring', *Punjab Government Records (1847-1849)*, VI, 414.

villages on the lake-side, the government collected three-fourths of the total produce, commuting a part of it into cash.[69]

Pasture lands formed yet another source of revenue.[70] Grazing tax, known as *tirnī* was collected in Dera Ismail Khan, and from the lower Sindh Sagar, Chaj, lower Rachna and lower Bari Doabs.[71] In fact, grazing tax was a common incidence in the plains as well as the hills.[72] Although, income per unit area

[69] *Singhāra*, an edible water root which was found in great quantities in the Wular Lake was an article of considerable consumption. It was of two descriptions: the '*sabzjinsee*' collected in May and the '*komaie*' collected during November-May. Each 'zumeendar' on the lake-side was bound to collect 100 *kharwārs* of *singhāra* annually as the share of the government which sometimes amounted to a lakh of *kharwārs*: 'Diary of R.G. Taylor', *Punjab Government Records (1847-1849*), VI, 96. See also, Diary of P.S. Melvill,' ibid., 221; Mir Ahmad, *Dastūr al-'Amal-i-Kashmir*, ff 80b-81a.

[70] Although *gāo-shumārī* or census of the cattle and *kāh-charāī* or grazing tax, were both known in the Mughal times, it was Sawan Mal under Maharaja Ranjit Singh, who developed *tirnī* as an important source of income to the state. *Cf.* G.W. Hamilton, 'On the Tirnee Tax of Jhung, *Selections PCPA*, I, No. 9, 103.

Diwan Sawan Mal first took one goat and one camel from every herd, but after the census of cattle, fixed the following annual rates in cash :

camel (female)	:	Rs. 2-0-0
camel (male)	:	Re. 1-0-0
buffaloe	:	Re. 1-0-0
cow	:	As. 0-6-0

Ibid., 104. For every goat and sheep one anna was the rate. Concession was given to cows and to the cattle coming for grazing from Bahawalpur. Also, villages on the bank of the Satlej did not pay any *tirnī* if the animals grazed in the lands belonging to the villages themselves. *Tirnī* was paid only by the rich owners of cattle who used to graze them in the jungle: Munshi Hukm Chand, *Tārīkh-i-Multan*, 712.

[71] 'SSR Lower Sindh Sagar, Lower Rachna and Bari Doabs', *Foreign/Secret Consultation*, 28 April 1848, Nos. 64-65; *Gazetteer of Gujrat* 102; Diary of H.B. Edwardes', *Punjab Government Records (1847-1849*), V, 197; 'Diary of L. Bowring', ibid., VI, 406 & 409; 'Diary of A Cocks', ibid., 435-36. See also, Munshi Hukm Chand, *Tārīkh-i-Multan*, 712; *Khālsa Darbār Records*, Bundle 3, Vol. IV, 03-15.

[72] For example, the spontaneous jungle products in the Kangra hills, such as grass, herbs and trees, were treated as a distinct source of

from pasture lands was much smaller than the income from land under cultivation, nevertheless the amount of grazing tax collected from different areas in itself was fairly considerable. The wandering tribes on the banks of the Chenab, for example, paid 50,000 rupees a year as *tirnī* on 20,000 buffaloes, 10,000 cows, 10,000 sheep and 4,000 camels.[73] In Mitha Tiwana, the proportion of *tirnī* amounted to a fourth of the total revenues, and the single town of Nurpur yielded 7,000 rupees by way of grazing tax on camels and cows.[74]

The burden of the cesses or *abwāb* traditionally levied from the cultivators by government officials or intermediaries was perhaps neither increased nor much reduced by the Sikh rulers. The 'percentages' of *qānūngos*, *chaudharīs*, *muqaddams* and *patwārīs* were generally deducted from the share of the government, but not always. In the upper Bari Doab, for instance, the cultivators contributed towards the *in'ām* of the headmen in some villages.[75] The perquisites of the *munshīs* and *mutasaddīs* connected with the canals, having grown into a virtual rule, were considered 'as a part of their salary'.[76] In Kashmir, additional levies were made on account of the expense of collection and the fees of the *kārdār*, the *qānūngo*

income and were grouped under the name of '*banwazeree*', 'which as the name implies, was the control exercised by the state directly or by the agency of farmers over the wastes and forests of the district': G.C. Barnes, Deputy Commissioner, Kangra, to John Lawrence, *Foreign/Political Proceedings*, 31 December 1847, 2393, para 2. The items and amounts of the '*banwazeree*' differed greatly in different *ta'alluqas*.

In Kashmir, the grazing tax on sheep ranged between seven and eight rupees per hundred and that on cows was generally eight annas a head: 'Diary of P.S. Melvill', *Punjab Government Records (1847-1849)*, VI, 206, 215, 216, 217, for example. *Cf.* Mir Ahmad, *Dastūr al-'Amal-i-Kashmir*, f 84a.

[73] *Foreign/Secret Proceedings*, 18 November 1845, No. 17.

[74] 'SSR Lower Sindh Sagar Doab', *Foreign/Secret Consultatian*, 28 April 1848, No. 65. *Tirnī* was a source of considerable income in the *bārs* or uplands of the Panjab where people mainly depended on cattle: see, for example, *Gazetteer of Gujrat*, 102.

[75] 'SSR Upper Bari Doab', *Foreign/Secret Consultation*, 28 April 1848, No. 61, para 7.

[76] R. Napier, 'Report on the Shah Nehr or Husli Canal', ibid., No. 62.

and others.[77] The number and incidence of *abwāb* varied from place to place. Some of them were introduced by the local authorities 'to bewilder the government as well as the people'.[78] The incidence of *abwāb* at places was inversely related to the rates of assessment : 'where the rate of the government share was high, cesses were few; where the rate was low, cesses were many'.[79]

One of the most important cesses of the Sikh times was *nazr* or *nazrāna* for the *kārdārs*, the *daftarīs* and the like.[80] Some of the other cesses were *jama'bandī*, for the preparation of the rent roll; *nazr-i-muharrir*, to start weighing; *muhāsilī*, for the field watchman; *bhāra*, for carriage hire; *khurāk*, towards feeding the measurers; *chilkāna*, to make up the difference between the standard and other rupees; *sarrāfī*, for testing the money paid as revenue; *nazr-i-muqaddamī*, for good harvests; *shukrāna*, for rise in prices after commutation; compensation for *bhūsā* not taken in kind; a fixed amount per plough for not sowing *zabtī* crops, money commutation for fodder, *begār*, and for a skin, a blanket and a pair of shoes; and *nazr-i-kanjan*, a cess on each *kāmil* well of eight yokes.[81] This list is by no means an exhaustive one. Nor were all these

[77] 'Diary of P.S. Melvill, '*Punjab Government Records* (*1847-1849*), VI, 204-07, 213, 215, 216 & 217. The incidence of the *abwāb* or *kharch* in Kashmir varied from locality to locality. However, it generally ranged from 2 *traks* to 6 *traks* in a *kharwār*, sometimes leaving the cultivators only a little more than one-third of the total produce : 'Diary of R.G. Taylor', ibid., 80.

[78] A. Cocks, 'SSR Lower Rachna Doab', *Foreign/Secret Consultation*, 28 April 1848, No. 64, para 4.

[79] Edward O'Brien, *SR Muzaffargarh*, 84. Brien is saying this with reference to Diwan Sawan Mal's administration in Muzaffargarh but this was equally true of the other areas under the Diwan.

[80] *Khālsa Darbār Records*, Bundle 3, Vol. IV, 31, 53 & 55 ; Munshi Hukm Chand, *Tārīkh-i-Multan*, 656. The rate of *nazrāna* for the *kārdārs* in Chhachh for example, was four rupees, and for other *mutasaddīs*, two rupees : 'SSR Upper Sindh Sagar Doab', *Foreign/Secret Consultation*, 28 April 1848, No. 66.

[81] For comprehensive lists of these cesses see, for example, *Gazetteer of Multan*, 124-25; *Gazetteer of Gujranwala*, 71; *SR Thanesar*, 32-33, 171. See also, Mir Ahmad, *Dastūr al-'Amal-i-Kashmir*, Part 2, f 59a; Munshi Gopal Das, *Tārīkh-i-Peshawar*, II, 387; *SR Ludhiana*, 171.

cesses levied at a single place.[82] Where the produce from land was actually *batāied*, the equivalent of extra cesses was taken out before the produce was divided between the cultivator and the government.[83] Collected in cash or grain, on the whole, these extra charges amounted to only 'a moderate percentage of the revenue', generally not exceeding ten per cent.[84]

The cultivator paid certain quantities of grain from his own share to individuals performing different services for him in the village.[85] The most important of these were the carpenter and the ironsmith. The *chamār* or the saddler used to get as much as the carpenter or the ironsmith in some villages.[86] Some of the others mentioned are the musicians (*mutrib* and *rabābī*), the *faqīrs* of the village *takia*, the *mullas* of the mosque and the *sādhs* of the *dharmsāla*.[87] Thus, on the whole, the cultivator paid on three accounts : the stipulated share of the government, extra cesses to officials and

[82] In the *Khālsa Darbār Records*, the longest list of cesses for one *ta'alluqā* is as follows : *sar-i-dehī*, *sar-i-chāhī*, *muttasaddīana*, *faslāna*, *nazrāna*, *kārdārī*, *chobdār-i-kotwālī*, *langar*, *kirāya*, *mu'āfī-i-chāt*, *thānadārī*, *dharat*, *muhrāna* and *chautara* : Bundle 2, Vol. VI, 59-60.

[83] In Multan, for instance, grain was taken out on account of *zamīndārī*, *dabīrī*, *muhāsilāna*, '*amlāna*, etc., before the heap was divided : Munshi Hukm Chand, *Tārīkh-i-Multan*, 656.

[84] C.F. Mackeson, 'SSR Cis-Satlej', *Foreign/Political Consultation*, 31 December 1847, No. 1832, para 32. In the Jalandhar Doab, these additional demands even in the 1840s amounted to about 7 per cent of the total revenues from land : Vansittart to John Lawrence, ibid., No. 2444, para 5. In Chhachh, all the *rasūm* or cesses other than the *nazrāna* amounted to 4½ per cent of the revenues : 'SSR Upper Sindh Sagar Doab', *Foreign/Secret Consultation*, 28 April 1848, No. 66. In Kot Kamalia, Satghara, Dipalpur, Haveli, Hujra, Qabula and Jhang, about 60,000 rupees were collected as extra cesses, forming about 8 per cent of the total revenues : 'SSR Lower Rachna and Bari Doabs', ibid., No. 64, para 2.

[85] It may be pointed out that the cultivators paid about 5 per cent of the grains as *sep* or *lāg* to these village servants. It was called *haqūq-i-kamiāna* : *SR Lahore*, 61; *Gazetteer of Sialkot*, 57; *Gazetteer of Shahpur*, 56; *Gazetteer of Jullundur*, 39; *Gazetteer of Montgomery*, 80.

[86] Ghulam Muhammad, *Dastūr al-'Amal*, f 15a. The potter was also an important village servant.

[87] Loc. cit. The *sayyid* and the *mirāsī* may also be included in this list. It is probable that they were paid before the division of the *dherī* : see, for example, Munshi Hukm Chand, *Tārīkh-i-Multan*, 637.

intermediaries, and payment for services rendered by professional individuals in the village.

From the evidence available for the Sikh times, it appears that after paying what was due to the government and the village professionals and what was exacted from him by the officials and the intermediaries, an average cultivator was able to keep nearly half of the produce for himself.[88] The incidence of *abwāb* ranged from 5 per cent to 10 per cent of the revenue,[89] and the rate of revenue ranged from 33 per cent to 40 per cent on the average.[90] Thus, the cultivator normally parted with less than half of his produce.

The Sikh rulers were anxious to increase cultivated area by bringing more and more waste or pasture lands under

[88] However, this does not seem to be true in the case of Kashmir under Sikh rule: see, for example, 'Diary of R.G. Taylor', *Punjab Government Records (1847-1849)*, VI, 80; 'Diwan Kishan Lal's Account of Kashmir', *Foreign/Secret Proceedings*, 31 March 1848, No. 68. However, it may not be without interest to note that in Kashmir under Akbar, in spite of the imperial regulations, more than two-thirds of the produce was being collected at times: see, for example, Irfan Habib, *Agrarian System*, 224. There is little information about the intervening period but there is also no reason to believe that any appreciable reduction in the share of the government had been introduced by the Afghan rulers of Kashmir. In fact, some of the *abwāb* or *kharch* in Kashmir appear to be a legacy of the intervening Afghan rule: Kirpa Ram, *Gulzār-i-Kashmir*, 256-57.

[89] *Cf.* Kohli, 'Land Revenue Administration', *JPHS*, 84; Hardit Singh Dhillon, 'Taxation System', *Maharaja Ranjit Singh*, 136.

[90] This at any rate appears to be the norm. Even one-half share of the government was equivalent to about 40 per cent of the gross produce: see, for example, Henry Lawrence, *Adventures of an Officer in the Service of Ranjeet Singh*, I, 50. The demand, though 'not excessively low', was based on the principle of nowhere raising the assessment nor (generally) depriving any one of anything which he has heretofore enjoyed': G. Campbell, 'SSR Cis-Satlej', *Foreign/Political Consultation*, 31 December 1847, No. 1832, para 44. Further, the 'Sikh demand was full but that it was not excessive is proved by the fact that it was realised without force . . . and that the country flourished': C.F. Mackeson, ibid., para 42. This was true of nearly the whole of the core dominions of Ranjit Singh. In any case, when the early British administrators talk of excessive demands and oppression, they talk generally of the 1840s and not of the reign of Ranjit Singh.

cultivation.[91] During the reign of Ranjit Singh, as during the Mughal times, lenient rates of assessment were imposed on wasteland brought under cultivation.[92] Revenues from land were granted to those who promoted the extension of agriculture.[93] The peasant proprietors, who had run away from their villages during the period of political turmoil were induced to come back and

[91] The standing order of the Maharaja to his officials was to always keep in mind the well-being of the subjects and the prosperity of the government:

آبادئ رعایا وافزنئ مالِ سرکار

Kohli, 'Land Revenue Administration', *JPHS*, 80.

It was one of the foremost duties of a *kārdār* or of an *ijāradār* to increase the land under cultivation and was also mentioned in the undertaking given by him : see chapter IV, 77 & n 65. To advance *taqāvī* loans to needy cultivators and to supply materials for the repair of wells or even dig new canals was a part of this policy. The *jāgīrdārs* occasionally laying out money for the improvement of their *jāgīrs*, especially their ancestral possessions, are also on record : 'Diary of John Lawrence', *Punjab Government Records* (*1847-1848*), III, 436.

It may be added that the founding of new villages was an important feature throughout the period of Sikh rule, particularly under Ranjit Singh. For a typical description of colonization, see Baden Powell, *Land Systems of British India*, II, 678-81.

[92] For instance, in the case of a newly dug or reopened well, all revenue was excused for the first year, for the second year a fifth of the produce was taken, and for the third year a fourth 'and so on' until the revenue gradually came to be fixed at the standard rate of the locality : Diwan Dina Nath, quoted in 'Diary of Henry Lawrence', *Punjab Government Records* (*1847-1848*), III, 235.

As a result of 'temporary remissions' in case of natural calamities and 'a light and equitable' *jama*', Misar Rup Lal was able to reclaim large tracts in the Jalandhar Doab and convert 'a perfect wilderness' into the 'Garden of the Punjab': John Lawrence, 'SSR Jullundur Doab', *Foreign/Political Proceedings*, 31 December 1847, No. 2443, para 7. See also, *SR Hoshiarpur*, 126-27. In Multan, Diwan Sawan Mal also did much to restore the prosperity of a country which had been desolated by 'a century of anarchy' : Douie, *Punjab Settlement Manual*, 20.

[93] In most parts of the Sikh dominions, the *chaudharīs* and *muqaddams* were allowed a deduction of a fourth from the share of the government, known as *takhfīf-i-chahāramī-i-zamīndārān* : see, for example, *Khālsa Darbār Records*, Bundle 3, Vol. I, 317; Bundle 20, Vol. IV, 3.

resettleon their lands.[94] 'Many of the cattle feeders, and inhabitants of the grazing tracts' were encouraged to settle permanently as cultivators.[95] In fact, 'throughout the Sikh rule', one of the 'principal means' of increasing the revenue was 'encouragement given by the rulers to the families of more industrious cultivators to settle in their villages'.[96] Settlers who possessed capital and enterprise were encouraged 'to sink wells, dig canals and cultivate the lands of the nominal owners'.[97] They were allowed hereditary and transferable rights both in the well or irrigation channel and in the cultivation of the land irrigated from it.[98]

However, there was a limit set on the extension of agriculture not merely by the available capital or manpower, or the quality of soil,[99] but also by the available means of irrigation. Lack of irrigational facilities in many parts of the Sikh dominions placed an insurmountable limitation on the extension of agriculture.[100] Conversely, cultivation of land in all

[94] See, for example, *Gazetteer of Gujranwala*, 11; *Gazetteer of Gujrat*, 101-02.

[95] G.W. Hamilton, 'On the Tirnee Tax of Jhung', *Selections PCPA*, Vol. I, No. 9, 105.

A large number of colonists were settled in Jhang and Muzaffargarh by Diwan Sawan Mal. The *bār* nomads were settled down to agriculture in Gujranwala : 'SSR Lower Rachna Doab', *Foreign/Secret Consultation*, 28 April 1848, No. 64, para 35; *SR Muzaffargarh*, 53; *Gazetteer of Gujranwala*, 9, respectively.

[96] A. Kensington, *SR Ambala*, 78.

[97] Edward O'Brien, *SR Muzaffargarh*, 92.

[98] D.G. Barkley, 'Character of Land Tenures', *Report on the Administration of the Punjab (1872-1873)*, 14-15.

[99] The soil was divided both according to its quality and the mode of irrigation. For a discussion of the deterioration of the soil with time, see Munshi Hukm Chand, *Tārīkh-i-Multan*, 521 & 522.

[100] For example, the first British settlement officer in the lower Sindh Sagar Doab found only half of the land under cultivation; in the Chaj Doab, however, it was a little more than half. But even in the latter, there were 'vast tracts of jungle, extending for miles and miles, without a *beegah* of cultivation'. What was needed in this case was 'solely good irrigation' : L. Bowring, 'SSR Lower Sindh Sagar and Chaj Doabs', *Foreign/Secret Consultation*, 28 April 1848, No. 65. See also, Harbans Singh, 'Agriculture in the Punjab during the Maharaja's Reign', *Maharaja Ranjit Singh*, 145.

those areas where rainfall was 'small and uncertain' was possible only with one or another mode of irrigation.

Various means of irrigation were available in different parts of the Sikh dominions. In areas of scanty rainfall, cultivated land could be divided into three categories according to the modes of irrigation used. In the river-side belt, cultivation depended upon *sailāba* or autumnal floods from the river and was partly protected by wells; in the intermediate belt, it depended upon inundation canals and wells, and in the submontane belt, it depended upon mountain torrents which came in floods after storms and during the monsoons, and were held up by embankments.[101] Wells, however, formed the most important single means of irrigation nearly all over the Panjab.[102]

It is difficult to ascertain the total revenue from land in the Sikh dominions at any given point of time. It is even more difficult to discern any pattern for the period as a whole. However, estimated or exact figures are available for the various parts or the entire dominions of Ranjit Singh and the researcher is obliged to base his estimates or conjectures on these figures.[103] According to these, the total annual revenues from

[101] J.B. Lyall, *Selections from the Records of the Financial Commissioner's Office*, No. 37 (New Series Nos. 11 & 16), 839-45, paras, 3, 4, & 6-9; 'SSR Lower Rachna and Lower Bari Doabs', *Foreign/Secret Consultation*, 28 April 1848, No. 64, paras 34 & 47; 'Memorandum of the First Eight Years' of British Rule in the District of Hoosheearpore', *Selections PCPA*, Vol. III, No. 4, 284-85.

For detail of the irrigated and unirrigated area in each *pargana* of Kashmir, see Mir Ahmad, *Dastūr al-'Amal-i-Kashmir*, Part 2.

[102] Wells were the only means of artificial irrigation in the uplands between the river valleys all over the Panjab. Wells were plentiful across the Satlej also and irrigated about one-sixth to one-fourth of the cultivated land: 'SSR Cis-Satlej', *Foreign/Political Consultation*, 31 December 1848, No. 1830, para 13.

[103] According to a contemporary estimate, the total revenues from land in the dominions of Ranjit Singh around 1830 amounted to about 2,33,00,000 rupees: Prinsep, *Origin of the Sikh Power*, 146. About a decade later, Shahamat Ali estimated the total revenues from land at 2,84,11,762 rupees: *Sikhs and Afghans*, 23. The figures given by

land in the dominions of Ranjit Singh ranged between 2 and 3 crores of rupees; and, on the average, they were more than 2½ crores of rupees.[104]

Taking the figures available for the different parts of the dominions of Ranjit Singh, we find similar variations from time to time and from source to source. For Kashmir, the average of these figures comes to over 34 lakhs of rupees a year.[105] The average for Multan works out to about 41 lakhs of rupees a year.[106] The average for those parts of the five

Cunningham are only about 5 lakhs less, amounting to 2,79,00,000 rupees: *A History of the Sikhs*, 387, Appendix XXXVIII.

[104] In the dominions of the Sikh rulers, a very large number of different kinds of Sikh and non-Sikh coins were current. 'First and foremost, purest in substance most widely known, came the Nanak-Shahi rupee, of which in the space of forty-two years, no less than six and a half crores had been coined at the Lahore and Amritsar mints. But of this kind alone there were no less than 50 different varieties : 'The Administration of the Punjab' (anon.), *Calcutta Review*, Vol. XXI, No. XLI, 240. For more information, see C.J. Rodgers, 'On the Coins of the Sikhs', *JASB*, Vol. L, Part I, No. 1, 71-93.

It may be added that the Nanak-Shāhī coin struck in Sammat 1884-85 was the final standard coin, containing 11 *mashas* and 7 *rattīs* of silver and equal to 15 annas of the English rupee. The Kashmiri or Hari Singhi rupee, first struck in Kashmir during the *nizamat* of Hari Singh Nalwa in the early 1820s, was equal to 10 annas of the standard Nanak-Shāhī coin : Kohli, 'Land Revenue Administration', *JPHS*, 90.

[105] For Kashmir, Kohli gives 40,67,861 Kashmiri or 25,42,413 Nanak-Shāhī rupees, as the revenue from land in 1821: Loc. cit. For 1824, the figure given in the *News of the Court of Ranjit Singh* is 37,00,000 rupees : *News(1825)*, 359. It is not mentioned, however, whether or not this figure is in Kashmiri rupees. Baron Schonberg gives 42,00,000 rupees as the land revenue of Kashmir in the early 1830s : *Travels in India and Kashmir*, II, 97. Writing in 1838, Shahamat Ali gives 36,75,000 rupees : *Sikhs and Afghans*, 22. However, Cunningham writing in 1844, gives only 30,00,000 rupees for Kashmir : *A History of the Sikhs*, 384, Appendix XXXVIII.

[106] For Multan, the amount of annual revenue given for 1821 by Kohli is only 5,80,975 rupees : 'Land Revenue Administration', *JPHS*, 90. The later figures for the enlarged province of Multan are several times higher, Shahamat Ali gives 38,98,550 rupees for 1838 : *Sikhs and Afghans*, 21. For 1844, Cunningham gives 45,00,000 rupees : *A History*

doābs which were covered by the former Mughal province of Lahore comes to over 95 lakhs of rupees a year.[107] The average for the three provinces of Kashmir, Multan and Lahore adds up to 1 crore and 60 lakhs of rupees a year.[108] Subsequent increase in the revenues of the Lahore Darbar is understandable in terms of the revenues from territories across the rivers Satlej and Indus,[109] expansion of cultivation in the latter half of the reign of Ranjit Singh,[110] and the increased *mushakhasa*[111]

of the Sikhs, 384, Appendix XXXVIII. According to John Lawrence, the gross revenues of Multan in 1846 amounted to 44,43,755 rupees: 'Statement of the Acting Commissioner and Superintendent', *Foreign/Secret Consultation*, 26 December 1846, Nos. 1236-38.

[107] For the former Mughal province of Lahore, Sita Ram Kohli gives 27,39,579 rupees as the land-revenue for 1821. But this figure is for the *khālisa* only, lands worth one crore of rupees in all being given in *jāgīr* at this time: 'Land Revenue Administration', *JPHS*, 90. John Lawrence gives 79,66,190 rupees for the revenues of the four *doābs* excluding the Jalandhar Doab: 'Statement of the Acting Commissioner and Superintendent', *Foreign/Secret Consultation*, 26 December 1846, Nos. 1236-38. According to another report, the annual revenues from the four *doābs* before 1849 were 74,44,244 rupees: *GRAPP (1849-1851)*, 83. See also, *Khālsa Darbār Records*, Bundle 3, Vol. II, 1. For the Jalandhar Doab alone, John Lawrence's figures are 23,13,672 rupees: 'SSR Jullundur Doab', *Foreign/Political Proceedings*, 31 December 1847, No. 2443, para 39. Shahamat Ali's estimate is, however, 18,72,902 rupees: *Sikhs and Afghans*, 21. Cunningham's figures for the same region are 22,00,000 rupees: *A History of the Sikhs*, 384, Appendix XXXVIII.

[108] This roughly is the amount given by Kohli for Kashmir, Multan and Lahore in 1821: 'Land Revenue Administration", *JPHS*, 90.

[109] The revenues of the 'conquests and grants' of Ranjit Singh across the Satlej amounted to a little over 4 lakhs of rupees: Lepel Griffin, *Minor Phulkian Families*, 607. According to John Lawrence, the trans-Indus territories excluding those in the province of Multan yielded the gross revenues of 13,39,407 rupees: 'Statistical Notes on the Punjab', *Foreign/Secret Consultation*, 26 December 1846, Nos. 1325-27.

[110] See 111 & nn 91-92.

[111] 'The revenues of various districts had greatly increased since Maharaja Ranjit Singh's time': Diwan Dina Nath, quoted in 'Diary of Henry Lawrence', *Punjab Government Records (1847-1848)*, III, 235. Lawrence refers to the *mukshahasa* of the *ta'alluqas* of Khai, Mitha (Tiwana?) and Dipalpur, which was respectively 8,000, 32,000 and 32,000 (?) rupees, had been raised to 40,000, 70,000 and 1,02,000 rupees

in the 1840s to meet the increasing expenditure of the state.[112] The average of 2¼ crores of rupees a year as the revenue from land in the entire dominions of Ranjit Singh may be treated as reasonably reliable. In certain good years, the land-revenue could amount to 2½ crores of rupees or even more.

Turning to the figures available for the provinces of Lahore, Multan and Kashmir during the Mughal times, the average *jama*' on the basis of the ten different sources from the reign of Shah Jahan to that of Muhammad Shah works out respectively to 2,35,73,083 rupees, 60,50,650 rupees and 51,38,815 rupees.[113] The total revenues of the three Mughal provinces thus amounted to nearly 3½ crores of rupees.[114] The larger income from land in the Mughal times is generally explained in terms of the larger extent of the *sūba* of Multan[115] and of the greater peace and prosperity.[116] It is equally possible,

in the post-Ranjit Singh period. In the Jalandhar Doab, Shaikh Ghulam Muhiyuddin and his son Imamuddin, had raised Misar Rup Lal's assessment by 25 per cent : *Gazetteer of Jullundur*, 9.

[112] For a discussion of the financial difficulties of the kingdom of Lahore after 1839 see, for example, Kohli, *Sunset of the Sikh Empire*, 39-41 & 85-87.

[113] See, for example, Irfan Habib, *Agrarian System*, 403-05, Appendix D; Noman Ahmad Siddiqi, *Land Revenue Administration*, 167-69, Appendix E.

[114] The average of the figures given for the total revenues of these provinces in the *Khulāsat-us-Siyāq* compiled in the Punjab in the 41st year of Aurangzeb's reign, and in the *Dastūr al-'Amal-i-Ghulam Muhammad*, compiled in 1748, also comes to 143 crores of *dāms* or a little over 3½ crores of rupees, even assuming that 40 *dāms* of the *jama*' figures represented a rupee : see Irfan Habib, *Agrarian System*, 388, Appendix C.

[115] Of the three *sarkārs* in the Mughal *sūba* of Multan under Akbar, the territory covered by the *sarkār* of Bhakkar and some *mahāl* even of the sarkār of Multan were outside the kingdom of Ranjit Singh : see, for example, Abul Fazl, *Ā'īn-i-Akbarī*, II, 331-36.

[116] For example, Prinsep notices that in the figures given by Murray, the total revenues from the dominions of Ranjit Singh were nearly equal to the figures of land-revenue given in Mughal records for the province of Lahore. He is inclined to accept the figures given by Murray as reliable on the argument that, 'considering that Kashmir, and some territory south of the Satlej', was included in the dominions of Ranjit Singh, 'the correspondence of amount is in favour of the correctness of the estimate, for the province cannot be so productive

however, that the lower income of the Sikh times was due partly at least to the lower rates of assessment.[117]

under the Sikhs as it was in the peaceable times of the Moghal dominion': *Origin of the Sikh Power*, 146.

[117] It is interesting to note that on taking the rates of assessment as two-fifths, the total produce of the dominions of Ranjit Singh amounts to 6.25 crores of rupees (2½x5/2). The corresponding amount for the Mughal times is seven crores (3½x2/1), if we assume the rate of assessment to have generally been one-half. It is obvious that the income of the state was substantially altered by the difference in the rate of assessment.

6

The Jagirdars

According to contemporary estimates, one-third to one-half of the total revenues of the kingdom of Lahore were alienated by way of *jāgīrs* and charitable grants.[1] By far the bulk of this proportion was alienated in favour of those who served the state. Service *jāgīr* was, in fact, more important than the *dharmarth* grants and all other categories of *jāgīrs* put together —the *pattīdārī*, the *chahāramī*, the *in'ām* and the *jāgīrs* for subsistence.[2]

Service *jāgīr* may be conceived as being primarily either military or civil. When a *jāgīrdār* was required to serve with a certain number of horsemen he was assigned *jāgīrs* not only for his personal services but also for the maintenance of those horsemen. The civil *jāgīrdār* was paid only for his personal services. Thus, the difference between civil and military *jāgīr* hinged around the fact that the military *jāgīrdār* maintained troopers and was paid for maintaining them.

Recruitment and maintenance of a fixed number of men by the *jāgīrdār* was the most important condition of a military *jāgīr*. Even a commander like Hari Singh Nalwa was not allowed to disregard it, so meticulously insistent was Maharaja

[1] See, for example, Prinsep, *Origin of the Sikh Power*, 146; Shahamat Ali, *Sikhs and Afghans*, 23; [Cunningham, *A History of the Sikhs*, 387, Appendix XXXVIII. For specific figures, see 144-45 n 97.

[2] *Cf.* Prinsep, *Origin of the Sikh Power*, 28-29; Kohli, *Catalogue of Khālsa Darbār Records*, II, 302-03; Gupta, *A History of the Sikhs*, I, 132; Fauja Singh, *Military System of the Sikhs*, 125.

Ranjit Singh on this condition.[3] Periodical inspection of the *jāgīrdārī* troops was necessary to ensure the maintenance of the stipulated number and there are frequent references in contemporary records to the muster of troops.[4] Aware of the tendency among the *jāgīrdārs* to maintain a lower number, the Maharaja decided in the early 1830s to introduce the branding of horses.[5] He was concerned also about the turnout of the horsemen of the *jāgīrdārs*.[6]

Ranjit Singh and his successors insisted also on some other norms of service expected from the military *jāgīrdārs*. Mehtab

[3] In fact, this incident presents a typical instance. In 1828, Hari Singh Nalwa requested the Maharaja to inspect his troops, and the Maharaja discovered that the *sardār* had maintained only 450 horsemen and not 600 which was the number stipulated. Hari Singh failed to give any satisfactory explanation. The Maharaja ordered the *mutasaddīs* of the office to calculate the amount overpaid to the *sardār*. Consequently, he was asked to pay 5 lakhs of rupees; and having been placed under guard for a few days, he agreed to pay 2 lakhs. He was allowed to go, but shortly afterwards, the Maharaja ordered that this fine should be collected from him and, if he showed any reluctance, revenues from the territories under his management should be collected directly for the royal treasury: Sohan Lal, *Umdat*, II, 375 & 381.

[4] See, for example, *Events* (*1810-1817*), 263, 272 *et passim*; *News* (*1825*), 345; Sohan Lal, *Umdat*, II, 375; III, (ii), 258-59; (iv), 482 & (v), 37. *Cf.* Fauja Singh, *Military System of the Sikhs*, 125-29 & 134-36. Fauja Singh has emphasized the importance of musters, descriptive rolls and branding in what has been called the regular army of Ranjit Singh but he does not refer to the musters of the *jāgīrdārī* troops.

[5] Sohan Lal, *Umdat*, III, (ii), 258-59. See also, Ram Sukh Rao, *Srī Fateh Singh Partāp Prabhākar*, f 222b. Inspecting the troops of the Sandhanwalias in 1835, the Maharaja had remarked that the *sardārs* were enjoying large *jāgīrs* but maintaining only small number of troops. Sohan Lal refers to the branding of the horses of Karam Singh, Charhat Singh Atariwala, Attar Singh Atariwala and Wasawa Singh Sandhanwalia, for example: Sohan Lal, *Umdat*, III, (ii), 262 & 263.

[6] Sohan Lal alludes to a very interesting incident in this connection. On 19 May 1838, the Maharaja inspected the troops of the Jamwal Rajas and noticed their shabby appearance. He recalled the practice of his father Mahan Singh who used to have such defaulters bastinadoed. Raja Dhian Singh had to apologize and to assure the Maharaja that such a thing would not be allowed to happen again: ibid., III, (iv), 518.

Singh, a dependant of Raja Dhian Singh, lost his *jāgīr* for his refusal to go to Ladakh with his troops.[7] Gurmukh Singh Lamba, who had served Ranjit Singh with devotion and distinction, lost a substantial chunk of his *jāgīr* in 1835-36 because of a personal quarrel with Raja Fazl Dad Khan who was himself deprived of his *jāgīr* for going to Jammu instead of repairing to Lahore as ordered.[8] Ratan Singh Garhjakhia suffered heavily for constructing a fortress without the permission of the Maharaja.[9]

That the military *jāgīrdār* was paid on two accounts, for the maintenance of horsemen (*dar wajah-i-naukarī-i-sawārān*) and for personal service (*dar wajah-i-naukarī*), is evident from contemporary records.[10] John Lawrence also states that every *jārgīrdār* received a portion of his *jāgīr* as 'personal' and the rest 'for the support of his contingents'. He clarifies the position by suggesting that a *jāgīrdār* receiving 50,000 rupees a year, received 20,000 for his 'personal' service and 30,000 for

[7] *Foreign/Secret Consultation*, 8 April 1842, No. 37. A fine of 30,000 rupees was imposed on some other *jāgīrdārs* who had refused to go to Kashmir. Some time later, some *jāgīrdārs* were fined a sum of 25,000 rupees for leaving Peshawar without permission: *Foreign/Political Consultation*, 26 December 1846, Nos. 1169-72.

[8] Ibid., 29 December 1849, No. 49A(20); *Tārīkh-i-Sikhān* (anon.), I, 415-16 & II, 417-18, respectively.

[9] Sohan Lal, *Umdat*, III, (iii), 277-78 & 280. After some time, Ratan Singh went over to the British territories and his *jāgīr* worth 21,000 rupees was given over to Ventura: ibid., 286. He was persuaded by Captain Wade to return to Lahore to be reinstated. But in 1843, his *jāgīr* was again confiscated on the charge of fomenting trouble: ibid., IV, (iii), 42. On the other hand, Kirpa Ram, a grandson of Diwan Mohkam Chand, did not lose his *jāgīrs* when he went to Banaras without the Maharaja's permission: Griffin & Massy, *Chiefs and Families*, II, 163. This, however, was rather exceptional. Griffin explains the Maharaja's attitude with reference to Kirpa Ram's brother Shiv Dayal and his adopted son Dhan Raj who were still serving the Maharaja. It is probable that regard for the services rendered by Diwan Mohkam Chand and his grandson Ram Dayal to the Lahore Darbar also influenced the Maharaja's decision in this case.

[10] See, for example, *Khālsa Darbār Records*, Bundle 3, Vol. II, 323; Bundle 5, Vol. XIII, 9.

maintaining 100 horsemen.[11] The basic position is amply confirmed by the detail of 'personal' and 'service' *jāgīrs* available for a large number of the principal *jāgīrdārs* of the Lahore Darbar.[12]

However, John Lawrence's assumption that a *jāgīrdār* was paid uniformly at the rate of 300 rupees a trooper is not borne out by contemporary evidence. Mangal Singh Sandhu, for example, was paid at the rate of 300 rupees a year for 50 horsemen and at the rate of 250 rupees for 70 horsemen.[13] Similarly, Ram Singh Jallewasia was given a *jāgīr* at 300 rupees a trooper for 5 horsemen, and at 250 rupees for 12 horsemen.[14] In another case, the variation is still more interesting. Raja Fazl Dad Khan received 300 rupees for two horsemen, 250 rupees for one and 225 rupees for the fourth.[15] Furthermore, the *jāgīrdār* appears to have enjoyed the freedom of enlisting troopers on his own terms. It was not necessary for the *jāgīrdār* therefore to pay to a trooper the whole amount received from the government.[16] The *jāgīrdār* could, and very

[11] *Foreign/Secret Proceedings*, 25 February 1848, No. 60.

[12] *Foreign/Political Proceedings*, 3 April 1850, No. 280; *Foreign/Political Consultation*, 29 December 1849, No. 49A (Abstract); *Foreign/Secret Consultation*, 26 May 1849, Nos. 68-70.

It may be added that though there are *jāgīrdārs* with personal *jāgīrs* only, there is hardly a *jāgīrdār* holding a service *jāgīr* who, at the same time, does not hold a 'personal' *jāgīr* which in his case connoted the emoluments given to him for *his* services and for the maintenance of *his own* establishment. We may also be sure that the term service *jāgīr* is used in the early British records for a *jāgīr* given for the purpose of maintaining the stipulated number of men.

[13] *Foreign/Political Consultation*, 29 December 1849, No. 49 A (21).

[14] Ibid., No. 49A (20).

[15] Ibid., No. 49A (17).

[16] *Cf.* Fauja Singh, *Military System of the Sikhs*, 126-27.

In fact, according to John Lawrence, the *jāgīrdār* saved 'a lot of this sum', paying 'some a half, and some two-thirds, and perhaps a few cadets of the family, the full sum': *Foreign/Secret Consultation*, 25 February 1848, No. 60. See also, W. Moorcroft, *Travels (1819-1825)*, I, 98. According to Moorcroft, a *jāgīrdār* had to spend 250 rupees annually on an efficient horseman, whereas he got a *jāgīr* worth 500 rupees for each trooper maintained by him.

often did, pay his troopers through sub-assignments from his *jāgīr*.[17]

What the state paid to the *jāgīrdār* for a trooper was not substantially less than what was paid to the horseman (*ghurchara*) directly recruited by the state. Even towards the end of Ranjit Singh's reign, the annual pay of a *ghurchara* ranged from 250 to 300 rupees.[18] In 1846, when there were over 10,000 *ghurcharas* in 19 *deras* receiving in all 32 lakhs of rupees, every fifth *ghurchara* was paid in *jāgīr*. The average pay of a *ghurchara*, even after the Anglo-Sikh War in 1846, works out to about 300 rupees a year.[19] The *jāgīrs* of the *sawārān-i-ghurcharāhā-i-khās* were spread over all the Doabs.[20]

The total amount of pay received by a military *jāgīrdār* and the variations of pay depended generally on the number of his

[17] The instances of further alienation of portions of *jāgīrs* are so numerous indeed that they indicate a general practice. To cite a few examples, Sardar Sher Singh Atariwala ordered the resumption of the assignments of those horsemen who failed to join him during the Multan campaign : *Parwānajāt-i-Atariwala*, II, 7; Sardar Lehna Singh Majithia appointed Mihan Singh Bhagowalia as the *thānadār* of Amritsar during the Peshawar campaign and gave him a *jāgīr* worth 3750 rupees : Griffin & Massy, *Chiefs and Families*, II, 3; Sardar Jawand Singh Maukal gave four villages out of his *jāgīr* in Dipalpur to Farid who was serving him : Munshi Bakhtawar Lal, *Tārīkh-i-Montgomery*, 8.

[18] Kohli, 'Organization of the Khalsa Army', *Maharaja Ranjit Singh*, 84-85. *Cf.* Charles Hugel, *Travels in Kashmir and the Panjab*, 330 & 350 n.

[19] *Foreign/Secret Proceedings*, 26 December 1846, No. 1038. See also, *Foreign/Political Proceedings*, 27 September 1850, No. 73 A; ibid., 7 January 1853, No. 228; *Khālsa Darbār Records*, Bundle 4, Vol. VII, 362. *Cf.* Chopra, *Sovereign State*, 66 n 2.

[20] *Khālsa Darbār Records*, Bundle 5, Vol. XIII, 33-327.

This particular volume has been misleadingly called 'mutafarriqa', and in the *Catalogue* prepared by Sita Ram Kohli, it is listed along with the volumes relating to *dharmarth* grants : *Catalogue of Khālsa Darbār Records*, II, 303. This has presumably stood in the way of the historian getting hold of this useful information on the *jāgīrs* of the *ghurcharas*. It may also be pointed out that another volume in Bundle 5, listed as Vol. XVIII, in fact, is a part of Vol. XIII, and contains information on the *jāgīrs* of individual *ghurcharas* : see, for example, 3, 5, 13, 21, 23, 25 & 33.

men. For instance, in 1846, Karam Singh Chhina was receiving 21,600 rupees and maintaining 25 horsemen; earlier, when he was maintaining 70 horsemen, he was receiving 50,000 rupees.[21] Sometimes, what was saved from the reduction of horsemen was added to the personal *jāgīr* of the *jāgīrdār*.[22] In exceptional circumstances, a *jāgīrdār* was compensated for having incurred unexpected but unavoidable expenditure on the same number of horsemen as he was normally expected to maintain.[23] In some cases, however, the personal *jāgīr* of a military *jāgīrdār* remained much larger than his service *jāgīr*.[24]

Though one and the same person could be asked

[21] Griffin & Massy, *Chiefs and Families*, I, 522.

[22] In 1848, Nihal Singh Chhachhi was allowed to reduce the number of his horsemen from 13 to 8, but the pay of 5 horsemen at the rate of 250 rupees a year, was added to his personal *jāgīr* : *Foreign/Political Cansultation*, 29 December 1849, No. 49 A (16). According to John Lawrence, however, the government also gained in the case of reduction in the number of horsemen because 50 per cent of the pay due to them was kept by the government : *Foreign/Secret Consultation*, 25 February 1848, No. 60.

[23] Fauja Singh, *Military System of the Sikhs*, 129.

Another kind of concession was not to deduct anything from the *jāgīr* but to allow the *jāgīrdār* to maintain a smaller number than the stipulated number of horsemen. Sardar Sardul Singh Man, for example, on account of his great debt, was excused from furnishing 20 of his *sawārs* for five years: *Foreign/Political Consultation*, 29 December 1849, No. 49 A(14).

[24] Some of the princes, for example, held *jāgīrs* bearing no relationship to the troops they maintained. Similarly, the *jāgīrdārs* of long standing and high status, like Jamadar Khushal Singh and Raja Tej Singh, held larger personal *jāgīrs* than service *jāgīrs*. The Sandhanwalia *sardārs*, who were the collaterals of the Sukarchakias, appear to have received liberal grants of personal *jāgīrs*. Also, *jāgīrdārs* who rendered long and meritorious service to the Lahore Darbar, like Kahan Singh Atariwala and Gulab Singh Pahuwindia, received larger personal *jāgīrs*. This was true also of some of the smaller *jāgīrdārs* like Sardul Singh Man and Mian Waris Khan. To these may be added a few of the *jāgīrdārs*, like Sodhi Nihal Singh, who were holding considerable *jāgīrs* by way of *dharmarth* before getting small service *jāgīrs*. For some detail, see *Foreign/Political Consultation*, 29 December 1849, No. 49 A (27); *Foreign/Political Proceedings*, 3 April 1850, No. 280.

alternatively to perform non-military and military duties,[25] the contemporaries made a clear distinction between a person with administrative ability and a man of the field.[26] In any case, a considerable number of administrators performing duties largely of a civil nature were generally paid in *jāgīr*. Misar Beli Ram of the royal *toshakhāna*, for example, received *jāgīrs* worth 60,000 to 70,000 rupees.[27] Similarly, Diwan Dina Nath was at one time enjoying a *jāgīr* worth nearly 50,000 rupees.[28] It may be safely presumed, in fact, that the *dīwāns*, not only of Ranjit Singh and his successors, but also of the other Sikh rulers were normally paid in *jāgīr*.[29] The majority of *kārdārs*

[25] Some of the known civil administrators were employed on military duties in certain situations. For example, while Faqir Azizuddin conquered Wazirabad and settled the country, Ganda Singh Safi, a military *jāgīrdār* was asked to prepare *kāghaz-i-zabtī*: Sohan Lal, *Umdat*, II, 101-02; Ratan Singh Garhjakhia was asked to perform the civil duties of an *'adālatī*: Amar Nath, *Zafarnāma*, 224; Har Sukh Rai served first as an *'adālatī* and then as a commander: Griffin & Massy, *Chiefs and Families*, II, 121; Ralia Ram was first a commandant then a *kārdār* : *Foreign/Political Proceedings*, 3 April 1850, No. 194(11); Nanak Chand Daftari led expeditions against the recalcitrant Rajas of the Khakha and the Bamba in Kashmir : Amar Nath, *Zafarnāma*, 135.

[26] When, for example, the Maharaja asked the *sardārs* about the difference between Avitabile and Ventura, they were unanimous that the former was essentially a civil administrator and the latter a man of the field : Sohan Lal, *Umdat*, III, (iii), 308. Tej Singh, on the other hand, was regarded as essentially a soldier unsuitable for civil administration : ibid., (ii), 303.

[27] Ibid., (i), 153 & (iii), 398. See also, Shahamat Ali, *Sikhs and Afghans*, 35 & 130.

[28] *Foreign/Political Proceedings*, 22 November 1850, No. 117 A. See also, *Foreign/Political Consultation*, 31 December 1847, Nos. 195-98; Sohan Lal, *Umdat*, V, 91. It may be added that of these *jāgīrs*, lands worth 6,000 rupees were assigned to Diwan Dina Nath in the province of Kashmir : Shahamat Ali, *Sikhs and Afghans*, 36.

[29] Some of the important *dīwāns* of Ranjit Singh besides Dina Nath were Devi Das, Bhawani Das, Ajudhya Parshad, Kirpa Ram, Sukh Dayal, Shiv Dayal and Shankar Das : Raja Ram Tota, *Gulgashta-i-Panjab*, ff 233 a & 236b. See also, Griffin & Massy, *Chiefs and Families*, II, 163. Kidar Nath, Amar Nath, Hukm Chand, Shankar Nath, Ganga Bishan, Bishan Singh and Daulat Rai were some of the *dīwāns* enjoying *jāgīrs* in the period after Ranjit Singh : ibid., 6 September 1850, No. 31 A. In the ‹ d before Ranjit Singh, Diwan Shiv Dayal, for example, received

in the Sikh dominions received payment for their services through *jāgīrs*.[30] Several other categories of employees received *jāgīrs* for the personal service they rendered to the Sikh rulers, like the *qānūngos*,[31] persons employed in diplomatic service,[32] the employees of the postal and customs departments,[33] the *'adālatīs* and the *qāzīs*.[34]

a *jāgīr* from Charhat Singh, Diwan Gulu Mal from Gujjar Singh Bhangi and Diwan Sulakhan Mal and his sons, Radha Kishan and Kishan Chand, from Milkha Singh of Rawalpindi : *Chiefs and Families*, II, 198. Tek Chand was holding *jāgīrs* as the *dīwān* of the Nakais : *Khālsa Darbār Records*, Bundle 5, Vol. XII, 45.

[30] For example, even in the late 1840s, there were more than twenty-five *kārdārs* receiving nearly 85,000 rupees a year, of which 53,000 rupees were paid in *jāgīr* : *Foreign/Political Proceedings*, 3 April 1850, No. 194 (Abstract). Contemporaneously with Ranjit Singh, Fateh Singh Ahluwhlia paid his *kārdārs* in *jāgīr* : Ram Sukh Rao, *Srī Fateh Singh Partāp Prabhākar*, ff 324b & 341b; also *Foreign/Political Consultation*, 14 March 1851, No. 113 C. Even a minor chief like Bhup Singh of Ropar gave *jāgīrs* to his civil employees : ibid., No. 113 E.

[31] This has already been noted in a previous chapter. See chapter IV, 82 & n 97.

[32] Rai Anand Singh Bhandari and his sons, Rai Gobind Jas and Rai Kishan Chand, for example, were employed in diplomatic service and were given large *jāgīrs* : Sohan Lal, *Umdat*, III, (iii), 347 & 352; (v). 13. See also, *Bhandārī Collection*, PS A, Patiala; *Foreign/Secret Consultation*, 31 December 1849, Nos. 195-98.

More conspicuous and important was the family of the Faqir brothers who received *jāgīrs* for serving the Lahore Darbar as diplomats and civil administrators. For some detail of the *jāgīrs* of Faqirs Azizuddin, Imamuddin, Nuruddin and Tajuddin, see Shahamat Ali, *Sikhs and Afghans*, 48; *Events (1810-1817)*, 259; Mir Ahmad, *Dastūr al-'Amal-i-Kashmir*, f 186b; *Foreign/Political Proceedings*, 22 November 1850, No. 117 (case nos. 2-13). See also, Fakir Waheeduddin, *Real Ranjit Singh*, 39-47.

[33] See, for example, *Foreign/Political Proceedings*, 3 April 1850, No. 194; Griffin & Massy, *Chiefs and Families*, I, 310.

[34] Misar Harcharan Das, for example, received a *jāgīr* worth about 4,000 rupees while serving as the *'adālatī* of Lahore : *Foreign/Political Proceedings*, 3 April 1850, No. 194 (31). More numerous than the *'adālatīs* were the *qāzīs* who continued to administer justice throughout the Sikh period, in some cases their *jāgīrs* (*arāzī-i-maurūsī*) and office coming down from the Mughal times. For example, Qazi Karam Bakhsh's service *jāgīr* (*dar naukarī*) in Ramnagar had been

The number of civil *jāgīrdārs* was inflated by the employees of various offices and the *khidmatgārs* of the royal household. In the mid-1840s, the *munshīs* of the Lahore Darbar were receiving nearly 80,000 rupees in salary and of this amount, over 54,000 rupees were paid in *jāgīr* to 16 persons.[35] The *jāgīrs* of some of the important *munshīs* and their staff (*kār pardāzān-i-munshīān-i-huzurī*) are detailed in the *Khālsa Darbār Records*.[36] *Jāgīrs* given to the male and female attendants of the royal household were numerous. Among the *khidmatgārs* were included *mistrīs*, *lāngrīs* *pālkī*-bearers, tailors and barbers.[37] Several other categories of persons got *jāgīrs* for serving in the royal household: *gadwaīs*, *chhāta-bardārs*, *chaurī-bardārs*, *farrāshes*, *bhishtīs*, *musicians*, gardeners, kennel-keepers, table-bearers, nurses of children, sweepers, falconers, ironsmiths, keepers of chains, store-keepers, etc.[38]

Raja Dina Nath informed the British Administrators in 1847 that the Darbar had returns of the revenues of every section (*pattī*) of a village.[39] It was possible also to know the

held by his father Qazi Abdul Rahman in the late eighteenth century. The family also had hereditary land (*arāzi-i-maurūsī*), apparently coming down from the Mughal times: *Khālsa Darbār Records*, Bundle 5, Vol. XI, 406, 407 & 409.

[35] *Foreign/Political Proceedings*, 3 April 1850, No. 194 (Abstract). Of these, Ratan Chand Darhiwala was getting 13,600 rupees in *jāgīr* and his brother Mangal Sain only rupees 1000. Ratan Chand Duggal was getting over 10,000 rupees; Ram Chand was getting over 5000; Devi Ditta Mal and Sohna Mal each over 4000. At the lower rungs, one Mohan Lal was getting only 730 rupees and Shiv Dayal 720. It may be added that Devi Ditta Mal was a *parwāna-nawīs* and Shiv Dayal a *muharrir*.

[36] *Khālsa Darbār Records*, Bundle 5, Vol. XV (also listed under *mutafarriqa*), 13-18. See 122 n 20.

[37] See, for example, ibid., Bundle 5, Vol. XI, 7; Vol. XII, 31; Vol. XIII, 161 & 165; Vol. XIV (listed under *mutafarriqa*) 43 & Vol. XV (also listed under *mutafarriqa*), 289, 291, 297, 309, 313, 317, 335, 339, 343, 345, 347 & 349-98.

[38] *Foreign/Political Proceedings*, 7 January 1853, No. 231.

Sometimes a servant of the royal household got substantial *jāgīrs* as in the case of Manglan, the maid in attendance upon Rani Jindan: *Khālsa Darbār Records*, Bundle 5, Vol. XV, 289. See also, Sohan Lal, *Umdat*, V, 19.

[39] John Lawrence to H.M. Elliot, *Foreign/Secret Consultation*, 30 October 1847, No. 95.

area, its value in terms of revenue and the length of time for which it had been held by a *jāgīrdār*.[40] In fact, the *jāgīrdārī* system could not have functioned without such records.[41] It was on the basis of these records that the accounts of *kārdārs* and *jāgīrdārs* could be examined and specific orders issued.[42] Such orders are numerous enough to support the view that the functionaries of revenue administration under Sikh rule were meticulously maintaining detailed records of the lands conferred in *jāgīr*.[43]

[40] See, for example, *Foreign/Political Proceedings*, 18 June 1852, Nos. 181-85 (case nos. 34, 79, 81, 85, 93 & 95).

[41] It has been possible to make this statement after examining the voluminous *Khālsa Darbār Records* at the Punjab State Archives, Patiala.

It may however be pointed out that occasionally a *jāgīr* was not entered in the Darbar records: see, for example, *Foreign/Political Proceedings*, 22 November 1850, No. 117 A. But these *jāgīrs* generally happened to be the ancestral holdings of the *jāgīrdārs* with their houses etc., on the estates, and nearly in all such cases, hereditary possessions were allowed to continue.

[42] For example, in an order of Maharaja Ranjit Singh dated 28 Baisākh 1886, addressed to Sardar Desa Singh Majithia, it is stated that one-fourth of a well, worth 26 rupees a year, in the village Naushehra Nangal, was granted to a *jogī* called Rala Rawal with effect from the *kharīf* harvest of Sammat 1885; he was to be paid 13 rupees from each of the *kharīf* and the *rabī*' crops; and the accounts of Sardar Desa Singh Majithia were to be credited accordingly in the *daftar-i-mu'alla* on producing a written receipt from the grantee: ibid., 23 August 1850, No. 35 C. In an order of Maharaja Dalip Singh, dated 6 Hār 1904, the *ijāradārs* of the village Wadala Sandhuan were told to pay 2681 rupees a year to eight assignees, for each of whom the specific amount to be paid is mentioned, and the *ijāradārs* were required henceforth to pay 2681 rupees less than the stipulated amount of 6000 rupees: *Foreign/Political Consultation*, 29 December 1849, No. 49 A.

[43] Direct orders were issued by the rulers to the *zamīndārs* also to ensure that they readily paid the revenues due to the assignees mentioned in those orders and entered in the records. When a whole village was given in *jāgīr* to an assignee he was to deposit the excess into the government treasury or it was adjusted at the time of taking accounts: see, for example, ibid., 49 A; *Foreign/Political Proceedings*, 22 November 1850, No. 117 A. When a *jāgīr* was given with retrospective effect from the previous harvest, the *kārdārs* were sometimes ordered to

The conferment of a *jāgīr* entitled the assignee to receive or collect revenues from the lands assigned to him by way of *jāgīr*, without involving any change in the existing rights over land. Therefore, the amount of revenue to be received or collected from the given piece of land was specifically mentioned in the orders relating to the assignment of service *jāgīrs*. Any further alienation of revenue by the *jāgīrdār* in favour of others could not in theory last longer than his own tenure. This applied as much to the *dharmarth* grants made by the *jāgīrdār* as to the assignment of revenue to horsemen employed by him. In actual practice, however, many a *dharmarth* grant made by a *jāgīrdār* continued beyond his tenure because of the sentiment of piety attached to such grants. Even so, not all such grants were allowed to continue after the *jāgīrdār's* tenure.[44]

On the death of a *jāgīrdār*, his *jāgīrs* stood reverted to the *khālisa*. In fact, all his possessions were temporarily seized. When Sardar Budh Singh Sandhanwalia died, the Maharaja asked his brothers if they were prepared to pay 3 lakhs of rupees in order to remain in possession of the *jāgīrs* and troops of their deceased brother. They declined the offer and the *jāgīrs* of Sardar Budh Singh were resumed.[45] On the death of Jamadar Khushal Singh, all his *jāgīrs* were resumed but when his nephew, Tej Singh, made representation, the *jāgīrs* in Bajwat and Sialkot were given to him.[46] When Sardar Hari Singh Nalwa died, all his *jāgīrs* and possessions were taken over by the Lahore Darbar; his accounts were settled and then his son Jawahar Singh was given the *ta'alluqa* of Khanpur Duna in *jāgīr*.[47] Thus, it appears that possessions of a *jāgīrdār* were seized in order to ensure that nothing remained outstanding in his name. Once these accounts were settled, the ruler used his discretion regarding the property which was to be

pay a part of the amount in cash : ibid., 23 August 1850, Nos. 35 A & 35 C. Alienated revenues wrongly collected by another agency had to be returned to the assignee : ibid., 22 November 1850, No. 117 A.

[44] *Foreign/Political Proceedings*, 15 October 1852, No. 116; 14 January 1853, Nos. 212-23. See also, chapter VII, 154 n 33.

[45] Sohan Lal, *Umdat*, II, 381. See also, *Foreign/Political Consultation*, 29 December 1849, No. 49 A(2).

[46] ibid., No. 49 A(6).

[47] Sohan Lal, *Umdat*, III, (iii), 404, 407, 417 & 419.

allowed to pass on to the heirs of the deceased *jāgīrdār*.[48] The term escheat, therefore, cannot be appropriately used here.[49]

Jāgīrs given in perpetuity and hereditary *jāgīrs* were not unknown in the Sikh times. But they were not service *jāgīrs*. Lands held on the same basis as the service *jāgīr* but not against any office, or with any obligation to the state, may appropriately be termed *in'ām jāgīrs* and they were frequently given by the Sikh rulers by way of reward. Also, lands were given to individuals merely for subsistence without involving the idea of either reward or service.[50] Subsistence *jāgīrs*, like *in'ām jāgīrs*, were generally hereditary.

In'ām jāgīrs were generally given by Ranjit Singh and his successors either for past services or in recognition of a particular act of service. Misar Ralia Ram, for example, was given a *jāgīr* worth 1100 rupees as a reward for his discovery of a sulphur mine.[51] Lehna Singh Majithia was given a village in 1837 as a reward for supplying intelligence about the retreat of Muhammad Akbar Khan, the son of Dost Muhammad of Kabul.[52] Jhanda Singh Butalia was given two villages in

[48] *Cf.* Athar Ali, *Mughal Nobility Under Aurangzeb*, 63-68.

[49] *Cf.* Fauja Singh, *Military System of the Sikhs*, 129.

Fauja Singh refers to the law of escheat in connection with the *jāgīrdārī fauj*: 'Whenever a chief died his estate was confiscated, but his troops instead of being disbanded were transferred to the control of the state'.

[50] *Cf.* Irfan Habib, *Agrarian System*, 258-59 n 5; Athar Ali, *Mughal Nobility Under Aurangzeb*, 75 n 5. Both Irfan Habib and Athar Ali refer to the *jāgīrs* of Jahanara Begam and Raja Jai Singh as examples of *in'ām*. In spite of the use of the term *in'ām* in Jahanara's case, the *jāgīr* was not given by way of reward. Strictly speaking, it was not an *in'ām jāgīr*. However, Raja Jai Singh was given *in'ām* assignment in recognition of his services at a time when he had attained to the highest *mansab* permitted to any noble and when, consequently, the only way of honouring and rewarding him could be the grant of *in'ām jāgīr*. In any case, we have used the term *in'ām* to cover only those cases which did involve the idea of reward and not merely of subsistence.

[51] *Foreign/Political Proceedings*, 3 April 1850, No. 194(29).

[52] Ibid., No. 280. It may be interesting to know that Diwan Devi Sahai was assigned a *jāgīr* in Shahpur in 1838 for collecting information on the military and mercantile resources of the Presidency of Bombay : Griffin & Massy, *Chiefs and Families*, II, 198-99.

perpetuity from his own service *jāgīr* for defending the fort of Attock, bridging the Indus and keeping the roads open.[53] A village was granted to Kahan Singh Majithia as a reward for boldly attacking a lion with his sword.[54] According to Captain Wade, the British Political Agent, Ranjit Singh was 'prompt to reward and scatter his bounties on those who attracted his notice by their gallantry, skill or devotion to his service'.[55] But *in'ām jāgīrs* were not confined to acts of valour or service. The Maharaja gave a *jāgīr* worth 500 rupees a year to Chaudhari Khuda Bakhsh Chaththa who had presented an excellent horse to him.[56] Revenue-free lands were sometimes given by way of *in'ām* to those who brought wasteland under cultivation.[57]

[53] *Foreign/Political Consultation*, 29 December 1849, No. 49A(10). It may be added that Fateh Sher and Saadullah got a village worth 700 rupees a year in the Rawalpindi area for having furnished supplies for the armies of the Maharaja at Attock : *Foreign/Political Proceedings*, 9 January 1857, Nos. 229-30.

[54] Sohan Lal, *Umdat*, III, (i), 44-45. It may be interesting to know that a *kahār* was given the daily allowance (*yaumia*) of one rupee for showing courage in a hunt in which the Maharaja killed a tiger : *News (1825)*, 79.

[55] *Foreign/Miscellaneous*, No. 206, para 194.

[56] Sohan Lal, *Umdat*, III, (iv), 493.

Osborne refers to the detachment of about 150 dancing girls at the court of Ranjit Singh who 'are allowed a small daily subsistence, and there are few of them who have not succeeded in obtaining small grants of villages from Runjeet Sing. . . . as marks of his favour' : *Court and Camp of Runjeet Sing*, 96.

[57] This was obviously done to encourage cultivation. Ilahi Bakhsh of the *top-khāna*, for example, was given a village when he offered to get it cultivated : Sohan Lal, *Umdat*, III, (v), 102. One Gurdit Singh whose father was a *jama'dār* in the army of Ranjit Singh, was granted a village, consisting only of one hut, for bringing it under cultivation; Ratta Misar was similarly given half a village in *jāgīr* for having founded one and for bringing it under cultivation : *Foreign/Political Consultation*, 14 March 1851, No. 113. Earlier instances of such grants are also known. Jassa Singh Ramgarhia and Jai Singh Kanhiya, for example, granted the uninhabited village of Burhanpur to Misar Diwan Singh for the purpose of being peopled; Diwan Singh received a fourth of the revenues for having reclaimed the village : *Foreign/Political Proceedings*, 15 October 1852, No. 116. It may be added that some of the *dharmarth* grantees also received grants for reclaiming wastelands and these appear to

With regard to *jāgīrs* for subsistence, charity may be said to have begun at the royal homes. Many a close relation of the ruling chief enjoyed subsistence *jāgīr*.[58] It was a considered policy of Ranjit Singh to alienate villages also in favour of the dispossessed chiefs and their dependants.[59] And Ranjit

have been given in perpetuity like some of the *in'ām* grants : ibid., 28 June 1854, Nos. 204-05 ; *Foreign/Political Consultation*, 14 March 1851, No. 113 A; ibid., 27 March 1853, Nos. 201-03.

[58] To cite a few examples, the mother of Prince Kharak Singh was given several villages by Maharaja Ranjit Singh for her maintenance; Rani Daya Kaur, the mother of Prince Kashmira Singh, also enjoyed subsistence *jāgīr* for over thirty years : Sohan Lal, *Umdat*, III, (iv), 591 & (iii), 344, respectively. Maharaja Sher Singh gave grants of revenue-free lands to his wife Rani Partap Kaur : *Foreign/Political Consultation*, 14 March 1851, No. 113. Raja Ala Singh of Patiala gave thirty villages to his wife : Karam Singh, *Baba Ala Singh*, 236-39 & 243. Gujjar Singh Bhangi gave subsistence *jāgīr* to his father-in-law and Bhup Singh of Ropar gave one to his mother-in-law : Griffin & Massy, *Chiefs and Families*, II, 97; *Foreign/Political Consultation*, 14 March 1851, No. 113 E, respectively. The rulers of Kalsia gave similar grants to their relatives and their dependants : Nagina Ram, *Ravī Parkāsh*, III, 946; Inaitullah, *Administrative History of Kalsia State*, f 159 a.

[59] Ranjit Singh ejected a large number of chiefs from their territories either immediately or having kept them up as vassals for sometime. Almost in all cases, he gave subsistence *jāgīrs* irrespective of their religious affiliation. To cite a few typical instances, Sarfaraz Khan, the eldest son of Nawab Muzaffar Khan of Multan, was given the *pargana* of Sharafpur, besides cash allowance, for his maintenance Sohan Lal, *Umdat*, II, 225; Ahmad Shah, *Tārīkh*, 476. Sagri Khan of Makhad and Ahmad Khan of Isa Khel were granted one-eighth share in the revenues of their former possessions for subsistence : Griffin & Massy, *Chiefs and Families*, II, 258 & 286, respectively. The dispossessed Rajas of Jaswan, Datarpur, Kutlehr and Basohli also received *jāgīrs* for maintenance : Sohan Lal, *Umdat*, II, 184; Hutchison & Vogel, *Panjab Hill States*, I, 212 ; Bute Shah, *Tārīkh*, V, f 271a; Kahan Singh Balauria, *Tawārikh-i-Rājputān* 77-78, respectively. Even when Sahib Singh Bhangi, one time rival of the Sukarchakias, was shorn of his territories, the *ta'alluqa* of Bajwat was allowed to remain with him : Ahmad Shah, *Tārīkh*, 411-12. Numerous indeed are instances of the Sikh and other chiefs receiving subsistence *jāgīrs* from Ranjit Singh. For some detail, see the author's *Agrarian System of the Sikhs (1759-1849)*, Ph.D. Thesis, Guru Nank University, Amritsar 1974, 369-85.

Singh was not the only Sikh ruler to adopt this policy.[60] Outside the royal homes, the dependants of the *jāgīrdārs* of the ruling chiefs received probably the largest share of subsistence *jāgīrs*.[61]

Much more important than the holders of subsistence and *in'ām jāgīrs* were the category of individuals called *pattīdārs*, literally shareholders or cosharers, who enjoyed certain hereditary rights. Their numbers in the early nineteenth century were strikingly large. In Ambala and Thanesar, they were so numerous that it was ' impossible as in the case of ordinary maafeedars to insist on their making appearance at the tehsildaree once a year for the purpose of having their existence

In several cases, the minor sons and widows of the dispossessed chiefs were also given *jāgīrs* for maintenance: *Khālsa Darbār Records*, Bundle 5, Vol. XII, 13, 51, 59, 63, for example. However, there are instances of such *jāgīrs* being given even during the lifetime of the chief. When Raja Agar Khan was ejected from Rajauri and imprisoned in Lahore, his sons were given Narowal : Amar Nath, *Zafarnāma*, 141-42. When the dislodged Rajas of Guler and Nurpur refused the *jāgīr* offered, and continued opposing the Sikhs, it was nevertheless granted to their dependants: Sohan Lal, *Umdat*, II, 129-30, 150-51 & 184, 190, respectively. See also, Hutchison & Vogel, *Panjab Hill States*, I, 206-07 & 264 respectively.

[60] Jassa Singh Ahluwalia, for example, gave a *jāgīr* to Rai Ibrahim whose territories of Kapurthala had been taken over by the Ahluwalia chief: Ram Sukh Rao, *Srī Fateh Singh Partāp Prabhākar*, f 80a. Bhai Desu Singh gave several villages in *jāgīr* to Niamat Khan after the latter was dispossessed of his share of the Kaithal territory: *Gazetteer of Karnal*, 38. Gurbakhsh Singh Kalsia gave villages in *jāgīr* to some persons without any condition of service: Inaitullah, *Administrative History of the Kalsia State*, f118a.

[61] For example, the wives and dependants of Misar Diwan Chand, Colonel Shaikh Basawan, Jawand Singh Maukal, Diwan Bhawani Das, Lala Devi Sahai and several others were among the recipients of such *jāgīrs*: *Khālsa Darbār Records*, Bundle 5, Vol. XII, 15, 53, 97, 119, 143, 181 & 253. Sohan Lal refers to the grant of a village worth 1200 rupees to the wife of General Cortlandt, and worth 2500 rupees to the daughter of General Ventura: *Umdat* III, (iii), 325 & (iv), 430, respectively.

It may be added that the dependants of the individual troopers also were sometimes given subsistence *jāgīrs*: *Khālsa Darbār Records*, Bundle 5, Vol. XII, 69 & Vol. XIV, 163, for example.

recorded'.[62] *Pattīdārs* were not confined to the region between the Satlej and the Jamna.[63] To outside observers, their position appeared to vary from that of a *jāgīrdār* to that of an autonomous chief.[64]

The *pattīdārs*, without the slightest doubt, were a legacy of the initial stages of conquest made by the Sikhs. In the words of Prinsep :

> When the Misals acquired their territorial possessions, it became the first duty of the chiefs to partition out the lands, towns, and villages amongst those who considered themselves as having made the conquest *Shamil* or in common. Every *Sarkarda* or the leader of the smallest party

[62] *Foreign/Political Consultation*, 26 September 1851, No. 118. According to a settlement officer, in the Ambala district alone, 'in addition to the 33 leading families with *jāgīr* revenues of Rs. 260,000' there were 'over five thousand lesser *pattīdārī jāgīrdārs* dividing over three lakhs a year' : A. Kensington, quoted in Griffin & Massy, *Chiefs and Families*, I, 53.

[63] In the Jalandhar Doab, for example, there were several hundred villages held by families whose ancestors had originally conquered them : *Foreign/Political Consultation*, 9 November 1846, Nos. 2185-97. In some of the early British records, the *pattīdārīs* in Hoshiarpur are referred to as 'conquest jagirs' and equated with the *pattīdārīs* of the region across the Satlej : *Foreign/Political Proceedings*, 1 May 1857, No. 459.

[64] To a British administrator, the rights of the *pattīdārs* appeared to be 'something more than and distinct from civil and proprietary rights'. He goes on to say that 'we will not call the Putteedars sovereign or independent Rulers, but the rights which they are permitted to exercise, their hakimi rights do not greatly differ from Government rights. They collect revenue and taxes and impose fines for penal offences and exercise all other rights belonging to a Government in their respective Puttees, save the powers of life and death' : C.F. Mackeson, Commissioner & Supdt. Cis-Satlej, to H.M. Lawrence, *Foreign/Political Consultation*, 26 December 1846, Nos. 598-601. To another administrator, the *pattīdārs* appeared to be 'different from any body of men' he had 'met with or read of'; they most nearly resembled 'the jagheerdars and great maafeedars' in the North Western Provinces : W. Wynyard, settlement officer, to C.F. Mackeson, ibid., 12 May 1849, No. 142. To the Court of Directors also the *pattīdārs* appeared distinctly to possess territorial rights of 'a political nature' : Despatch to the G.G.-in-Council, ibid., 28 March 1849, No. 12.

> of horse that fought under the standard of the Misal demanded his share in proportion to the degree in which he had contributed to the acquisition, and, as they received no pay from the chief, and he had no other recompense to offer for their services, there was no recourse but to adopt this mode of satisfying them. The *Sirdari* or chief's portion being first divided off, the remainder was separated into *Pattis* or parcels for each *Sarkarda*, and these were again subdivided and parcelled out to inferior leaders, according to the number of horse they brought into the field. Each took his portion as a cosharer, and held it in absolute independence.[65]

Prinsep goes on to add that reciprocal aid for mutual protection and defence was 'the relation on which a Pattidar stood in other respects to the Sirdar, and the only condition of his tenure'.[66]

Prinsep's observations find ample support in other contemporary evidence which indicates, moreover, that the *pattīdārs* were gradually reduced to the status of hereditary holders of subsistence *jāgīrs*. This may be illustrated with reference to the history of the Kalsia chiefs. Gurbakhsh Singh Kalsi made initial conquests conjointly with Karam Singh and Budh Singh and divided the conquered territories into three equal shares. From his own share, Gurbakhsh Singh gave lands to other cosharers (*hissadārs*), according to the number of troops commanded by each. All his kinsmen who received lands from Gurbakhsh Singh in this way were his *pattīdārs* and their only obligation was to render military service when required.[67] At this stage, the position of the *pattīdār* was very similar to that of an autonomous chief. However, his lands were not inherited

[65] *Origin of the Sikh Power*, 26.

[66] Ibid., 28.

[67] Nagina Ram, *Ravī Parkāsh*, I, 42; II, 527-28 & 531-32 ; III, 945. Nagina Ram goes on to add that if any of the *pattīdārs* 'rebelled' against the chief, the latter could reduce or confiscate his territory. For detail of the division of villages between Sardar Gurbakhsh Singh himself and his *pattīdārs*, see Inaitullah, *Administrative History of the Kalsia State*, ff 14a-b & 15a-b ; also, 88b, 91a-b & 95 a.

by one single heir. In fact, failing all male heirs or collaterals, even widows and daughters and mothers succeeded to the holding.[68] The hereditary character of the *pattīdārī* holdings is hardly questionable and here they were distinct from service *jāgīrs*.[69] Ranjit Singh obliged some of the *pattīdārs* to render military service without receiving additional *jāgīrs*. In other words, he was asserting a right which had belonged to their former chiefs.[70] However, when *pattīdārī* holdings were divided

[68] For example, a *pattīdār* named Amar Singh died issueless and his widow, Malan, succeeded to the estate. After her death, the estate went to a lady called Saddan whose mother had been adopted by Malan as a daughter : Inaitullah, *Administrative History of the Kalsia State*, ff 91a-b & 92b. In the case of another *pattīdār* who died issueless, the estate went to his daughter and her descendants : ibid., f 92b. There are also instances of a widow succeeding to her husband's share even when the husband's brothers were alive and were holding their own shares of the *pattī*: *Foreign/Political Consultation*, 1 April 1853, Nos. 207-17. See also, ibid., 14 March 1851, No. 113; ibid., 11 June 1852, Nos. 109-14.

[69] A contemporary *Dastūr al-'Amal* makes a clear distinction between the *pattīdārs*, some of whom did not acknowledge the authority of the *sardār*, and the '*jāgīrdārs* and *tabi'dārs*' over whom the *sardār* exercised 'full authority regarding their service and other obligations' : Ghulam Muhammad, *Dastūr al-'Amal*, f 14a. The chronicler of the Kalsia chiefs is also explicit about the four categories of *jāgīr* tenures :

mu'āfīdār (the *dharmarth* in our terms)
guzārakhwār (the subsistence *jāgīr*)
jāgīrdār (the service *jāgīr*)
pattīdār

Nagina Ram, *Ravī Parkāsh*, III, 945-46.

[70] The *pattīdārs* rendered service to Ranjit Singh and paid *nazrāna* at the same time. According to John Lawrence, 'Maharaja Ranjit Singh was, to the day of his death, gradually resuming the lands of all the descendants of the conquering class and where he left them in possession, steadily increased their burden so as by degrees to assimilate their condition with that of the rest of the country'. After exacting military service, the Maharaja added 'so much per saddle'. Consequently, the petty *jāgīrdārs* who were collectively holding lands worth 5 lakhs and furnishing 700 horsemen 'paid in this ways Rs. 39,079 per annum' : 'SSR Jullundur Doab', *Foreign/Political Proceedings*, 31 December 1847, No. 2443, para 57.

In fact, Ranjit Singh was only completing a process started earlier. Many an original conqueror among the Sikhs was obliged to accept

and subdivided among a large number of heirs, many of them were not in a position to render any service because of their inadequately small holdings, and their position became similar to that of the subsistence *jāgīrdārs*.[71]

Jāgīrs were mostly managed by the *jāgīrdārs* either directly or indirectly through their agents. There was many a petty *jāgīrdār* who could not and did not have the services of an agent. Even if he himself was absent on duty, the other members of his family looked after the *jāgīr*. Even a big *jāgīrdār* sometimes preferred the management of his *jāgīrs* by a kinsman rather than a hired agent.[72] At times, a *jāgīrdār* managed his own *jāgīrs* directly because they fell within the administrative area under his jurisdiction.[73] Many dispossessed chiefs remained present as *jāgīrdārs* in a part of their former territories.[74] Those who had large *jāgīrs* scattered over a number of places had no option but to employ managers or

the status virtually of a hereditary *jāgīrdār* with the passage of time. In the territories of the Ahluwalia chiefs, for example, many *pattīdārs* were virtually reduced to this position : *Foreign/Political Consultation*, 14 March 1851, No. 113 C. For some other examples, see Griffin & Massy, *Chiefs and Families*, I, 151, 158, 164 & 167.

It may be interesting to note that in the areas which came under British protection the *pattīdārs* were deliberately reduced to the status of hereditary *jāgīrdārs* : *Foreign/Political Consultation*, 12 May 1849, No. 142.

[71] It may be pointed out that on succession of a widow a *pattī* did not necessarily become a subsistence *jāgīr*. The widow was required to maintain horsemen wherever the share was large enough to support them : see, for example, Sohan Lal, *Umdat*, IV, (i), 61 ; *Foreign/Political Consultation*, 29 December 1849, No. 49A (16).

[72] For instance, when Sardar Diwan Singh Ramgarhia was given a *jāgīr* worth 65,000 rupees in Qadian while serving in Kashmir, this *jāgīr* was managed by his son Mangal Singh : Sohan Lal, *Umdat*, III, (i), 76.

[73] For example, Fateh Singh managed his *jāgīrs*, in Shergarh when he was the '*hākim*' of Shergarh itself : Munshi Bakhtawar Lal, *Tārīkh-i-Montgomery*, 23.

[74] In the lower Bari Doab, for example, the sons of Rup Singh Kingra managed 24 villages which had been left to them in *jāgīr* : ibid., 47-48.

agents for the collection of revenues from their *jāgīrs*.[75] Many an absentee *jāgīrdār* gave his *jāgīr* on farm.[76]

Conflict between the various claimants to produce from land was not uncommon during the Sikh times.[77] The administrators appointed by the rulers were instructed to take cognizance of disputes and to obviate them.[78] Disputes between the assignees themselves were not infrequent, and they were settled by the disputants mostly without reference to the ruler.[79] More

[75] See, for example, *Foreign/Political Consultation*, 26 December 1846, No. 598.

[76] For instance, in 1832, Diwan Dina Nath received the village of Rattar Chattar, worth 1500 rupees in *jāgīr* and gave it in farm to the local *zamīndārs* (peasant proprietors) at 1590 rupees a year. In another case, he gave two villages worth 1000 rupees in farm to local *zamīndārs* at 1270 rupees a year. In yet another case, however, he farmed out wells worth 200 rupees a year at only 180 rupees : *Foreign/ Political Proceedings*, 22 November 1850, No. 117 A(1). For some other examples, see ibid., 6 September 1850, No. 31 A; *Foreign/ Political Consultation*, 29 December 1849, No. 49 A (2).

[77] In order to obviate disputes, John Lawrence argued in favour of defining the position of the *jāgīrdār* in relation to the government and his rights and privileges in relation to the proprietors and the cultivators. He strongly felt that the powerful *jāgīrdārs* in Sikh times ground the proprietors and the cultivators to dust; the weak *jāgīrdārs*, on the other hand, failed to get what was due to them; and where the power was fairly balanced, bloodshed and violence at the time of harvest were of common occurrence: 'SSR Jullundur Doab', *Foreign/Political Proceedings*, 31 December 1847, No. 2443, para 59.

[78] Tej Singh, for example, was instructed not simply to help the collectors against recalcitrant *zamīndārs* of the *pargana* but also to ensure that the new grantees got possession of their *jāgīrs* without undue delay on the part of the old grantees to hand over the charge : Sita Ram Kohli, 'A Note on Some Khalsa Darbar Parwanas', *The Indian Archives*, IV, 2-6. Orders were frequently issued to the *kārdārs* against interference with the lands legitimately held in *jāgīr*. Sardar Kahan Singh Majithia, for example, was ordered in 1822 that there should be no interference with the *jāgīr* of Man Singh and Kahan Singh, and the *sardār* on his own part, passed similar orders to his subordinates : *Foreign/Political Proceedings*, 7 May 1853, No. 228. See also, ibid., 3 April 1850, No. 194.

[79] In 1834, a dispute arose between Diwan Sawan Mal and Raja Gulab Singh over their *jāgīrs* and the Maharaja had to intervene : Sohan Lal, *Umdat*, III, (ii), 207 & (iv), 391. Similarly, a dispute arose between

common were the disputes between the *jāgīrdārs* and the peasant proprietors. In some areas, the *jāgīrdārs* were powerful enough to oppress the peasantry.[80] But in some other areas, the proprietors were strong enough to resist even the legitimate demands of the *jāgīrdārs*.[81]

The Sikh *jāgīrdārī* system was by no means a creation of Ranjit Singh. His father, Mahan Singh and his grandfather, Charhat Singh gave *jāgīrs* to those who served them in civil or military capacity.[82] *Jāgīrs* for service were given also by the

Jamadar Khushal Singh and Sardar Wasawa Singh Sandhanwalia and resulted in some bloodshed on both sides. When the matter was reported to the Maharaja he remarked that if he had been informed of the dispute in time there would have been no violence. Khushal Singh replied, significantly, that such matters were usually settled by the disputants without reference to the Maharaja. But Khushal Singh had to apologize when the Maharaja retorted that disputes and quarrels were on the increase precisely because they were not reported to him: *Umdat*, III, (iii), 320.

[80] It was surmised that such disputes were in the beginning frequent and troublesome because the 'jageerdar used to consider the jageer as his private property, the people on it as his serfs' : John Lawrence to H.M. Elliot, *Foreign/Political Consultation*, 31 December 1847, No. 2288, para 5. Some of the *jāgīrdārs* appeared to have gradually ousted the proprietors from their lands : ibid., Nos. 2216-17. See also, *Events* (*1810-1817*), 99; Sohan Lal, *Umdat* III, (iii), 326.

[81] For example, in three villages in the *jāgīr* of Sardar Gulab Singh Pahuwindia, the *zamīndārs* had insisted upon sharing the produce rather than paying the revenue in cash, in accordance with the office records. Sardar Gulab Singh had eventually to request the transfer of his *jāgīr* from these villages : *Foreign/Secret Consultation*, 30 October 1847, No 95.

[82] Charhat Singh, for example, gave the town of Kunjah in *jāgīr* to Dal Singh and the '*ilāqa* of Kalra and Kuthala to Himmat Singh : Ganesh Das, *Chār Bāgh*, 130. The ancestors of Jiwan Singh Chhachhi, Jhanda Singh Butalia and Kishan Singh Lumba were among the earliest *jāgīrdārs* of Charhat Singh. He gave *jāgīrs* worth 65,000 rupees to Sahib Singh Kalianwala for maintaining 80 horsemen for service: *Foreign/Political Consultation*, 29 December 1849, No. 49 A (case nos. 8, 10, 35 & 12, respectively). In one of his orders addressed to the *pīrs* of Tilla Gorakh Nath (seen in translation through Prof. B.N. Goswamy's courtesy), the addressees are the *jāgīrdārs* as well as the *kārdārs* of the Jehlam area. Mahan Singh generally confirmed the *jāgīrs* given by Charhat Singh. In the cases of Lal Singh Kalianwala and Kahan Singh Man, the *jāgīrs* were not only confirmed but

chiefs of the petty principality of Kalsia.[83] Neither the powerful Sukarchakias nor the petty Kalsia chiefs were exceptional in this respect. The well-known names like Hari Singh Bhangi, Jassa Singh Ahluwalia, Jai Singh Kanhiya, Gujjar Singh Bhangi, Gulab Singh Bhangi, Ala Singh of Patiala, and the names, of less-known chiefs like Ran Singh Nakai, Bhag Singh Hollowalia, Sudh Singh Dodia, Sangat Singh Nishanwala, Jassa Singh Dulu and the Bhais of Kaithal can easily be added to the list.[84] John Lawrence was struck by the number of *jāgīrs* in

also increased by Mahan Singh: *Foreign/Political Consultation*, 29 December 1849, No. 49 A (case nos. 12 & 14); *Foreign/Political Proceedings*, 7 January 1853, No. 228, respectively. Mahan Singh also gave fresh *jāgīrs* of his own. Rangpur, for instance, was wrested from the Bhangis and given in *jāgīr* to Chaudhari Man Sahai : Munshi Amin Chand, *History of Sialkot*, 4. Griffin & Massy refer to several cases of service *jāgīrs* given by Mahan Singh : *Chiefs and Families*, II, 34, 104, 105, 108, for example.

[83] Gurbakhsh Singh Kalsia gave several villages by way of service *jāgīr* (*b'wajah-i-naukarī*) to those who were serving him as *sawārān-i-khās* in his conquests across the Satlej: Inaitullah, *Administrative History of the Kalsia State*, ff 82b, 103b & 126b. When he conquered Chhachhrauli he appointed Tek Singh as the *tahsīldār* of the *'ilāqa* and paid him in *jāgīr*: ibid., f 129a. Jassa Singh and Ganda Singh received 11 villages for maintaining 15 horsemen and Badan Singh received 4½ villages for service (*mulāzmat*) as a commander: ibid., ff 84a-b & 120b. Sometimes, a single village was held by several persons in *jāgīr* : ibid., f 120b. See also, Nagina Ram, *Ravī Parkāsh*, III, 947-1040.

Nagina Ram has a very interesting observation to make on the categories of *jāgīrs* given for service by the Kalsia rulers: one, those which were given only for the lifetime of the grantee; two, which descended to the heirs of the grantee generation after generation. The term used for the latter was *wāguzār* : ibid., 945.

[84] For example, Jassa Singh Ahluwalia gave four villages worth 4000 rupees in *jāgīr* to Jagat Singh, Prem Singh and Des Raj on condition of furnishing four *sawārs* and protecting the 'frontier': *Foreign/Political Consultation*, 12 March 1852, No. 95. Across the Satlej, Bhai Lal Singh of Kaithal gave lands worth nearly 1000 rupees to Lehna Singh for maintaining 10 horsemen; Bhai Karam Singh gave a village in *jāgīr* to Tej Singh for 13 or 14 *sawārs*; Bhai Udai Singh gave three villages to Qalandar Bakhsh Risaldar for maintaining 32 horsemen; and Bhai Desu Singh of Kaithal had given several villages in *jāgīr* to Budhu Khan for furnishing hundred *sawārs*: ibid., 14 March 1851, No. 113 A. Raja Ala Singh granted more than 3000 *ghumāons*

the Jalandhar Doab coming down from the days prior to its conquest by Ranjit Singh.[85] We may safely infer that during the late eighteenth century, as in the early nineteenth, the Sikh rulers paid their servants largely through *jāgīrs* rather than in cash.

Maharaja Ranjit Singh took over the old system and developed it systematically with men drawn from several sources. Already in the late eighteenth century, some of the minor chiefs were being reduced to the status of *jāgīrdārs*.[86] Ranjit Singh completed this process by systematically reducing the largest number of chiefs to the status of *jāgīrdārs*. To serve him as *jāgīrdārs* at some time in their lives were Nahar Singh Chamiariwala, Bhag Singh Hallowalia, Chait Singh Bhangi of Lahore, Gurdit Singh Bhangi of Amritsar, Milkha Singh of Rawalpindi, Dasaundha Singh and Jhanda Singh of Dallewal, Ran Singh Nakai of Bharwal, Nidhan Singh Wadalia, Jodh Singh Saurianwala, Bhag Singh Muraliwala, Dal Singh Akalgarhia, Karam Singh Rangar Nangalia, Prem Singh

of land in service *jāgīr* to each of the 'Semeke and Sardulkian *jats*': Karam Singh, *Baba Ala Singh*, 127. The servants and officials of the Patiala state were paid largely in *jāgīr* : Griffin, *Rajas of the Punjab*, 126, 129, 130 & 138.

For further detail on the *jāgīrs* granted by the early Sikh rulers see, for example, *Foreign/Political Consultation*, 29 December 1849, No. 49 A ; ibid., 5 September 1856, Nos. 109-15; *Foreign/Political Proceedings*, 27 March 1857, Nos. 233-37. Griffin & Massy, *Panjab Chiefs*, II, 41 ; Munshi Bakhtawar Lal, *Tārkīh-i-Montgomery*, 21; Munshi Amin Chand, *History of Sialkot*, 10.

[85] 'SSR Jullundur Doab', *Foreign/Political Proceedings*, 31 December 1847, No. 2443, para 55.

[86] The ancestors of Sardar Fateh Singh Man who served Ranjit Singh as a *jāgīrdār*, present an interesting example in this connection. Karam Singh Man had conquered territories worth over a lakh of rupees jointly with the Bhangi chiefs. He was succeeded in those territories by his sons Ram Singh and Sham Singh. The former was obliged to pay tribute to Mahan Singh. After his death, Mahan Singh took away the larger part of his territories from his younger brother Sham Singh who was allowed to subsist on lands worth 20,000 only. Ranjit Singh obliged Sham Singh to maintain 15 horsemen. It was this position to which Fateh Singh Man was allowed to succeed in the beginning of his career : *Foreign/Political Consultation*, 29 December 1849, No. 49 A (14). Likewise, Mahtab Singh, a minor chief who had conered over 50 villages in his own right, was obliged by the Bhangi chiefs

Khundawala, Jassa Singh Dulu and Jodh Singh Kalalwala.[87] Several Muslim chiefs were also made to serve the Maharaja as *jāgīrdārs* including Qutubuddin Khan and his nephew Fatehuddin Khan of Qasur, Ahmad Khan Sial of Jhang, Fateh Khan of Sahiwal, Ahmad Yar Khan Tiwana of Nurpur and Hafiz Ahmad Khan of Dera Ismail Khan.[88] Some of the *jāgīrdārs*

Jhanda Singh and Ganda Singh to render service to them with a fixed number of horsemen maintained on the revenues of his villages : Griffin & Massy, *Chiefs and Families*, II, 52. Similarly in Dipalpur, the Nakai chief Qamar Singh overpowered Sahai Singh, another Nakai chief, and reduced him to the status of a *jāgīrdār* : Munshi Bakhtawar Lal, *Tārīkh-i-Montgomery*, 3-4.

[87] Ganesh Das mentions that Nahar Singh Chamiariwala and Bhag Singh Hallowalia, 'each of whom in his own right claimed sovereign status, were uprooted and given *jāgīrs* strictly in accordance with the pleasure (of Ranjit Singh) and were made subject to his command' : *Chār Bāgh*, 146. Chait Singh Bhangi of Lahore was given the *ta'alluqa* of Wainki in *jāgīr* and was required to supply a contingent to the Maharaja : Ahmad Shah, *Tārīkh*, 410. Gurdit Singh, the son of Gulab Singh Bhangi of Amritsar, rendered the service of only five horsemen and was placed under Hari Singh Nalwa : Aliuddin, *'Ibratnāma*, 297. Milkha Singh of Rawalpindi, who ruled over a territory worth 3 lakhs of rupees, became a *jāgīrdār* of the Maharaja and was given 700 horse and foot to command : Amarnath, *Zafarnāma*, 32.

For further detail, see ibid., 32-33; Aliuddin, *'Ibratnāma*, 306-07 & 381; Munshi Bakhtawar Lal, *Tārīkh-i-Montgomery*, 11; Bute Shah, *Tārīkh* V, ff 163 a-b & 255 b; Griffin & Massy, *Chiefs and Families*, II, 7-8, 45 & 65.

[88] The territories of the Qasur chiefs were worth about 8 lakhs of rupees when Qutubuddin Khan accepted Mamdot in *jāgīr* subject to the service of 100 horsemen; his nephew Fatehuddin Khan also accepted a *jāgīr* on a similar condition. The value of Fatehuddin Khan's *jāgīr* in 1826 is given as 29,000 rupees : *Foreign/Political Consultation*, 29 December 1849, No. 49 A (15). Ahmad Khan Sial, the chief of Jhang, who had been dislodged from his territory worth 4 lakhs of rupees, was given the *pargana* of Merowal in *jāgīr* for service (*jāgīr dar khidmat*): Sohan Lal, *Umdat*, II, 212. See also, Amar Nath, *Zafarnāma*, 28-29. The Barakzai brothers, Sultan Muhammad, Pir Muhammad and Sayyid Muhammad, were given Kohat and Hashtnagar, worth 3½ lakhs of rupees : Sohan Lal, *Umdat*, V, 66 & 70. *Cf.* Amar Nath, *Zafarnāma*, 241; Charles Hugel, *Travels in Kashmir and the Panjab*, 306; Shahamat Ali, *Sikhs and Afghans*, 266.

For further detail regarding these and some other Muslim chiefs turned *jāgīrdārs*, see ibid., 276; Amar Nath, *Zafarnāma* 248;

of the dispossessed chiefs were also taken into service by Ranjit Singh and paid through *jāgīrs*. Mohkam Chand and Hukma Singh Chimni, the Majithias and the Atariwalas present only the most conspicuous examples of such *jāgīrdārs*.[89] However, a large number of individuals and families who came to serve the kingdom of Lahore with distinction were picked up all afresh and patronized by Ranjit Singh on the basis of their merit or promise.[90] In fact, the *jāgīrdārs* of Ranjit Singh were drawn from different racial and religious groups and also from differant regions in his kingdom.[91]

Prinsep, *Origin of the Sikh Power*, 93; Griffin & Massy, *Chiefs and Families*, II, 178, 187-88, 195, 270 & 300.

[89] Mohkam Chand had served Dal Singh Akalgarhia and Sahib Singh Bhangi before joining the service of the Maharaja in 1806 : Sohan Lal, *Umdat*, II, 67. Hukma Singh Chimni, who served Ranjit Singh with distinction, had for some time been a *jāgīrdār* of the Bhangi chiefs : Munshi Amin Chand, *History of Sialkot*, 5. Nihal Singh Atariwala and his cousin Jodh Singh had served Sahib Singh Bhangi before receiving service *jāgīr* from Ranjit Singh : Aliuddin, *'Ibratnāma*, 305 & 309. Hukm Singh and Jagat Singh, sons of Tek Singh Atariwala, abandoned Sahib Singh Bhangi for receiving the honour of appropriate '*mansabs*' from the Maharaja : Ganesh Das, *Chār Bāgh*, 147. For further detail, see ibid., 147-48 & 149; Griffin & Massy, *Chiefs and Families*, I, 469, 472 & 495; II, 39, 41, 117, 142 & 320.

[90] The case of the Jamwal brothers before they were created *rājas* is well-known. From within the Panjab plains came Hari Singh Nalwa, Misars Diwan Chand, Beli Ram, Megh Raj, Sukh Dayal and Misar Rup Lal, Ralia Ram Chopra, Nanak Chand Daftari, Diwan Sawan Mal, 'Karnail' Mihan Singh, the Faqir brothers Azizuddin, Imamuddin and Nuruddin, Shaikh Ghulam Muhiyuddin and his son Imamuddin, Ilahi Bakhsh, Sultan Muhammad, Gulab Singh Pahuwindia and his son Ala Singh, Diwan Lakhi Mal, Diwan Amir Chand, and several others.

[91] In the *Umdat-ut-Tawarīkh*, and in the *Events at the Court of Ranjit Singh*, the names of the important courtiers of Ranjit Singh are given from time to time and the statement made here is amply borne out by that evidence. A specimen may, however, be given from the *News of the Court of Ranjit Singh* : On 5 March 1825, among the courtiers present with the Maharaja were Jamadar Khushal Singh, Lehna Singh Sandhanwalia, Jawand Singh Maukal, Jawala Singh Naherna, Partap Singh Atariwala, Hardas Singh Doabia, Diwan Singh Roparwala, Sobha Singh Kalsia, Attar Singh Faizullapuria, Diwan Bhawani Das, Diwan Moti Ram, Misar Diwan Chand, Diwan Ganga Ram, Kirpa Ram, Sukh Dayal, Sarb Dayal, Faqir Azizuddin, Faqir Nuruddin and th *Sāhibān-i-Farānsīs* : *News* (*1825*), 21.

They were not confined to the Panjab either.[92] If several families served the Sikh rulers successively for more than one generation, it was largely because service to the state was an important criterion for selection and the heirs of a *jāgīrdār* were generally selected for service.[93]

A clear distinction between the *khālisa* and the *jāgīr* lands existed during the Sikh times.[94] Just as lands from the *khālisa* were alienated in favour of the *jāgīrdārs*, so were the lands once given in *jāgīr* taken back into the *khālisa*. The known examples indicate that while certain areas remained in the *khālisa* all the time, the position of the areas given in *jāgīr* alternated between the *jāgīr* and the *khālisa*.[95] No distinct term

[92] To come from outside the Panjab plains to serve the Maharaja with distinction were Diwan Bhawani Das, Diwan Ganga Ram, Diwan Ajudhiya Parshad, Diwan Dina Nath, Jamadar Khushal Singh and his nephew Tej Singh. Some of the European officers of the Maharaja, such as Ventura, Avitabile, Allard and Court, were also paid at least partly in *jāgīr*.

[93] That was how several families of *jāgīrdārs* came to serve the Sikh rulers for more than one generation. The instances of the heirs of Nihal Singh Atariwala, Diwan Mohkam Chand and Desa Singh Majithia being taken into service by the Maharaja are rather well-known. Parts of ancestral possessions and *jāgīrs* were continued to the sons and successors also of Sham Singh Butalia, Jawand Singh Maukal, Dhanna Singh Malwai, Kirpal Singh Kunjahia and several others: *Foreign/Political Consultation*, 29 December 1849, No. 49A; *Foreign/Political Proceedings*, 15 October 1852, No. 116; ibid., 7 January 1853, No. 228; ibid., 10 June 1853, No. 217.

It may be pointed out that the heirs of a deceased *jāgīrdār* paid the 'customary *nazr*' before they were allowed to succeed to his position or property: see, for example, Sohan Lal, *Umdat*, III, (i), 12.

[94] For example, for the dominions of Ranjit Singh, Shahamat Ali, a British functionary, also gives the revenue figures separately for the *khālisa* and the *jāgīr* lands: *Sikhs and Afghans*, 23. Ahmad Shah refers to the papers related to the *khālisa* and *jāgīr* lands in the territories of the Ramgarhia chiefs: *Tārīkh*, 472. Aliuddin mentions the territories given in *jāgīr* by Tara Singh Dallewalia as a category distinct from the *khālisa*: *'Ibratnāma*, 333-34.

[95] This may be illustrated with reference to the area covered by the Sialkot district after its conquest by Ranjit Singh. The Maharaja gave Daula in *jāgīr* to Misar Diwan Chand first and then to Hari Singh Nalwa. It reverted to the *khālisa* before it was given in *jāgīr* to

appears to have been used, however, for the land reverting to the *khālisa* and waiting to be assigned in *jāgīr*.[96] For the entire dominions of Ranjit Singh, the land given in *jāgīr* appears to have been less than the land retained in the *khālisa*.[97] Transfer

Ganda Singh of Batala. Bal was given in *jāgīr* to Surat Singh and Jamadar Khushal Singh before it reverted to the *khālisa*. Lalah was given in *jāgīr* by Ranjit Singh to Dharam Singh, Jamadar Khushal Singh and Gulab Singh one after the other before it became *khālisa* : Munshi Amin Chand, *History of Sialkot*, 9 & 12; also, 5-15.

In fact, a number of places were given in *jāgīr* to more than one person at different times and also reverted to the *khālisa* from time to time. For further detail, see, for example, Griffin & Massy, *Chiefs and Families*, II, 216 ; Sohan Lal, *Umdat*, III, (ii), 261 & 289-90; (iii), 234-35.

96 Under the Mughals, areas due for assignment, but not yet assigned in *jāgīr*, bore the technical name of *pāibāqī* : Irfan Habib, *Agrarian System*, 258-59 & 259 n 6.

97 No exact figures are readily available for the period of Sikh rule to determine the precise proportion of revenues alienated in *jāgīr* at any given time. Figures are available however to give us some idea of the proportions involved. The figures given by Prinsep for the 1830s do not give the *khālisa* and *jāgīr* revenues separately. He gives the figures for *jāgīr* and *dharmarth* together, and those for the *khālisa* and tribute from the vassals together. In these figures, the revenues alienated by the Maharaja in favour of all kinds of grantees amount to about 47 per cent of the total revenues from land, including tribute:

Land Revenue and Tribute from the Vassals :	1,24,03,900
Customs :	19,00,600
Muhrāna :	5,77,000
Jāgīrs and *Dharmarth* :	1,09,28,000

Origin of the Sikh Power, 146.

In Shahamat Ali's figures for 1838, *jāgīr* and *khālisa* revenue are given separately and the proportion of *jāgīrs* to the total revenues from land comes to about 31 per cent :

Khālisa :	1,96,57,172
Jāgīrs :	87,54,590
Kharājguzārs :	12,66,000
Transit duties :	5,50,000

Sikhs and Afghans, 23.

The absolute figures given by Cunningham for the year 1844 are larger than those of Shahamat Ali and his proportion of *jāgīrs* to the total revenues from land is about 35 per cent :

Tributary States :	5,65,000
Farms :	1,79,85,000

of *jāgīrs*, in part or whole, was by no means uncommon, though certain areas remained in the *jāgīr* of a particular person for a very considerable length of time.[98] In the case of persons holding large *jāgīrs*, enough care was taken as a rule not to allow the concentration of their *jāgīrs* in one area.[99] In exceptional cases, when the bulk of the *jāgīrs* did lie in one area, they were not allowed to become contiguous.[100]

A considerable portion of the *jāgīrs* went to the princes and some prominent individuals and families.[101] The first

Eleemosynary :	20,00,000
Jāgīrs :	95,25,000
Customs, etc :	24,00,000

A History of the Sikhs 387, Appendix XXXVIII. See also, *GRAPP (1849-1851)*, 161.

According to John Lawrence's Report on the Jalandhar Doab, nearly 50 per cent of the total revenues of the region had been alienated in *jāgīrs* by the rulers of Lahore : 'SSR Jullundur Doab', *Foreign/Political Proceedings*, 31 December 1847, No. 2443, para 53; also, para 8.

[98] For example, very early in his reign, Naunar in the *pargana* of Sialkot, was given by Ranjit Singh in *jāgīr* to Amir Singh Sandhanwalia whose family enjoyed it for the rest of the reigns of Ranjit Singh and his successors : Munshi Amin Chand, *History of Sialkot*, 15.

[99] For example, Gurmukh Singh Lamba held *jāgīrs* in the Sindh Sagar, Chaj and the Bari Doabs : *Foreign/Political Consultation*, 29 December 1849, No. 49 A (20). Similarly, Sardar Shamsher Singh Sandhanwalia got *jāgīrs* in the Bari, Rachna and Sindh Sagar Doabs and also in the region across the Indus : ibid., 49 A (2). Diwan Dina Nath held *jāgīrs* in Adina Nagar, Lahore, Qasur, Shaikhupura, Wazirabad, Gujrat and Peshawar : *Foreign/Political Proceedings*, 22 November 1850, Nos. 117 & 117 A. Griffin's observation that Ranjit Singh gave new *jāgīrs* to dispossessed chiefs and entrusted their former territories to his own devoted dependants has to be considered also in the light of the Maharaja's policy of not leaving large chunks of contiguous territory in the hands of any *jāgīrdār* : see, *Rajas of the Punjab*, 88 & 90.

[100] For example, Sardar Lehna Singh Majithia got most of his *jāgīrs* in the upper Bari Doab but his *jāgīrs* did not form a contiguous territory : *Foreign/Political Proceedings*, 3 April 1850, No. 280.

[101] It is not clear if, as in the Mughal *mansabdārī* system, there was a strict hierarchy of *jāgīrdārs* even in the reign of Ranjit Singh. Amar Nath refers to the conferment of the title of *sardār*, along with a *jāgīr*, upon several individuals in 1804: *Zafarnāma*, 32. The conferment of the 'rank of Sirdar' was accompanied by 'usual khillut of investiture': 'Diary of Henry Lawrence', *Punjab Government Records*,

among the princes to receieve large *jāgīrs* was Kharak Singh, followed by Prince Sher Singh, and his own son Naunihal Singh.[102] The other princes also got *jāgīrs* but on a much smaller scale.[103] Among the leading *sardārs* who received large *jāgīrs* were the Sandhanwalias, the Majithias, the Atariwalas, Sardar Hari Singh Nalwa, Jamadar Khushal Singh and his nephew Tej Singh, the family of Diwan Mohkam Chand and the Kalianwala *sardārs*.[104] There were several other individuals

(*1847-1848*), III, 128.

Just as the former chiefs, generally called '*sardārs*', were being reduced to the status of *jāgīrdārs*, so the newly created *jāgīrdārs* were being raised to the status of *sardārs*. Obviously, every *jāgīrdār* did not enjoy that status. Amar Nath refers to Desa Singh Majithia being raised to the status of a *sardār* in 1804; before that he was a mere '*khidmatgār*' : *Zafarnāma*, 31. In the *Khālsa Darbār Records* the principal *sardārs* were classified into *sardārān-i-nāmdār* and *sardārān-i-kalān* : Kohli, *Catalogue of Khalsa Darbar Records*, II, 302-03. Amar Nath refers to the *sardārān-i-'umūm* : *Zafarnāma*, 32. It is not clear, however, if this category was not really covered by the two mentioned in the *Khālsa Darbār Records*. In any case, these terms appear to have been used to indicate the general position of the *sardārs* rather than any strict ranking.

[102] For the *jāgīrs* of Prince Kharak Singh and other princes, see Sohan Lal, *Umdat*, II, 70-71, 98, 108-10, 192, 205, 245 & 362; IV, (i) 11 & 58 ; Ahmad Shah, *Tārīkh*, 454 & 463 ; Amar Nath, *Zafarnāma*, 140, 149, 176 & 188; Ganesh Das, *Chār Bāgh*, 153 & 154; Prinsep, *Origin of the Sikh Power*, 102; Charles Hugel, *Travels in Kashmir and the Panjab*, 385; Shahamat Ali, *Sikhs and Afghans*, 110 & 198.

[103] For example, Prince Kashmira Singh found the income from his *jāgīr* insufficient even to meet 'his necessary expenses' and was reported living upon the sale of his jewellery : Sohan Lal, *Umdat*, III, (iii), 344.

[104] Some idea of the *jāgīrs* enjoyed at differeet times by the leading *sardārs* of the Lahore Darbar may be formed from the figures given in the following : *Khālsa Darbār Records*, Bundle 5, Vol. XV (listed under *mutafarriqa*), 4-12, 33-84, 207-22 & 239-76 : *Foreign/Political Consultation*, 29 December 1849, No. 49 A; *Foreign/Political Proceedings*, 22 November 1850, No. 117 A; ibid., 3 April 1850, No. 280; *Foreign/Secret Consultation*, 31 December 1847, Nos. 195-98; ibid., 26 May 1849, Nos. 68-70; Cunningham, *A History of the Sikhs*, 385-86; Appendix XXXVIII; Shahamat Ali, *Sikhs and Afghans*, 35, 45, 48 & 55; Mir Ahmad, *Dastūr al-'Aml-i-Kashmir*, f 186b; *Events* (*1810-1817*), 259. It may be added that the *jāgīrs* of the 'principal' *sardārs*

who enjoyed considerable *jāgīrs* from time to time.[105] One does not get the impression, however, that a very large proportion of the revenues alienated by Ranjit Singh and his successors in *jāgīrs* was concentrated in the hands of a few individuals or families. [106] Nor does one get the impression that the revenues alienated in favour of a considerable number of small *jāgīrdārs* formed any large proportion of the total revenues from land.[107]

ranged from 25,000 to over 8 lakhs. Hari Singh Nalwa came to have *jāgīrs* worth 8,52,000 rupees before his death. Jamadar Khushal Singh got *jāgīrs* worth 4,37,315 rupees; Diwan Kirpa Ram got *jāgīrs* worth 3,07,000. Raja Tej Singh's *jāgīrs* amounted to 2,41,679 rupees. Among those who received *jāgīrs* worth over one lakh of rupees, were Atar Singh Kalianwala, Chatar Singh Atariwala, Diwan Mohkam Chand and Lehna Singh Majithia. Receiving *jāgīrs* inversely ranging from about 20,000 to 72,000 rupees were Mangal Singh Sandhu, Shamsher Singh Sandhanwalia, Lal Singh Muraria, Surjan Singh Maukal, Partap Singh Sandhanwalia, Ranjor Singh Majithia, Kahan Singh Majithia, Gurmukh Singh Lamba, Gulab Singh Pahuwindia and Kahan Singh Man.

[105] The instances of such *jāgīrdārs* are numerous : see, for example, *Foreign/Political Consultation*, 29 December 1849, No. 49 A; *Foreign/ Political Proceedings*, 3 April 1850, No. 280; *Foreign/Secret Consultation*, 26 May 1849, Nos. 68-71.

[106] The total revenues alienated to the 'principal' *jāgīrdārs* of the kingdom of Lahore in the mid 1840s, according to the British records stated above, amounted to nearly 25 lakhs.

[107] If, as the traveller Masson says, 'there was scarcely a Sikh who was not a *jāgīrdār*' (*Journal*, 174), we may be sure that by far the majority of even the Sikh *jāgīrdārs* held petty assignments. See also, 'Statement of the Yearly Expenses of the Lahore Army from the time of Maharaja Ranjit Singh ', Henry Lawrence to H.M. Elliot, *Foreign/Secret Proceedings*, 31 December 1847, Nos. 334-36.

7

Dharmarth

The Sikh dominions came to be regarded at one time as the land *par excellence*, of *mu'āfīdārs* and *jāgīrdārs*.[1] In Gujranwala 'alone, the early British administrators confirmed over 16,000 revenue-free grants of the Sikh times.[2] The number of such grants in the Jalandhar Doab too ran into thousands.[3] Prinsep in the 1830s found '*faqīrs*' located in and around every town and village in the Panjab, 'each having his Takiah to which were assigned a few bigahs of land'.[4] The number of persons and institutions enjoying revenue-free land by way of charity (*dharmarth*) was very large indeed.

Since ancient times in India, rulers had been giving grants of revenue-free land to religious personages and institutions.[5] The immediate predecessors of the Sikh rulers had been rather liberal in matters of *madad-i-ma'āsh* grants not only to *sayyids* and *shaikhs* but also to non-Muslims of known religious sanctity.[6] The vassal chiefs of the Mughal empire had been free to

[1] Baden Powell, *Land Systems of British India*, II, 698-99.

[2] *SR Gujranwala (1866-1867)*, 12.

[3] *Foreign/Political Consultation*, 31 December 1847, Nos. 2185-97.

[4] *Origin of the Sikh Power*, 167.

[5] See, for example, D.C. Sircar, *Landlordism and Tenancy in Ancient and Mediaeval India as Revealed by Epigraphical Records*, 6-9, 11, 27, 31, 33, 36, 42-43 & 53-56. It may be added that in certain respects revenue-free grants in ancient times appear to be very similar to what we find in Mughal or Sikh times.

[6] See, for example, B.N. Goswamy & J.S. Grewal, *Mughals and the Jogis of Jakhbar*, 17-46 & 47-188. For references to Aurangzeb's

make *dharmarth* grants from their territories. The *jāgīrdārs* of the Mughal emperors had tended to imitate their masters within the *jāgīrs* assigned to them and some of the grants given by them initially for their own tenure actually continued to be enjoyed by the grantees even later.[7] Consequently, wherever the Sikhs made their conquests they found many a plot of land held in '*dharmarth*'.

The Sikh rulers, from the very beginning confirmed grants given by the former masters of the territories they occupied.[8] The *Khālsa Darbār Records* contain numerous references to *madad-i-ma'āsh* grants coming down from olden times (*az qarār-i-qadīm*).[9] There are also references to grants being confirmed in accordance with the former practice (*b'dastūr-i-sābaq*).[10] The Sikh *kārdārs* were instructed repeatedly not to interfere with grants of 'the olden times'.[11] The early British records contain numerous instances of confirmation of old grants by the Sikh rulers in the districts of Lahore, Amritsar, Gujranwala, Sialkot, Jhang, Multan, Jehlam, Hazara, Shahpur, Rawalpindi, Khangarh, Peshawar, Kangra, Ferozepur, Ludhiana and Ambala, among others.[12]

grants to Hindu and Jain temples, see Athar Ali, *Mughal Nobility Under Aurangzeb*, 98-99 n 1.

[7] Irfan Habib, *Agrarian System*, 298-316.

[8] Hakumat Singh's order of 1752 confirms a revenue-free grant given by the Mughal rulers to the *mahants* of Pindori. Sada Kaur's orders confirm some other grants originally received by the *mahants* during the Mughal times : *Pindori Documents*, XVIII, XIX & XXXI.

A grant made by the Mughal emperor Muhammad Shah for the support of a *dharmsāla* is confirmed in an order of Ranjit Singh, and it may be safely assumed that it had been confirmed by the intervening rulers as well : see, *Foreign/Political Consultation*, 27 March 1857, Nos. 245-47.

[9] Bundle 5, Vol. XI, 3-6, 11-12, 15, 19, 387, 557, 575, for example.

[10] Ibid., Vol. XI, 627, for example.

[11] See, for example, *Foreign/Political Proceedings*, 15 October 1852, No. 116, containing scores of cases where the *sanads* of the Sikh rules refer to *qarār-i-qadīm*.

[12] See, for example, ibid., 9 January 1857, Nos. 221-38. This volume contains 433 pages and hundreds of instances of revenue-free tenures in the districts of Sialkot, Rawalpindi, Ferozepur, Lahore and

Ranjit Singh's charities are fairly well recorded by his contemporaries,[13] but far from being exceptional, he was a rather typical Sikh ruler in this respect. Numerous indeed were the Sikh rulers who alienated land revenue by way of charity. On the basis of the early British records which are amply confirmed by the *Khālsa Darbār Records*, it is possible to mention nearly fifty names of such rulers, including not only the well-known chiefs like Jassa Singh Ahluwalia, Jassa Singh Ramgarhia and Hari Singh Bhangi, but also the rather unknown chiefs like Sudh Singh Dodia, Bhag Singh Muraliwala and Mali Singh Guraya.[14] It may indeed be difficult to find a Sikh ruler worth the name who did not either confirm an old *madad-i-ma'āsh* or give a fresh grant of his own. The example of the rulers was

Amritsar where the old grants, even those by *lambardārs*, *chaudharīs* and *zamīndārs*, made mostly to *takias*, *khānqāhs*, *sarāis*, temples, *dharamsālas* and to the *udāsīs*, *faqīrs*, and *brāhmans*, were allowed to continue undisturbed by the Sikh rulers. See also, ibid., 27 March 1857, Nos. 239-40 & 242-43.

[13] See, for example, Sohan Lal, *Umdat*, II, 215, 261, 267, 314, 322, 335, 388, 391, 398-99 *et passim*.

[14] *Foreign/Political Proceedings*, 15 October 1852, No. 116; ibid., 14 January 1853, Nos. 212-23; ibid., 10 June 1853, No. 217.

Some of the other chiefs giving *dharmarth* grants are Jhanda Singh, Ganda Singh and Gulab Singh Bhangi, Gujjar Singh and Sahib Singh Bhangi, Lehna Singh and Chait Singh Bhangi, Tara Singh and Khushal Singh Ramgarhia, Mali Singh, Jodh Singh and Diwan Singh Ramgarhia, Jai Singh, Gurbakhsh Singh and Sada Kaur Kanhiya, Haqiqat Singh and Jaimal Singh Kanhiya, Mehtab Singh and Fateh Singh Kanhiya, Amar Singh and Budh Singh Bagga, Ran Singh and Kahan Singh Nakai, Jodh Singh, Wazir Singh and Gian Singh Nakai, Baghel Singh Karora Singhia, Tara Singh Dallewalia, Nahar Singh Chamiariwala, Bhag Singh Hallowalia, Milkha Singh Rawalpindiwala, Karam Singh Dulu, Tara Singh and Jai Singh Chainpuria, Amir Singh and Gurbakhsh Singh Dodia, Sahib Singh Vegalia, Jodh Singh Saurianwala, Natha Singh Shahid, Budh Singh Faizullapuria, Tara Singh Pathankotia, Sahib Singh Dorangla, Dal Singh Akalgarhia, Amar Singh Kingra, Bhup Singh of Ropar, Gurbakhsh Singh and Daya Kaur of Ambala, Karam Singh Shahid, Sudh Singh Chhina, Sahib Singh Sialkotia, Tara Singh Kathgarhia, Dharm Singh Qadirabadia, Nidhan Singh Daskewala, Gajpat Singh and Bhag Singh of Jind, Gurbakhsh Singh and Jodh Singh Kalsia and the Bhais Desu Singh, Lal Singh and Udai Singh of Kaithal.

followed by other members of the ruling family and even by their *jāgīrdārs*.[15]

The terms most commonly used for *dharmarth* grants in the orders of the Sikh rulers are *mu'āf* and *wāguzār*, that is, exempt from the payment of revenues.[16] The land given in grant was *khārij-az-jama'* because the revenue due from it to the state was not to go to the government treasury.[17] It was to go to the grantee. Other cesses (*rasūmāt*) were also remitted to him, besides exemption from forced labour (*kār-o-begār*).[18] Tolls and customs were also remitted sometimes.[19] The payment of what was due to the grantee was sometimes made in kind (*ghalla*).

[15] For the grants of princes and *rānīs* see, for example, *Pindori Documents*, XXXVIII, XL, XLIII, XLIV & XLV. See also, *Foreign/Political Proceedings*, 10 June 1853, No. 217; *Foreign/Political Consultation*, 27 March 1853, Nos. 201-03; ibid., 17 March 1854, Nos. 195-97; ibid., 25 September 1856, Nos. 243-46.

A *jāgīrdār* by the very nature of his position could give grants of a permanent nature only from a *jāgīr* held in perpetuity. The majority of *dharmarth* grants therefore were initially given only for the tenure of the *jāgīrdār*. However, since the grants were connected with sentiment of piety, they appear to have been allowed to continue often by the succeeding *jāgīrdārs* and administrators. That precisely was the reason for the continuance of such grants into the British times.

The *Khālsa Darbār Records* and the early British records contain references to *jāgīrdārs* granting land in *dharmarth* even before the reign of Ranjit Singh. In any case, numerous grants were given by *jāgīrdārs* like Hari Singh Nalwa, General Ventura, Dina Nath, Moti Ram, Karam Singh and Gurmukh Singh Chahal, Gurmukh Singh Lamba, Hukma Singh Chimni, Amir Singh and Atar Singh Sandhanwalia, Wasawa Singh, Kehar Singh and Ajit Singh Sandhanwalia, Nihal Singh and Sham Singh Atariwala, Atar Singh and Thakur Singh Atariwala, Jodh Singh, Uttam Singh and Dal Singh Kalianwala, Desa Singh, Lehna Singh and Uttam Singh [Majithia, Mitha Singh Padhania, Fateh Singh Man, Dhanna Singh Malwai, Jawand Singh, Bela Singh and Surjan Singh Maukal, Budh Singh and Lal Singh Muraria, Sham Singh Sultanwindia, Ratan Singh Saurianwala, Kahan Singh Kunjahia and Budh Singh and Baj Singh Bhagowalia.

[16] See, for example, *Pindori Documents*, XXIV, XXVI, XXX, XXXI & XL.

[17] Ibid., XXXVIII.

[18] Ibid., XXX. See also, B.N. Goswamy, *Painters at the Sikh Court: A Study Based on Twenty Documents* (cited hereafter as *Painters at the Sikh Court*), Document I.

[19] *Pindori Documents*, XXV.

Generally the collection of revenues due to the state was made directly by the grantee.[20] Sometimes it was made for him by the agents of the state.[21] When a piece of culturable waste (*zamīn-i-banjar uftādah*) was given to a grantee, he became its proprietor. When the grantee himself got the land cultivated as a proprietor, he was entitled to the entire produce.[22] Many hereditary holders of *madad-i-ma'āsh* land had come down from the Mughal times and continued to enjoy those rights during the Sikh rule.[23]

The land granted was generally given in terms of *ghumāons* and *kanāls*.[24] Presumably, in all such cases, land was measured and clearly demarcated.[25] The monumental *Dastūr al-'Amal* of Kashmir contains not only the names of villages and grantees but also specified areas of both irrigated and unirrigated land given by way of *madad-i-ma'āsh*.[26] Though much less frequently, land was given also in terms of wells and ploughs.[27]

[20] *Pindori Documents*, XXXI & XXXV. In these documents it is explicitly stated that the *mu'āmala* (revenue) or the *hāsilāt* is to be collected by the grantee himself.

[21] Ibid., XXVI & XXVIII.

[22] Ibid., XXXIII. In this document there is a clear reference to the land held in grant as *khud-kāshta* and the instruction against interference relates not only to *hāsilāt* but also to the land in question. See also, *Painters at the Sikh Court*, Documents, IV & V.

[23] See, for example, *Pindori Documents*, XVII, XX & XXI. The phrase used in these documents is 'proceeds and proprietorship' (*mālkīat-o-mu'āmala*), which unambiguously alludes to the enjoyment of hereditary right over the land held in *madad-i-ma'āsh*.

[24] In Mughal documents, the unit of area generally mentioned is *bigha* which consisted of 2 *kanāls*. A *ghumāon* consisted of 4 *bighas*. For some detail, see chapter V, 90-91 n 9.

[25] *Pindori Documents*, XIX, XXII, XXVII, XXXII & XLIX. In these documents there is no explicit reference to a specified measured area but that is precisely because the fact was taken for granted. In Document XXIX for example, it is specified in the 'detail' given that 9 *ghumāons* of the grant were adjacent to the *bāolī* and 9 adjacent to the well. In Document XLIX, which relates to a fresh grant, it is clearly stated that the area of land granted is to be measured and handed over.

[26] Mir Ahmad, *Dastūr al-'Amal-i-Kashmir*, f 215 a.

[27] See, for example, *Pindori Documents*, XXXIII; *Foreign/Political Proceedings*, 14 January 1853, Nos. 212-23.

Sometimes, a whole village or half a village or a fourth of a village too was given in grant.[28]

Although no tenure was specified for *dharmarth* grants given by the Sikh rulers, the use of the phrase 'year after year and harvest after harvest' (*sāl b'sāl fasl b'fasl*), particularly when the *madad-i-ma'āsh* lands given by the Mughal rulers had become hereditary, suggests that the *dharmarth* grants were given practically in perpetuity.[29] This was certainly true of the wastelands made *khud-kāshta* and held as revenue-free grants. It is understandable, therefore, that the practice of selling or mortgaging *madad-i-ma'āsh* land continued.[30] Also, the *dharmarth* grantees sometimes gave a part of their land in dowry.[31] In no case, however, did *dharmarth* grants disturb the existing rights over land.[32] Also, the Sikh rulers could and did,

[28] See, for example, *Pindori Documents*, XXIII & XXIV; *Foreign/Political Proceedings*, 9 January 1857, Nos. 221-38.

[29] In 1690, Aurangzeb made all existing *madad-i-ma'āsh* grants hereditary through a special *farmān*: Irfan Habib, *Agrarian System*, 306. By the middle of the next century, the character of the *madad-i-ma'āsh* holders had changed and they now 'enjoyed the right to sell or transfer land as gifts in the same way as the *zamīndārs* did' and 'were owners of land granted to them': Noman Ahmad Siddiqi, *Land Revenue Administration*, 125.

It may be of some interest to note that when George Lawrence expressed surprise over the *madad-i-ma'āsh* holders in Peshawar inheriting their charitable grants, he was informed by Diwan Hakim Rai that, 'in the Punjab it was always so': 'Diary of Henry Lawrence', *Punjab Government Records (1847-1848)*, III, 186.

[30] See, for example, Grewal, *In the By-Lanes of History*, Document II; *Pindori Documents*, XIV & LII.

[31] Sodhis Ram Singh, Nand Singh, Uttam Singh and Surjan Singh of Anandpur, for instance, gave a village each out of their grants to their daughters in dowry: *Foreign/Political Consultation*, 14 March 1851, No. 113 E.

It may be interesting to note the case of Giani Gurdit Singh who received a village and two wells in *dharmarth* in the *pargana* of Chiniot from Maharaja Ranjit Singh. Gurdit Singh, on the marriage of his daughter, transferred one well to her husband Tehal Singh in dowry. Tehal Singh further gave that well away to his own son-in-law, Nain Singh: ibid., 12 March 1852, No. 98.

[32] This position is clarified in the early British records by the statement, wherever necessary, that the *jāgīrdār* (the *dharmarth*

though very rarely, resume *dharmarths* previously granted.[33]

The existence of old revenue records for villages and *parganas* and the continuance of the old local officials on whom the new rulers largely depended for procedural guidance and information, enabled the Sikh rulers to follow the practice of the Mughals. On his own inclination, or on the recommendation of someone who enjoyed his confidence, the ruler decided to give land in *dharmarth*, and this decision was often given the form of an official order in writing, even if he himself gave only a verbal order.[34] The smaller chiefs addressed their orders directly to *'āmils* or *kārdārs* or even to the *zamīndārs*.[35] Ranjit Singh sent his orders sometimes through his *dīwāns* and *nāzims*.[36]

grantee) was *not* the *zamīndār* (the proprietor) : see, for example, *Foreign/Political Consultation*, 14 March 1851, No. 113.

[33] In theory, the ruler always had the right to resume any *dharmarth* grant. That was why sometimes grants had to be got confirmed from a new ruler. There are numerous instances of Ranjit Singh confirming the grants given by the early Sikh rulers, His successors also confirmed nearly all the grants made by the Maharaja : see, for example, ibid., 29 December 1849, No. 49 A (case nos. 01-38). The following *sanad* of Maharaja Sher Singh (dated 10th Jeth 1898) adressed to the *'āmils* of Jandiala, only supports the view that the resumption of *dharmarth* was rare : 'Whereas, a well known as Padreewala valued at Rs. 100/- annually having been of old granted in Dharmarth to Misar Lachhman Das and was during the administration of Tek Chand resumed, is now graciously restored in Dharmarth. Considering that the well has been rendered waguzar the same is to suffer no loss or detriment. This is credited in accounts' : *Foreign/Political Proceedings*, 23 August 1850, No. 35 C. For another example of the resumption of an old revenue-free grant held by a *pīrzāda* in Shergarh and Hujra and its regrant by Ranjit Singh, see *Events (1810-1817)*, 38.

[34] See, for example, *Pindori Documents*, XX, XXV & XXXIII.

[35] For instances of the smaller chiefs addressing the *'āmils*, *kārdārs* and even the *zāmīndārs*, see ibid., XIX, XXI, XXV, XXVI, XXVIII, & XXXIV. For more such examples and those also of the *jāgīrdārs* addressing the *pargana* and *ta'alluqa* officials and even the *panches* of a village, see *Foreign/Political Proceedings*, 27 May 1853, Nos. 207-08; ibid., 10 June 1853, No. 217; also, ibid., 14 January 1853, Nos. 212-23.

[36] Maharaja Ranjit Singh's original *sanad* (dated 29th Poh 1885) granting 50 rupees in *dharmarth* in Khangarh *'ilāqa* to one Jai Ram was kept by Diwan Sawan Mal who issued its copy to the grantee,

The *'āmils* or *kārdārs* executed these orders with the help of the *qānūngos*, the *chaudharīs* and the *muqaddams*. Records of *dharmarth* grants were generally maintained not only locally but also at the centre.[37] However, there were cases of old *madad-i-ma'āsh* grants which were not entered in records though they were being enjoyed by the grantees.[38] Their rights never seem to have been questioned as they continued to hold grants throughout the Sikh period.

The rulers tried to ensure that the grantees received what was granted to them, forbidding all interference on the part of the officials, the *chaudharīs* or the proprietors. Abstracts of numerous *sanads* in the early British records leave no doubt about the conflict between the grantee and others during the period of Sikh rule. In contemporary *parwānas* there are references to interference by the proprietors, the *muqaddams*, the *chaudharīs* and even the *'āmils* or *kārdārs*.[39] We find the Sikh

together with one from himself confirming the grant : ibid., 30 April 1852, No. 100. In another case, Maharaja Ranjit Singh addressed his *sanad* (dated 1st Asuj 1882) to Sardar Budh Singh Sandhanwala asking him to pay 300 rupees to Dharam Singh Bungawala for the *deg*. On the receipt of this royal order, Sardars Budh Singh and Atar Singh Sandhanwalia issued a *parwāna* (dated 20th Bhadon 1883) granting in *dharmarth* a well in *mauza'* Chatiwind from *kharīf* 1879 Sammat to Dharm Singh: ibid., 10 June 1853, No. 217. In fact, such instances can be multiplied, but this does not mean that the Maharaja did not occasionally, when required, address his orders to the *'āmils*, *kārdārs*, small *jāgīrdārs* and even *zamīndārs*.

It may be pointed out that the formality of these orders increased with the passage of time : see, for example, *Pindori Documents*, XLI; *Painters at the Sikh Court*, Document VIII.

[37] This is evident from the dozens of volumes in Bundle 5 of the *Khālsa Darbār Records* which were maintained at the centre and are now available at the Punjab State Archives, Patiala.

[38] For continuance of the Mughal grants without any confirmatory *sanads* from the Sikh rulers see, for example, *Foreign/Political Consultation*, 25 February 1859, Nos. 172-74.

[39] For examples of the interference of the *zamīndārs* with *dharmarth* grants, see *Foreign/Political Proceedings*, 23 August 1850, No. 35 C; for that of the *chaudharīs*, see *Khālsa Darbār Records*, Bundle 5, Vol. III, 77-78; for that of the *jāgīrdārs*, see *Pindori Documents*, XL; and for the interference of the *'āmils* or *kārdārs*, see ibid., XLI and *Painters at the Sikh Court*, Document II.

rulers issuing orders against interference of any kind with the concessions given to the *dharmarth* grantees.[40]

Individuals and institutions belonging to the Sikh faith received the largest measure of *dharmarth* grants from the Sikh rulers. The most conspicuous of these grantees were the Sodhis.[41] As the collaterals of Guru Gobind Singh, they were patronized by the majority of rulers and several *jāgīrdārs*, and held revenue free lands in nearly all parts of the Panjab.[42] Many Sodhi families were in the active service of Maharaja Ranjit Singh.[43] The Maharaja attributed his success in politics and government to the blessings of Bhai Wasti Ram, and his regard for the Sodhis in general increased because of the Bhai.[44]

[40] See, for example, *Pindori Documents*, XXVI, XXXI, XXXII, & XXXIV. The British records also contain numerous abstracts of such 'letters of admonition'.

[41] According to Sohan Lal, leadership in both the spiritual and the temporal realms (*pīrī* and *mirī*) was associated with the Sodhis : *Umdat*, II, 16. They got *jāgīrs* not only because they came from the same stock as Guru Gobind Singh but also because they were active soldiers. Bute Shah provides fascinating information on grants received and enjoyed by Sodhi Nahar Singh, the great grandson of Guru Hargobind, and his descendants in the area of Anandpur : *Tārīkh* (SHR 1288), 445-60 & 463-64. Some of the Sodhis got their initial *jāgīrs* from Muslims who induced them to settle in their terriotry because the Sikhs 'did not attack a village where the Sodhis used to reside' : ibid., 490-91. See also, Griffin & Massy, *Chiefs and Families*, I, 210.

[42] See, for example, *Khālsa Darbār Records*, Bundle 5, Vol. IX, 01-158 & 667; Bute Shah, *Tārīkh* (SHR 1288), 464, 478-79, 480-82, 485, 487-90 & 492-93; *Foreign/Political Consultation*, 29 December 1849, No. 49 A (27); ibid., 19 March 1852, Nos. 67-68; 'SSR Jullundur Doab', *Foreign/ Political Proceedings*, 31 December 1847, No. 2443, para 56. See also, Inaitullah, *Administrative History of the Kalsia State*, f 132 b.

[43] For instances of the Sodhis serving Ranjit Singh, see Bute Shah, *Tārīkh* (SHR 1288), 460, 485-87, 490-91 & 493; Griffin & Massy, *Chiefs and Families*, I, 210 & 216; *Foreign/Political Consultation*, 29 December 1849, No. 49 A (27).

[44] Bhai Wasti Ram had come to enjoy a great reputation for his saintly character and his knowledge of medicine in the city of Lahore before he died in the early years of the nineteenth century without having accepted any grant from a Sikh ruler. Bhai Harbhaj Rai, the elder son of the Bhai, who specialized in medicine, was the first in the family to accept a *jāgīr* for having successfully treated

However, the most prominent family of the Sodhis during the Sikh period was that of Sodhi Badbhag Singh of Kartarpur who is referred to as *sāhib-i-jāgīr-o-mulk* by Bute Shah, and master of *sardārī-o-riyāsat* by Sohan Lal.[45] His son, Sodhi Sadhu Singh, received large *jāgīrs* from Maharaja Ranjit Singh.[46]

The Bedis, the descendants of Guru Nanak, were not far behind the Sodhis in receiving patronage from nearly all the Sikh rulers [47] and an equally large number of *jāgīrdārs*.[48] The

the Maharaja in 1806. After the death of Bhai Harbhaj Rai, two of his sons, Bhai Ram Singh and Bhai Gobind Ram, were patronized by the Maharaja and came to play a very important role in the affairs of the Lahore Darbar: Sohan Lal, *Umdat*, III, (i), 117; (ii), 162, 191, 201, 225-26 & 230; (iii), 391; (iv) 438, 441, 452-53 *et passim*. See also, Griffin & Massy, *Chiefs and Families* I, 269; Shahmat Ali, *Sikhs and Afghans*, 80; Kirpal Singh, *An Historical Account of Bhai Vasti Ram and Bhai Ram Singh, 13-26*.

[45] Bute Shah, *Tārīkh* (SHR 1288), 478; Sohan Lal, *Umdat*, II, 60.

[46] Sodhi Sadhu Singh succeeded his father in 1805 with the approval of Ranjit Singh, and remained in close association with the Maharaja throughout his reign, exchanging gifts and courtesies and receiving *jāgīrs*. A large number of villages were given in *jāgīr* also to the copy of the Ādī Granth in his possession: *Khālsa Darbār Records*, Bundle 5, Vol. I, 3-4. See also, Sohan Lal, *Umdat* III (Eng. tr.), 29, 51, 105, 106, 107, 178, 179, 183 *et passim*. For the detail of the lands of the Sodhis of Kartarpur, see Bute Shah, *Tārīkh* (SHR 1288), 479, 481 & 482.

[47] The *Khālsa Darbār Records* contain hundreds of instances of revenue-free land granted to the Bedis by the Sikh rulers: Bundle 5, Vol. III, 01-812. See also, *Foreign/Political Proceedings*, 14 January 1853, Nos. 212-23. Nearly all the Sikh rulers listed above (150 n 14), are on record to have given revenue-free lands to the Bedis. It may be of interest to note that the earliest known grant given to a Bedi by a Sikh ruler is that of Mansa Singh Guraya who gave two villages to Charhat Singh Bedi in 1756 in the *parganas* of Guraya and Shakargarh.

[48] Some of the *jāgīrdārs* who gave grants to the Bedis in the early nineteenth century were Atar Singh and Ajit Singh Sandhanwalia, Jawand Singh Maukal and his son Bela Singh & grandson Surjan Singh, Hari Singh Nalwa, 'Karnail' Mihan Singh, Jawala Singh Padhania, Jamadar Khushal Singh, Dhanna Singh Malwai, Desa Singh Majithia, Karam Singh and Gurmkh Singh Chahal, Nihal Singh and Sham Singh Atariwala, Jagat Singh and Ganda Singh Atariwala, Jhanda Singh Butalia, besides a host of minor *jāgīrdārs*

dharmarth lands of the Bedis were scattered all over the Panjab, particularly in the upper Bari, Rachna and the Jalandhar Doabs.[49] The most prominent family among them was that of Sahib Singh of Una who had risen to prominence in the last quarter of the eighteenth century.[50] His son, Bikram Singh, came to possess several strong forts and used to maintain large bodies of armed men.[51] According to one estimate, the Bedis and the Sodhis together enjoyed over forty per cent of the revenues alienated in *dharmarth* by the Lahore Darbar.[52]

As in the case of the Sodhis and the Bedis, there was hardly a Sikh ruler who did not alienate some revenue in favour of the Har Mandir (the Golden Temple) at Amritsar.[53] The Sikh *jāgīrdārs* too gave revenue-free lands to this, their central

and even *ghurcharas*. Some of the earlier *jāgīrdārs* to have granted revenues to the Bedis were Chuhar Singh under Jodh Singh Wazirabadia, Amir Singh under Nahar Singh Chamiariwala, Mohar Singh under Bhag Singh Muraliwala and Sham Singh Kunjahia under Charhat Singh Sukarchakia : *Foreign/Political Proceedings*, Nos. 212-23.

[49] Most of these land grants of the Bedis were situated in the *ta'alluqas* of Hoshiarpur, Dinanagar, Batala, Tarn Taran, Saurian, Dharmkot, Qasur, Gugera, Bhagowal, Qadian, Hujra, Sialkot, Wazirabad, Eminabad, Shakargarh, Talwandi, Hafizabad, Shaikhupura, Gujranwala, Ramnagar, Manawar, Sanktara, Qila Sobha Singh, Zafarwal, Pasrur and Daska : ibid., Nos. 212-23; 'SSR Jullundur Doab, ibid., 31 December 1847, No. 2443, para 56.

[50] For some of Ranjit Singh's grants to Bedi Sahib Singh, see Amar Nath, *Zafarnāma*, 61 & 180 ; Munshi Bakhtawar Lal, *Tārīkh-i-Montgomery*, 42-44.

[51] 'SSR Jullundur Doab', *Foreign/Political Proceedings*, 31 December 1847, No. 2443, para 56.

[52] Cunningham, *A History of the Sikhs*, 385, Appendix XXXVIII.

It may be added that the descendants of Guru Amar Das, the Bhallas, were also venerated by the Sikhs but they did not receive patronage in any way comparable with the grants of the Bedis and Sodhis. For their grants, see *Khālsa Darbār Records*, Bundle 5, Vol. IV, 01-126.

[53] *Foreign/Political Proceedings*, 10 June 1853, No. 217. There is no need to repeat their names. Nearly all of them have been mentioned already in connection with the *dharmarth* grants in general. However, it may be of interest to note that the Bhangi chiefs Hari Singh, Jhanda Singh and Ganda Singh appear to have been the earliest to give land grants to the Har Mandir.

shrine.[54] Indeed, the number of grants received was so large and the area covered so wide that separate *mutasaddīs* had to be appointed for collecting the revenues.[55] Detailed instructions issued by Maharaja Ranjit Singh in 1837 regarding the management of the Har Mandir are indicative of the nature of control exercised by the Maharaja over this establishment.[56] The *granthīs*, *ardāsias*, *rāgīs*, *rabābīs* and the *mutasaddīs* of the Har Mandir also enjoyed grants all over the Panjab.[57] Smaller establishments around the Golden Temple and shrines of local importance also received revenue-free grants.[58]

[54] The British records cited above contain, among others, the names of nearly all the 'principal' *jāgīrdārs*.

[55] For several references to these *mutasaddīs*, see *Foreign/Political Proceedings*, 10 June 1853, No. 217.

[56] It may be interesting to reproduce the relevant portions of Maharaja Ranjit Singh's *sanad* (dated 27th Poh 1894) addressed to Sardar Lehna Singh Majithia: You are requested to establish the following rule in the Akal Bunga and must be careful that it be not infringed. The offerings (*ardās*) and the proceeds (*jama*') of the *jāgīr* should be deposited in the same chest, and Sant Singh and both the Gurmukh Singhs should, on the first of Baisākh and at the Dipmala, open the said chest and dole out the collections as used to be done in the time of Desa Singh (Majithia) in the manner following: When there are hundred or fifty persons they ought to have their money allowances distributed to them personally and individually, at which time four *mutasaddīs* are to attend from Māgh 1894 who are to keep the accounts of the receipts and disbursements: ibid., 23 August 1850, No. 35 C.

It may be added that disputes regarding succession to different *gaddīs* were sometimes brought to the notice of the Maharaja for arbitration. For a dispute over the *gaddī* of Dera Baba Nanak, see Bute Shah, *Tārīkh* (SHR 1288), 501.

[57] *Khālsa Darbār Records*, Bundle 5, Vol. VIII, 01-244.

[58] Ibid., Bundle 3, Vol. III, 669-70. To have received revenue-free land in Amritsar were the shrines of Akal Bunga, Jhanda Bunga, Shahid Bunga, Ber Baba Sahib, Dera Baba Atal Sahib and Bibeksar. For the *dharmarth* of Darbar-i-Tahli-Sahib-i-Guru Har Rai and the shrine at Tarn Taran, see ibid., Bundle 5, Vol. X, 347 & 349-57. The Darbar Sahib at Ramdas was given revenue-free lands by Mahan Singh and Ranjit Singh in the Bari and Rachna Doabs: ibid., Vol. IV, 95-96 & 109-12. For grants given to Gurdwara Tahli Sahib at Dera Baba Nanak and the Gurdwaras of Keshgarh, Kiratpur, Kapal Mochan and Muktsar, see *Foreign/Political Consultation*, 14 March 1851, Nos. 113 E & F; *SR Gurdaspur*, 59.

The Sikh rulers gave extensive grants of revenue-free land to the *udāsī* and *nirmala sādhs*, the acknowledged missionaries of the Sikh faith. The *Khālsa Darbār Records* contain numerous entries of *dharmarth* in favour of individual *udāsīs* and *udāsī akhāras*, including the famous Brahmbuta in Amritsar.[59] The *udāsī mahants* had been receiving revenue-free land from the very beginning of Sikh rule.[60] The *dharmarth* lands of the *udāsīs* were scattered over all the Doabs.[61] Grants enjoyed by the *nirmala sādhs* were equally numerous and extensive.[62]

The *akālīs* and *nihangs* who figure in the colourful descriptions by contemporary Europeans as the militant protagonists of the Khālsa were yet another important category of grantees patronized by the Sikh rulers. The famous Akali Phula Singh was not the only *nihang* to enjoy the generosity of Maharaja Ranjit Singh. Sohan Lal refers to the confirmation of the grants of the *singhān-i-akālia* in the reign of Ranjit Singh.[63] Shahamat Ali notices extensive revenue-free lands of the fraternity of Sobha Singh Nihang near Hasan Abdal.[64] The *nihangs* of Bibeksar in Amritsar received *dharmarth* grants from

[59] *Khālsa Darbār Records*, Bundle 5, Vol. II, 43-46, 89-94, 117-18, 123-24, 145-46, 629-30, for example. Some of the *udāsī akhāras* or establishments mentioned in these pages are those of Basant Singh in Sri Hargobindpur, Baba Bhagwan Singh in Doda, Mahant Atma Ram in Narowal, Mahant Budh Das in Sanktara, Harprashad Udasi of Kuthala, Dera Shah Balawal in Batala and that of Santokh Das Udasi in Gujrat. For instances of *dharmarth* grants to the *udāsīs* in the Satlej-Jamna Divide, see Madanjit Kaur, 'The Origin of the Udasis, etc.', *Proceedings Punjab History Conference (1971)*, 128-31.

[60] Pritam Das Udasi, for instance, received revenue-free land, among others, from Jhanda Singh Bhangi, Bhag Singh Muraliwala, Amar Singh Bagga, Sahib Singh Bhangi, Fateh Singh Ahluwalia, Ranjit Singh, Kharak Singh, Rani Chand Kaur and Maharaja Dalip Singh : *Foreign/Political Proceedings*, 7 January 1853, No. 219.

[61] *Khālsa Darbār Records*, Bundle 5, Vol. II, 01-630.

[62] For example, the lands attached to Dera Bhai Pheru Sahib alone are given in nearly 50 pages : ibid., 153-200, 203-04, and 205-06. See also, *Foreign/Political Proceedings*, 23 June 1854, Nos. 204-05.

[63] *Umdat*, II, 351.

[64] *Sikhs and Afghans*, 259.

Ranjit Singh and his successors.[65] From other known instances, it is evident that his predecessors also gave revenue-free grants to the *nihangs* and *akālīs*.[66] They were also patronized for their active service in behalf of the rulers.[67]

Hindu religious establishments and individuals received extensive patronage from the Sikh rulers. *Purohits* and *brāhmans* in general figure prominently in the *Khālsa Darbār Records* as the recipients of *dharmarth* grants in all the Doabs.[68] The Darbar *pandits* Brij Raj and Madhusudan received lands worth thousands of rupees a year.[69] Maharaja Ranjit Singh confirmed religious grants enjoyed earlier by *brāhmans* and temples.[70] The Jawalamukhi temple in Kangra is only the best-known example of a Hindu establishment being patronized not only by Ranjit Singh and his successors but also by other Sikh rulers.[71] The *purohits* of Thanesar and Hardwar were

[65] *Khālsa Darbār Records*, Bundle 5, Vol. X, 207, 208, 209-10 & 330. For the *dharmarth* of some other '*akālīs* of the Darbar Sahib', see ibid., Bundle 2, Vol. VI, 84.

[66] See, for example, ibid., Bundle 3, Vol. III, 362-64 & 669-70; also, Bundle 2, Vol. VI, 83-84; Bute Shah, *Tārīkh* (SHR 1288), 466-70 & 472.

[67] Akali Phula Singh, the hero of the battle of Naushehra, is well-known for his active service to the state. Akali Sadhu Singh also distinguished himself in the successful expeditions against Multan and Kashmir. It seems that the Maharaja was gradually able to channelise the martial traditions of the *akālīs*. Forming 'a class by themselves' there were about 3000 *akālīs* actively engaged in behalf of the state : Fauja Singh, *Military System of the Sikhs*, 141 n 2 & 226. See also, Chopra, *Sovereign State*, 66-67.

[68] See, for example, *Khālsa Darbār Records*, Bundle 5, Vol. VIII. The *brāhmans* in Kashmir received their *dharmarth* in kind (*jins*) also. It included, among other things, grains, shawls, oil, salt, firewood, saffron, *singhāra*, *ghī* and milk : Mir Ahmad, *Dastūr al 'Amal-i-Kashmir*, ff 281 a-b; also, 202a-206a.

[69] *Khālsa Darbār Records*, Bundle 5, Vol VI, 489-502; Griffin & Massy, *Chiefs and Families*, I, 313, respectively.

[70] B.N. Goswamy & J.S. Grewal, 'Religious Land Grants from Kangra', *Essays in History, Literature, Art and Culture* (ed. K.S. Bedi & S.S. Bal), 89-97.

[71] 'Virtually every *pandā*' at the temple of Kangra and Jawalamukhi 'is in possession of some *pattā* or *parwāna* recording a grant to some ancestor of his by Maharaja Ranjit Singh': B.N. Goswamy, *Painters at the Sikh Court*, 54 n 117. It may be of interest to know that among

similarly patronized and it appears that every Sikh ruler had a family *purohit* and so had many a *jāgīrdār*.[72] Grants of land given specifically for the support of cows are also on record.[73] It may be added that the Sikh *jāgīrdārs* emulated the rulers in their patronage of Hindu establishments and *brāhmans* in general.[74]

The interest of the Sikh rulers in Hindu religious institutions is equally evident from the patronage they extended to the Shaiva *jogīs* and the Vaishnava *bairāgīs*. Besides the confirmation of their *madad-i-ma'āsh*, the Sikh rulers gave them fresh grants of revenue-free land and other concessions. The *jogī* establishment of Jakhbar in the upper Bari Doab was not the only *math* of the Gorakhnāthī *jogīs* to be patronized during this period.[75] The Tilla of Gorakh Nath in the Chaj Doab, which

other Sikh rulers, Ranjit Singh's father and grandfather had also been to Jawalamukhi on a pilgrimage and they had duly entered their names in the registers of the *pandās* : ibid., 37. The richly executed golden roof of both the large and small building of the shrine and its beautiful silver gates are also said to be an offering of Maharaja Ranjit Singh : ibid., 54 n 117. See also, Charles Hugel, *Travels in Kashmir and the Panjab*, 45 & 360.

This benevolent attitude was continued by Ranjit Singh's successors and also by others : Hakim Paras Ram, *Tārīkh-i-Mandir-i-Jwālāmukhī*, M/922, Punjab State Archives, Patiala. See also, *Gazetteer of Kangra*, 237; Ram Sukh Rao, *Srī Fateh Singh Partāp Prabhākar*, f 119b.

[72] For statements of the revenue-free lands of the *purohits* of the Lahore Darbar and also its 'principal' *jāgīrdārs*, see *Khālsa Darbār Records*, Bundle 5, Vol. VI, 489-502 ; *Foreign/Political Proceedings*, 7 January 1853, No. 225; ibid., 3 April 1850, No. 194. See also, Inaitullah, *Administrative History of the Kalsia State*, ff 147a & 164a; Nagina Ram, *Ravī Parkāsh*, III, 946 & 1041-45.

[73] *Foreign/Political Proceedings*, 22 November 1850, No. 117 A.

[74] For grants of Sardar Hari Singh Nalwa and so many other *jāgīrdārs* to *brāhmans*, see ibid., 15 October 1852, No. 116 ; ibid., 25 February 1859, Nos. 172-74.

[75] The *dharmarth* documents of the Jakhbar establishment have been studied recently. For some detail, see Goswamy & Grewal, *Mughals and the Jogis of Jakhbar*. See also, *Khālsa Darbār Records*, Bundle 5, Vol, VI, 435 & Vol. XIII, 383.

It may be interesting to note that Ranjit Singh granted a village by way of *kharch-i-dhūnī* (literally, expense of constant fire) for the *samādh* of the well-known Kashmiri Pandit, Mansa Ram Razdan who was a Shaiva and had settled in *mauza'* Kotla in *tappa* Waraich of the Chaj Doab : Ganesh Das, *Chār Bāgh*, 209.

in fact, was their premier *math* in the Panjab, received several entire villages in the districts of Jehlam and Gujrat, besides several minor grants of revenue-free land, cash and concessions on customs and salt.[76] Pir Sukal Nath, the *mahant* of the *jogī gaddī* at Kirana, also in the Chaj Doab, enjoyed revenue-free lands in Sahiwal, Mangowal, Gondal, Lalian and Jhang, besides the grant of salt from Bagh and cash from Pind Dadan Khan.[77] The *jogīs* of Pehowa near Thanesar received fresh grants of revenue-free land and other concessions from the Sikh chiefs of Kaithal.[78]

About the *bairāgī* establishment of Pindori in the upper Bari Doab, it has been said recently that it was 'more affluent in the Sikh times than ever before, or perhaps after'.[79] The Sikh rulers like Jai Singh Kanhiya and Ranjit Singh, and their successors, had given fresh grants to the *mahants* of Pindori, besides confirming their old grants.[80] However, Pindori was not the only Vaishnava establishment to attract the attention of the Sikh rulers. They gave large grants of revenue-free land to the *gaddīs* at Dhianpur and Dhamtal.[81] Numerous grants were

[76] In 1937, Pir Kala Nath, the *gaddī-nashīn* of Tilla Gorakh Nath, appealed to the Financial Commissioner of the Panjab 'to restore the confiscated muafis and jagirs which were granted and assigned to the gaddi during the time of Mohammadan and Sikh rulers'. Along with this petition, he submitted English translations of the *sanads* in his possession. A copy of that petition and *sanads* was given to Prof. B.N. Goswamy, Head of the Department of Fine Arts, Panjab University, Chandigarh, by the successors of Pir Kala Nath who are now settled in Ambala City. This material has been consulted through Prof. Goswamy's courtesy.

[77] *Khālsa Darbār Records*, Bundle 5, Vol. XIV, 155-57. It may be of some interest to note that a dispute regarding the *gaddī* of Kirana was referred to Maharaja Ranjit Singh and later to Maharaja Sher Singh: *Foreign/Political Consultation*, 22 February 1856, Nos. 191-94.

[78] The present *mahants* of Pehowa have a large number of documents in their possession which have been seen through Prof. Goswamy's courtesy. The information given here comes from those documents.

[79] Goswamy & Grewal (ed.), 'Introduction', *Pindori Documents*, 32.

[80] Ibid., XXII, XXIII, XXVII, XXXVI—XXXIX, XLIV, XLVI & XLVIII. See also, *Khālsa Darbār Records*, Bundle 5, Vol. VI, 251-56 & 261.

[81] Ibid., Bundle 5,Vol. VI, 219; *Foreign/Political Proceedings*, 14 January 1853, No. 215; *SR Gurdaspur*, 60. The Dhianpur establishment

given by the Sikh rulers also to individual *bairāgīs* and *thākurdwāras*.[82] Put together, the Sikh patronage of Hindu religious institutions and individuals was very considerable indeed.

A partial view suggests that Muslim *pīrzādas* suffered loss or diminution of their *madad-ma'āsh* during the Sikh period.[83] It may be readily conceded that some Muslim religious establishments and individuals lost a part or the whole of their old grants. It is more to the point however, that the Muslim grantees received essentially the same treatment from the Sikh rulers as the Hindu or Sikh grantees. The Gardezi *sayyids* of Multan retained much of their wealth and influence though some of their lands were resumed.[84] The descendants of Shaikh Farid at Pakpatan received fresh grants of revenue-free land in addition to their old *madad-i-ma'āsh*.[85] In Kashmir, the number of Muslim grantees of all categories ran into thousands, including the famous shrines of Hazratbal and Shah Hamdan.[86]

was founded by Baba Lal whose dialogues with Dara Shukoh have been preserved for posterity.

[82] See, For example, *Khālsa Darbār Records*, Bundle, 5, Vol. VI, 7, 17, 61, 81, 109, 325-27; *Foreign/Political Proceedings*, 15 October 1852, No. 116. Some of the rulers to make these grants were Jassa Singh Ramgarhia, Lehna Singh and Gujjar Singh Bhangi, Jai Singh, Jaimal Singh, Jodh Singh and Fateh Singh Kanhiya, Bhag Singh Hallowalia, Nahar Singh Chamiariwala and Bhag Singh Muraliwala. Some of the grantees were Bairagis Mahesh Das, Amar Das, Ajodhiya Das, Thakur Das, Baba Baldev Das, Lachhman Das, Sarup Das, Baba Sahaj Ram, Mangal Das, Baba Hira Das, Baba Baikunth Das and Gosain Ramji.

[83] Prinsep, *Origin of the Sikh Power*, 166. Also, the shrines at Multan lost 'most of the valuable jagirs that had been assigned for their support' : Griffin & Massy, *Chiefs and Families* I, 306.

[84] Ibid., 314.

[85] *Foreign/Political Proceedings*, 28 June 1854, Nos. 204-05. In fact, in 1825, the *jāgīrdār* of Pakpatan was ordered by Ranjit Singh to respect all grants given to the celebrated shrine of Shaikh Farid.

It may be added that the *sāliyāna* of Hasan Shah, the *mujāwir* of the *khānqāh* of Baha-ul-Haqq in Multan was confirmed by the Maharaja, and the *nāzim* of Multan was informed accordingly : *News (1825)*, 91.

[86] Mir Ahmad, *Dastūr al-'Amal-i-Kashmir*, ff 184 a, 206 b, 207 b, 208 a-b, 209a & 283a; also, ff 326 a-341a.

Muhammad Shah Naqshabandi alone was given five villages.[87] In Peshawar, 'in every village there were one or more masjids to each of which was attached a small mafi, enjoyable by the Imam'.[88] All old grants enjoyed by the *sayyids*, the *'ulamā* the *qāzīs* and the *faqīrs* in Peshawar had been confirmed by Ranjit Singh.[89] The *sayyids* and *'ulamā* of Bannu were also 'exempt from taxation'.[90] The shrine of Sakhi Sarwar in Dera Ghazi Khan enjoyed the equivalent of over 40,000 acres of land in *dharmarth*.[91] Thus, to put it mildly, the Muslim grantees in the territories conquered by Ranjit Singh on the whole did not lose their old concessions.

In the core dominions of the Sikhs the *shaikhs* and *sayyids* were patronized from the very beginning and they enjoyed grants of revenue-free land in all the Doabs of the Panjab.[92] There are specific instances of the early Sikh rulers confirming old *madad-i-ma'āsh* in favour of *qāzīs* as well.[93] Numerous *khānqāhs* received *dharmarth* grants from the Sikh rulers.[94] The *shaikhs* of the *khānqāh* of Pir Mitha near Wazirabad enjoyed fifteen different concessions, including revenue-free lands, daily allowance in cash, dues from the mint, grain from Gujrat, rice from Kashmir and salt from Pind Dadan Khan.[95] It may

[87] Charles Hugel, *Travels in Kashmir and the Panjab*, 354.

[88] *Gazetteer of Peshawar*, 207-08.

[89] Sohan Lal, *Umdat*, III, (ii), 253.

[90] 'Diary of H. Edwardes', *Punjab Government Records (1847-1849)*, V, 162, 170, 179, 180, 213-14, 228, 265, for example. See also, *Gazetteer of Bannu*, 194 & 196.

[91] *Gazetteer of Dera Ghazi Khan*, 120.

[92] *Khālsa Darbār Records*, Bundle 5, Vol. XI, 3, 4, 11-15, 35, 101, 335, 353, 357, 387,399, 421, 449, 527, 597, for example; also, Bundle 3, Vol. I, 319-20; *Foreign/Political Proceedings*, 22 November 1850, No. 117 A; ibid., 7 January 1853, Nos. 231-34.

[93] *Khālsa Darbār Records*, Bundle 5, Vol. XI, 401 & 543, for example.

[94] Ibid., 371, 455, 485 & 575. See also, *Foreign/Political Proceedings*, 14 November 1851, No. 45; *Gazetteer of Shahpur*, 16, 42 & 85; *Gazetteer of Rawalpindi*, 116-17. Some of the *khānqāhs* to receive *dharmarth* grants from the Sikh rulers were those of Mastan Shah, Shah Bahlol, Wazir Shah, Sayyid Mahmud, Fateh Ali, Pir Adam Sultan, Shah Shams and Sultan Habib.

[95] *Khālsa Darbār Records*, Bundle 5, Vol. XIII, 615-16. Equally numerous are the grantors in this case including not only Maharajas Ranjit Singh, Sher Singh and Dalip Singh, but also the *jāgīrdārs*

only be added that Muslim grantees enjoyed the patronage of the Sikh *jāgīrdārs* as well.[96]

The great variety of *dharmarth* grants during the Sikh times is reflected in the grants given by a single *jāgīrdār*, namely, Sardar Lehna Singh Majithia. The categories of persons and institutions enjoying his munificence included *sadābarts*, *granthīs*, *pāthīs* and *ardāsias*, *brāhmans* and *purohits* of the Gangaji, Kurukshetra and Pehowa in particular, *sādhs*, *mahants* and *bhāīs* in general, the Sodhis and *akālīs* and *nihangs*, astrologers and astronomers, painters and poets, and lastly, the *sayyids*.[97] This list does not exhaust all the recipients. Grants of land were generally given to *dhādhīs* and *rabābīs* and sometimes also to the artists employed by the rulers and *jāgīrdārs*.[98] Grants for the support of hospitals and the maintenance of *bāolīs* and *samādhs* are also on record.[99]

Towards the end of Sikh rule at Lahore, according to a contemporary estimate, twenty lakhs of rupees were given in

like General Avitabile, Jamadar Khushal Singh, Sardar Hari Singh Nalwa, 'Karnail' Mihan Singh, Diwan Thakur Das Duggal and Shaikh Imamuddin.

[96] See, for example, *Foreign/Political Proceedings*, 7 January 1853, No. 234.

[97] Ibid., April 1850, No. 280(1).

These *dharmarths* amounted to 18,000 rupees and had been alienated out of a total *jāgīr* of 57,000 rupees. In 1847, the Lahore Darbar had reduced the *jāgīrs* of the *Majithia sardār* from 1,27,000 rupees to 57,000 rupees but granted the *sardār's* request to continue these grants for the lives of the holders and their heirs.

[98] For grants of the *dhādhīs*, *rabābīs* and *mirāsīs* see, for example, *Khālsa Darbār Records*, Bundle 5, Vol. XI, 17, 457, 479 & 581; *Foreign/Political Proceedings*, 7 January 1853, No. 234. For the grants of artists from the Kangra hills, see *Painters at the Sikh Court*, Documents I-VI, VIII-XII & XIV-XIX.

[99] Faqir Nuruddin received a village for support of a hospital: *Foreign/Political Proceedings*, 22 November 1850, No. 117 A. For grants for the maintenance of *samādhs* and *bāolīs*, see *Khālsa Darbār Records*, Bundle 5, Vol. II, 25-26, 35-38 & 39-40, respectively.

'religious grants'.[100] This amount formed nearly 7 per cent of the total revenues from land. The Sodhis and the Bedis received the largest share, the former receiving five lakhs and the latter four. The remaining 11 lakhs went to Hindu and Muslim as well as to the rest of the Sikh grantees. Even if the *dharmarth* grants of the Sodhis and the Bedis are excluded, the percentage of religious grants to the total revenues from land remains over 3½. The Sikh rulers alienated much larger shares of their revenues in favour of the religious groups than their Mughal predecessors.[101]

The consideration which the Sikh rulers gave to Sikh religious groups must be regarded first as an expression of their sense of piety. Their catholic outlook enabled them to accord similar treatment to non-Sikh religious groups. The piety and catholicity of the Sikhs is in marked evidence in the grants given by the Sikh *jāgīrdārs*. It must be added, however, that self-interest of the rulers dictated conciliation of all classes of their subjects and no other sections could serve better as vested interests than those that commanded influence with the subject peoples. Large grants given to the Sodhis and Bedis had a practical implication because of the veneration in which they were held by the Sikhs. It was politic to enlist their support. In any case, to rally influential individuals behind the new principalities was a necessity imposed by the situation in which a number of new rulers were trying to increase their power, or at least to maintain it. Extensive patronage of religious classes by the Sikh rulers was thus an expression as much of their practical good sense as of their sense of piety and catholic outlook.

[100] Cunningham, *A History of the Sikhs*, 385, Appendix XXXVIII.

[101] For the Mughal province of Lahore under Akbar this percentage has been suggested to be less than two : Irfan Habib, *Agrarian System*, 314.

8

Land Tenures

By far the largest bulk of our information on land tenures in the Sikh dominions comes from the early British administrators of the Panjab. The easiest way to be misled on the subject is to base oneself on only a part of this evidence. Furthermore, it is necessary to examine the evidence of the British administrators not only in its entirety but also in relation to information available from other sources.

The practical interest of the British rulers demanded a simple and rational classification of land tenures in the Panjab. They observed an 'infinite variety' of isolated tenures arising from 'the various social circumstances of the people and the past history of the administration of the different parts of the country'.[1] Some of them felt that it was impossible to classify them 'successfully' under 'a few general headings'.[2] Nevertheless, a general classification of land tenures was attempted and, with an eye on the major forms, three categories were discerned : the *ta'alluqdārs*, the peasant proprietors and the tenants.

The Persian chroniclers of the early nineteenth-century Panjab refer to the *ta'alluqdārs* as a category of *zamīndārs* between the vassal chiefs on the one hand and the peasant

[1] *General Report upon the Administration of the Punjab Proper (1849-50 & 1850-51)*, (cited hereafter as *GRAPP (1849-1851)*, 104.

[2] *Gazetteer of Multan*, 72.

proprietors on the other.[3] They were also known as *mālikān-i--a 'alā*, or superior owners entitled to a species of head-rent under several designations.[4] They were largely the descendants of former chiefs, *jāgīrdārs*, *ijāradārs* and other officials.[5]

> In a good many cases the superior owners are the descendants of persons who once exercised political sway or enjoyed a lordship over the soil, from which they were ousted during the dominion of the Sikhs, though they managed to collect at harvest with greater or less regularity some small proprietary fee such as a *ser* in every maund of the produce (*sermani*), from the persons in actual possession of the land. In other cases the connection of the ancestors of the present *talukdars* with the land was in its origin clearly official. They were revenue farmers or *jagirdars* who enjoyed under native rule large rights of management, which grew into rights of property. These two sources of *talukdari* right were often united in a single individual.[6]

[3] To this category, for example, belonged the *zamīndārs* of Gujrat, Dewa-Batala, Sahiwal, Makhad, Hasan-Abdal, Hazara, Dhanni and Pindi-Bhattian : Amar Nath, *Zafarnāma*, 82, 85, 100, 137, 139, 141, 149 & 151; Bute Shah, *Tārīkh*, V, ff 189a, 217b, 218a, 247a, 249b, 256b-257a, 266b, 272b & 274 a-b; Ganesh Das, *Chār Bāgh*, 310-11; Sohan Lal, *Umdat*, II, 53, 97, 98, 174-75, 177, 180, 181, 201, 202, 214, 238, 249 *et passim*.

[4] Baden Powell, *The Land Systems of British India* (cited hereafter as *Land Systems*), II, 641.

[5] For example, in the Kangra region, in some cases, representatives of the old ruling families enjoyed *ta'alluqdārī* rights : Douie, *Punjab Settlement Manual*, 71. In Muzaffargarh, some superior proprietors were the descendants of the *jāgīrdārs* and officials who had lost their position but were able 'to retain a small grain fee in the tract over which they once exercised power'. Some others were the descendants of *muqaddams* and the holders of *madad-i-ma'āsh* land. Most of them in Muzaffargarh were the descendants of the tribes who had come to the district for grazing at a time when it was not populated and occupied tracts without clearly defining the boundaries : *SR Muzaffargarh*, 91-92. When Kharak Singh resumed the *jāgīr* of the sons of Rup Singh Nakai, the proprietary right (*milkīat*) was allowed to remain vested in them and they became *mālguzārs* : Munshi Bakhtawar Lal, *Tārīkh-i-Montgomery*, 47-48.

[6] Douie, *Punjab Settlement Manual*, 68.

The early British administrators of the Panjab, anxious to preserve the holders of superior ownership, readily recognised their tenures which, consequently, were carefully 'investigated, defined and recorded'.[7] In the district of Lahore, it was noticed, there were some properties called *zamīndārī* which belonged to one or more individuals and which 'remained undivided and were held in common'.[8] In the district of Amritsar there were a few villages where *ta'alluqdārī* allowances were paid to the former Rajput owners who had been 'completely ousted' during the Sikh times by Jats, Kambos or Arains.[9] A small number of villages in Multan paid *haqq-i-zamīndārī*, or *haqq-i-muqaddamī*, to the former *zamīndārs*.[10] In Rawalpindi, a few of the *zamīndārī* villages were in the hands of a single individual; and some of the tribal chiefs held several villages in *zamīndārī*.[11] In Sialkot, however, there were only a few whole villages under *ta'alluqdārī* tenures.[12] In Hoshiarpur, only about 1 per cent of the estates were *zamīndārī*.[13] In Kohat, one Khattak chief enjoyed a great estate and many large estates were cultivated by the owners themselves; but omitting these, there were only 3½ per cent of the total land tenures 'in which the

[7] The following definition of *ta'alluqadārī* rights under the British is very nearly relevant for the Sikh times also :

> The taluqdars in the Punjab have no connection with the land nor any control over its cultivation, but receive an allowance fixed by Government in acknowledgement of rights formerly exercised but now obsolete. They are not intermediate between the proprietors and cultivators, and their dues are paid by a percentage on the Government demand.
>
> *Punjab Famine Commission Enquiries Report (1878-1879)*, II, 556.

[8] L.S. Saunders, *SR Lahore*, 65.

[9] J.A. Grant, *SR Amritsar*, 62.

[10] The *zamīndār* in this case was the original proprietor (or the descendant of an original proprietor) who had lost every other right to land than a small share in the produce because someone else started cultivating his land or sunk a well in it. The latter in due course became the *mālīk* while the former remained *a'alā mālik* but was entitled only to *zamīndārī* : Munshi Hukm Chand, *Tārīkh-i-Multan*, 630. See also, *Gazetteer of Multan*, 69.

[11] *Gazetteer of Rawalpindi*, 64.

[12] *Gazetteer of Sialkot*, 49-50.

[13] *Gazetteer of Hoshiarpur*, ix, Table XV.

co-parcener owners of the villages are not also the principal cultivators'.[14] In Jehlam and Shahpur also the percentage of *ta'alluqdārī* tenures was rather small.[15] Nowhere in the dominions of the Sikh rulers does the proportion of *ta'alluqdārī* tenures appear to have been even 10 per cent of the total.[16]

With an eye on the security and development of revenues, the Sikh rulers encouraged the actual cultivators as against the holders of superior ownership, which 'levelled down the differences and compelled an equality of the landlord and inferior'.[17] The 'industrious and frugal races' gradually acquired the rights of those 'whose lands they had been originally content to cultivate'.[18] Wherever the proprietors proved to be refractory, the Sikh rulers did not hesitate to farm the estate, 'locate cultivators with all the rights of property', and expel the former owners.[19] For want of support to the *zamīndārs*

[14] *Famine Commission Enquiries Report (1878-1879)*, II, 551-52.

[15] In Jehlam, 47 villages out of 979 were held by the *zamīndārs* possessing superior rights: *SR Jehlam*, 147-48. In Shahpur, there were numerous small *zamīndārs* but only one large village held by a *zamīndār* : *SR Shahpur*, 101.

[16] The proportion of area held by all the big and small *zamīndārs* in the total cultivated area in the Panjab was 10 per cent according to Baden Powell and even less than that according to Barkley : *Land Systems*, II, 569 n 2 & 617-18; 'Character of Land Tenures', *Report on the Administration of the Punjab and its Dependencies (1872-1873)*, (cited hereafter as 'Character of Land Tenures', *RAPD*), 9-10, respectivety.

Barkley adds that 'in the 30 districts (excluding Hazara and Kohat) from which returns of tenure have been received, only 435 villages with an area of 514½ square miles, are shown as held by superior proprietors collecting the Government revenue in addition to their own quit-rent; but this evidently does not include cases where the superior proprietors are also assignees of the Government revenue. There are also 13,169 holdings of superior proprietors who collect only their own quit-rent and are not responsible for the Government revenue. The latter are in many cases persons to whom the quit-rent was given in commutation of more extensive proprietary rights, of which they had been dispossessed in favour of the present holders' : ibid., 13-14.

[17] Baden Powell, *Land Systems*, II, 623.

[18] *GRAPP (1849-1851)*, 101.

[19] *Gazetteer of Rawalpindi*, 70.

during thc Sikh times, the cultivators assumed proprietary right in due course.[20] Ranjit Singh is believed to have completely ousted the *ta'alluqdārs* from certain parts of his dominions.[21]

Some *ta'alluqdārī* tenures were nonetheless a creation of the Sikh times.

> The Sikh *regime* did a good deal in some places to restrain this growth of landlord families, and yet it was good policy, and, indeed, a matter of necessity, to conciliate, in some way, the most prominent men. A certain number of the chiefs in Rawalpindi (for example) were made into 'jāgīrdārs', allowed a certain portion of the revenue of their ilāqa, and were expected to aid the ruler with a tribal force of horse and foot. But many others were reduced to being what was locally called 'chāhāramī'—allowed, that is, to receive a *fourth* part of the revenue of certain villages.[22]

Several persons in the north-western Panjab received *chahāramī* rights either from Ranjit Singh or his predecessors and successors.[23] Under this arrangement 25 per cent of the revenue due to the government went to the person who was given the right to *chahāram*, literally one-fourth. The arrangement was by no means confined to the north-western Panjab

[20] See, for example, *SR Thanesar*, 48.

[21] For example, the 'waris classes' in Hazara were said to have been 'crushed' by the Sikhs : *Gazetteer of Hazara* (1907), 89. In Jehlam also, Ranjit Singh is said to have completely ousted the *ta'ālluqdārs* and given every village either to its old '*wāris*' or to new cultivators : Mirza Muhammad Azim Beg, *Tārīkh-i-Jehlam*, 246-47. Apparently, the criterion was the ability and willingness to undertake cultivation and pay the share of the government.

[22] Baden Powell, *Land Systems*, II, 642. The practice of the Sikh administrators in this region is said to have been first to grant a *jāgīr*, to resume it later, granting in lieu a chahāram, and 'ultimately to absorb the chaharam, substituting for it an inam or two granted to the principal men of the tribe' : *Gazetteer of Rawalpindi*, 69.

[23] Rai Jalal in southern Rawalpindi, the Khattars, Ghebas and Jodhras in Attock and Fateh Jang, Umar Khan in Isa Khel, Fateh Khan Tiwana in Mitha Tiwana and Khushab, for example : Griffin & Massy, *Chiefs and Families*, II, 178, 261, 266, 273, 278-79 & 286. See also, *Foreign/Political Proceedings*, 7 January 1853, No. 228; ibid., 9 January 1857, Nos. 229-30.

or the territories of Ranjit Singh. In the area between the Satlej and the Jamna there were nearly a hundred estates which belonged to this category.[24] About the share, however, it is explicitly stated by Griffin that a person holding the *chahāramī* right was entitled to 'a quarter of the *gross produce*'.[25]

The *pattīdārs* who gradually came to be equated with the '*chahāramīs*' were originally distinct from the holders of *chahāramī* rights. In the third quarter of the eighteenth century, even a single horseman had sometimes got a share in conquest and thus become a sharer of territory with the chief. Such shares were divided amongst the descendants of the original co-sharers (*pattīdārs*) in accordance with the custom of the clan to which the *pattīdār* belonged.[26] Whereas the chief's territories, by and large, were inherited by one successor, the territory of a *pattīdār* was divided amongst his descendants.[27] The *pattīdār*, like the chief, respected old proprietary rights but asserted his right to a share of the produce. The descendants of a *pattīdār*, therefore, inherited their respective shares in produce from land held by others under various tenures. The prevailing custom was not to divide the land into horsemen's

[24] Lepel Griffin, *Rajas of the Punjab*, 200-01. See also, *Kitāb-i-Hālāt-i-Jind-wa-Dastāvezāt-i-Tārīkh Tā 1865 Īsvī* (anon.), f 27b; *Foreign/Political Proceedings*, 30 April 1852, No. 92. For the preponderance of the *chahāramīs* in the Jalandhar Doab, see Ram Sukh Rao, *Srī Fateh Singh Partāp Prabhākar*, ff 65a, 73b, *et passim*.

[25] *Rajas of the Punjab*, 200 n 1. The original 'chahāramīs' having 'in the course of years multiplied into numerous descendants (now called jagirdārs)', their allowance too was further divided into 'innumerable petty shares, and special rules have long been in force as to the succession by inheritance to such shares. The sharers in the jagir income (many shares are as low as one rupee) are called "pattidars" exactly as if it was a land share': Baden Powell, *Land Systems*, II, 683.

[26] For some detail on the *pattīdārs*, see chapter VI, 132-36 & nn 62-71.

[27] Either actual primogeniture or a tendency towards primogeniture is in evidence in the majority of houses whose chiefs lay claim to sovereignty. *Cf.* Lepel Griffin, 'The Law of Inheritance to Chiefships', *Panjab Past and Present*, VI, Part I, 146-50; Indra Krishen, *An Historical Interpretation of the Correspondence of Sir George Russel Clerk*, 26-34.

shares, each sharer attending at the harvest and taking his share of the government produce himself.[28]

By far the bulk of land in the Panjab during the Sikh times was held by small proprietors who cultivated their lands in whole or in part. In Lahore, for instance, over 27 lakh acres of land was cultivated by the proprietors themselves, while the land given to tenants amounted to over 3 lakh acres only.[29] In Jalandhar, over 66,000 proprietors held on the average only 12 acres of land or a little more.[30] In Rawalpindi, the peasant proprietors paid over 6 lakhs of rupees as revenue out of the total of over 7 lakhs.[31] Whether a village was labelled *bhaiyachāra* or *pattīdārī*, the bulk of the village land was held by the proprietors 'in severalty'.[32]

The most incontrovertible evidence in support of the individual's right to property is provided by the known deeds of sale and mortgage.[33] Before the Sikh rule was over, it was observed by a contemporary that land was a disposable property and fields as well as plots of ground were mortgaged and sold among the ordinary *zamīndārs* 'either with or without the concurrence of the local authorities'.[34] Even if such transactions were not very frequent or numerous,[35] the known

[28] W. Wynyard, Settlement Officer, Cis-Satlej, to C.F. Mackeson, Commissioner and Superintendent, Cis-Satlej, *Foreign/Political Consultation*, 12 May 1849, No. 142. It was further observed that hereditary proprietors of the soil had managed to preserve their rights under the *chahāramī jāgīrdārs* who were called 'puttidars who share with the Government, who were, in fact, the Government'.

[29] *SR Lahore*, 35.

[30] *Gazetteer of Jullundur*, 25.

[31] *Gazetteer of Rawalpindi*, 69.

[32] Douie, *Punjab Settlement Manual*, 65-66. Under the Sikh rule by and large, 'the land in each man's possession had to be recognised the measure of his liabilities, and also of his right in any common property or profits': ibid., 69.

[33] See, for example, *Pindori Documents*, IV, V, XIV; Grewal, *In the By-Lanes of History*, Documents II, VII & IX.

[34] C.F. Mackeson, 'SSR Cis-Satlej', *Foreign/Political Consultation*, 31 December 1847, No. 1829, para 10.

[35] In the Karnal district, for instance, shares of each household were carefully preserved, but 'the idea that the plot of land held by each

cases and references to mortgage and sale of landed property in contemporary records leave no doubt about the proprietary rights of the individual.[36]

Exceptions proved only the rule. Undivided interest in a part of the village lands was not uncommon. In the words of Barkley :

> Often all the cultivated land is held in separate ownership, while the pasture, ponds or tanks, etc., remain in common; in other cases the land cultivated by tenants is the common property of the community; and it frequently happens that the village contains several well-known subdivisions each with its own separate land, the whole of which may be held in common by the proprietors of the sub-division, or the whole may be held in severalty, or part in separate ownership and part in common.

The majority of the cultivators owned separate holdings in an estate and this separation extended so far that there

was his own to do what he pleased with' has been described as 'utterly foreign to ideas of the people': D.C.J. Ibbetson, *SR Karnal*, 96. In fact, 'if any of the proprietors wishes to sell his rights, or is obliged to part with them in order to satisfy demands upon him, the other members of the same community have a preferential right to purchase them at the same price as could be obtained from out-siders' : Barkley,'Character of Land Tenures', *RAPD*, 11. See also, 'SSR Cis-Satlej', *Foreign/Political Consultation*, 31 December 1847, No. 1832, para 29.

[36] There are numerous instances of the sale of land to individuals belonging to the same community as the vendor, or to outsiders when the collaterals had no objection : see, for example, *Customary Law of Lahore*, XIII, 46-50; *Customary Law of Pakpattan and Dipalpur Tehsils*, 92-110; *Customary Law of Attock*, XIV, 150-80; *Customary Law of Dera Ghazi Khan*, XVI, 41-43.

These instances are from the British period, but the practice of such sales during the earlier times may be safely assumed. In Dera Ghazi Khan, even the Hindu traders were 'always ready to advance money on land, and thus in time to become landed proprietors' : *SR Dera Ghazi Khan*, 76. Under the *hāthrakhāī* transaction in Multan, a village body placed themselves by a fictitious sale or transfer under the protection of a more powerful *zamīndārī* body. In some cases such 'protectors' absorbed the actual proprietary right and the protected then sank to the level of tenants : Baden Powell, *Land Systems*, II, 662. See also, *Gazetteer of Sialkot*, 50.

was 'no land susceptible of separate appropriation which is not the separate property of the individual or family'.[37] Naturally, an outsider was the 'full proprietor' of the piece of land purchased by him but was not given any share in the lands held in common.

The tribe as a whole was the true proprietary unit in the areas occupied by the Afghans, particularly across the Indus. Consequently, periodical redistribution of holdings was not uncommon, though the interval varied from 3 to 30 years. In some cases, only the land was exchanged; in others, the exchange extended to the houses as well. The term used for this arrangement was *vaish,* literally, a large block of land. It was not merely an adjustment of possessions according to shares but a complete exchange of property between one group of proprietors and others, followed by division among the proprietors of each group.[38] Nevertheless, these periodical redistributions were based on the original proprietary shares 'which were capable of transfer by sale or mortgage'.[39]

More or less quasi-proprietary tenures, known by various names, existed in different parts of the Sikh dominions.[40] In the Chaj Doab and in some other parts of the Panjab, a

[37] Barkley, 'Character of Land Tenures' *RAPD*, 11.

[38] Ibid., 12. See also, Baden Powell, *Land Systems*, II, 636-39. The settlement officer of Dera Ghazi Khan offers a rationale for such periodical redistribution : 'The Custom of "Vaish" is probably due to the fact that the lands irrigated by hill streams are of very different value. The lands with greatest facility of irrigation are the best and the lands least irrigated, the worst. The hill streams too are liable to change and land does not always retain the same character. The proprietors by dividing lands only for a time consider that they secure to each proprietor chance of holding good lands in turn : F.W.R. Fryer, *SR Dera Ghazi Khan*, 77.

[39] H.St.G. Tucker, *SR Kohat*, 86.

[40] Proprietary right was acquired through a variety of ways, such as *banjar shigāfī* or breaking the wasteland, purchase, payment of *nazrāna* to the government, digging a well in the waste, gift or offering, *jāgīr*, *mālguzārī*, hereditary possession, and through forcible occupation : Munshi Hukm Chand, *Tārīkh-i-Multan*, 631.

It may be interesting to note that the superior owners or *wārises* in Hazara found it convenient to associate with themselves on privileged terms any strong body of cultivators who could be located on

tenure called *mālik-i-qabza* entitled the holder to full ownership of the land he occupied but not to any share in communal rights.[41] In a large number of *vaish* villages across the Indus also there was a good deal of land held on *qabza* tenures.[42] The tenure known variously as *adhlāpī*, *taraddadkār*, *chakdār* and *sildār* was prevalent in Dera Ghazi Khan, Jhang, Muzaffargarh and Multan.

> A man who sinks a well in land which does not belong to him with the owner's permission becomes proprietor of half the land which it commands. He very commonly cultivates or arranges for the cultivation of the whole of the land, takes half of the proprietor's share of the produce and pays half the land revenue.[43]

The *chakdār* of Multan and Muzaffargarh, also called the *sildār*, enjoyed full proprietary rights but was regarded as inferior owner (*mālik-i-adna*).[44] In fact, he paid *haqq-i-zamīndārī* to the original proprietor (*mālik-i-a'alā*) as quit

the disputed land with a liability to military service only. They were called *lakbands*, that is to say, the men who girded their loins in the service of the *wārises* : *Gazetteer of Hazara*, 89.

[41] The number of such holdings in the Jehlam district was over ten thousand: *SR Jehlam*, 148. See also, *SR Shahpur*, 103; *Gazetteer of Gujrat*, 55.

The *mukarīdār* tenure in the Rawalpindi district was close to the *mālik-i-qabza* with the exception that the *mukarīdār* paid rent at fixed rates to the proprietors : *Gazetteer of Rawalpindi*, 72.

In Jehlam, Hazara, Rawalpindi, Gujrat and a few other places, the holders of this right had been the descendants either of the one-time proprietors borne down by incoming conquerers, or of the old settlers and tenants. In Jalandhar, however, they were the descendants of village servants who had held rent-free land for many generations and had 'by long possession gradually acquired proprietary rights' : W.E. Purser, *SR Jullundur*, 86.

[42] See, for example, *SR Kohat*, 87.

[43] Douie, *Punjab Settlement Manual*, 83. In Dera Ghazi Khan and Muzaffargarh, he was known as *adhlāpī*, and in Jhang as *taraddadkār*. His right was also known as *taraddadī* and he as *mālik-i-taraddadī* : Munshi Hukm Chand, *Tārīkh-i-Multan*, 629 & 631. See also, *Gazetteer of Multan*, 60; *SR Dera Ghazi Khan*, 75.

[44] The term *chakdār* was derived directly from *chak* or wooden frame on which the masonary cylinder of a well was built. The

rent.[45] Available descriptions underline the kinship of the *chakdār* with the *adhlāpī* and the *taraddadkār*.[46] The proprietary right of the holders of these tenures was underlined by the fact that they could get their lands cultivated by tenants.[47]

The number of tenants in the Sikh dominions was nearly

name was meant to express that the *chakdār* had acquired his rights in the land by having sunk the well. For this reason, he was also called *sildār* or owner of the bricks of the well. This particular form of tenure was introduced in Multan and Muzaffargarh by Diwan Sawan Mal. See also, *GRAPP* (*1849-1851*), 103-04; *Gazetteer of Multan*, 70; *SR Dera Ghazi Khan*, 75. The holder of the *chakdār* tenure in Rawalpindi was generally a trader who built a well with his own capital but did not himself cultivate the land irrigated from it : *Gazetteer of Rawalpindi*, 72.

[45] The *haqq-i-zamīndārī* in some cases was nominal amounting to an eighth to one seer in a maund, and at places, the *chakdārs* paid nothing to the original proprietors : Munshi Hukm Chand, *Tārīkh-i-Multan*, 630.

When the *chakdār* was an outsider introduced by the *zamīndār*, he paid the latter an installation fee variously known as *jhūrī*, *lungī*, *pag* or *saropā*. If he abandoned his land, it reverted to the *zamīndār*, not by virtue of any contract but only because the *zamīndār* was the owner of all the waste land. The full proprietary right of the *chakdār* was underlined by the fact that the *zamīndār* could cultivate the land of the *chakdār* only as the latter's tenant. In such a situation 'the original rights of the *zamīndār* were in no way influenced by his position as tenant' : *Gazetteer of Multan*, 70.

[46] Barkley's brief description of the *chakdārs* is worth reproducing : 'These are the owners of wells, or occasionally of irrigation channels, constructed at their expense in land belonging to others. They possess hereditary and transferable rights, both in the well or irrigation channel and in the cultivation of the land irrigated from it, but may be bought out by the proprietor repaying the capital they have expended. They are generally entitled to arrange for the cultivation, paying a small fixed proportion of the produce to the proprietor, and being responsible for the Government revenue. Sometimes, however, the management of the property has been made over to the proprietor, who pays the Government revenue, and the chakdār receives from him a fixed proportion of the produce, called *hakkasūr*' : 'Character of Land Tenures', *RAPD*, 14-15.

[47] The amount paid by the tenants to the *chakdār* was generally called *kasūr*. However, the term *kasūr* was used also for a small grain—fee in a different situation. One or two seers in a maund

half the number of proprietors.[48] The latter cultivated larger holdings and, therefore, the area cultivated by the tenants was less than even one-half of the area cultivated by the proprietors. In fact, the tenants cultivated only one-fourth of the total area under cultivation.[49] They were known by various names in the different parts of the Sikh dominions.[50] The terms on

went to the person who used his capital for *banjar-shigāfī*, irrespective of his proprietary position. He may be a *mālik*, a *chakdār* or a *muzāri'*. If the person cultivating that piece of land was different from the person who invested, he paid this *kasūr*. *Sāhūkārs* received *kasūr* in place of interest on loan: Munshi Hukm Chand, *Tārīkh-i-Multan*, 630. In Muzaffargarh and Dera Ghazi Khan, this grain-fee called *lichh*, was generally one or two seers in a maund or 1/17th of the gross produce and was known as *solh-satārī* : ibid., 631. See also, *SR Muzaffargarh*, 93; *SR Dera Ghazi Khan*, 75 & 80.

[48] Barkley, 'Character of Land Tenures', *RAPD*, 15. However, according to another report, a proprietor who cultivated a portion of his neighbour's holding in the capacity of a tenant he was returned as a tenant; and similarly, if he cultivated part of the common lands he did so as a tenant. Consequently, the 'true area of the cultivation of the tenant class, strictly so defined, was less than 44 per cent' : *Famine Commission Enquiries Report* (*1878-1879*), II, 552.

It may be pointed out that the proportion was reversed in the territories comprising the Sikh *sūba* of Multan, with nearly 34 per cent of the land cultivated by the proprietors and 66 per cent by the tenants. This was very largely due to the extention of cultivation during the period of Sikh rule. See also, *Gazetteer of Multan*, 76.

[49] The average size of 'tenancies of all descriptions' is said to have been 6 acres : *Famine Commission Enquiries Report* (*1878-1879*), II, 553.

[50] Even the general terms used for the tenants (*muzāri'ān*) in different parts of the Sikh dominions were many : *qadīmī* (old), *haqq-dār* (holder of a certain right), *chhapparband* (settlers), *khud-kāsht* (self-cultivating) and *pāhīkāsht* (non-resident cultivators). While 'residing in neighbouring villages', the *pāhī-kāsht* sometimes had 'marked and recognised rights': Douie, *Punjab Settlement Manual*, 99.

There were several local variations : *būtāmār* or *mundamār* (clearing jungle), *kuhmār* (sinking well), *latmār* (erecting embankments), *jhurī-band* (paying a *nazrāna* in cash or kind), *god-kash* (receiving a small fixed share which is transferable and getting the land cultivated by someone else), *lachhain* or *hatain* or *chārikār* (using

which they cultivated lands belonging to the proprietors also varied from place to place.[51]

The tenants of the Sikh dominions may be divided into two broad categories : *muzāri'ān-i-mustaqil* and *muzāri'ān-i-ghair-mustaqil*. The former may be further divided into three classes : *āsāmiān-i-qadīm*, who were coming down from the late eighteenth century; *mustaqil purānā*, who started cultivating around 1810; and *mustaqil jadīd*, who were the latest to start cultivation.[52] The proprietor had 'the power and right to evict any tenant, but such right was very seldom exercised lest the estate should be under-cultivated'.[53] The *mustaqil* tenants enjoyed greater security than the *ghair-mustaqil*, but if the proprietor wanted the land for his own use he could eject any tenant, irrespective of the length or the character of his tenancy.[54] The formal distinction which the British administrators

bullocks and seeds provided by the proprietor and getting a share), *rakh* , (receiving food and clothing and some cash twice during the year), and *miādī* (for a term). For further detail, see Munshi Hukm Chand, *Tārīkh-i-Multan*, 642-44.

[51] The variations can perhaps be explained in the following terms : the general condition and availability of land, fertility of the soil, means of irrigation, disposition of the administrator, and the clan composition and the relative strength of the proprietors and tenants: see, for example, *GRAPP (1849-1851)*, 103; *SR Dera Ghazi Khan*, 78-80; *SR Amritsar (1888-1893)*, 61; *SR Shahpur*, 103; *SR Kohat*, 90-92; *SR Jehlam*, 152; *SR Muzaffargarh*, 95-96.

[52] *SR Jehlam*, 149.

[53] *Papers connected with the Question of Tenant Right in the Panjab, Selections from Records of the Government of the Panjab*, Lahore, 1869 (cited hereafter as *Tenant Right in the Panjab, Selections PGR*), 67.

In fact, 'during the Sikh rule the tenants were tolerated by the proprietors without active resistance, and in most cases the proprietors were probably only too glad to be relieved of responsibility for cultivating and to get a trifling recognition of their proprietary right in the shape of a seer or two in the maund from the produce' : A. Kensington, *SR Ambala*, 78.

[54] The majority of the Lahore Committee, formed specifically to consider the question of tenant right, were of the opinion that 'however long a tenant might have resided or cultivated in the village, yet the proprietor, if he wanted the land for his own use, could eject him' : *Tenant Right in the Panjab, Selections PGR*, 67; also, ix & 39.

came to make between the occupancy tenant (*maurūsī*, literally hereditary) and the tenant-at-will (*ghair-maurūsī*, literally non-hereditary) was their own creation but it did have the informal precedent of the practice of the Sikh times.[55]

The preponderance of occupancy tenants in the British Panjab was in fact a corollary of the preponderance of the *mustaqil* tenants in the dominions of the Sikh rulers. Sikh rule had been favourable to 'the permanence of the cultivator's occupancy'.[56] Those who brought land under cultivation by clearing the jungle in Muzaffargarh during the Sikh times, for instance, were treated as occupancy tenants by the British.[57] Similarly, the *ābād-kārān* and *banjar-shigāfān* of Shahpur acquired occupancy rights because of their having broken up the wasteland or having sunk a well during the Sikh times.[58] In Dera Ghazi Khan, occupancy rights were acquired by erecting embankments for irrigation, improving the soil, clearing the jungle, or by sinking a well.[59]

In their dealings with the tenants, the Sikh rulers treated them essentially like proprietors, allowing them generally to 'share in the payment of revenue'.[60] So long as the tenants paid the revenue to the state and charges due to the village or the proprietor, they were not ejected from their lands. They could cut trees for agricultural or domestic purposes but

[55] In fact, this is emphatically stated in British records. For example : 'No useful purpose would be served by any detailing the grounds on which the occupancy rights of tenants have been awarded in the Settlement and Civil Courts. They have not been created by us on abstract grounds of policy; but are the Judicial and Legislative interpretation of the privileges which the older tenants possessed in the times immediately antecedent to our rule; an interpretation . . . arrived at by the majority of our Revenue Officers and Judges' : *Famine Commission Enquiries Report* (*1878-1879*) II, 553.

[56] J.E. Cracroft, *SR Rawalpindi* (*1864*), para 365.

[57] *SR Muzaffargarh*, 94.

[58] *SR Shahpur*, 101-02.

[59] *SR Dera Ghazi Khan*, 78-80.

[60] It may be interesting to note in this connection Baden Powell's comment that under Sikh rule, 'every land holder was treated as equal, being regarded as a revenue-producing machine' : *Land Systems*, II, 635.

they could not sell them. Their tenure was inheritable but they could not 'in any way transfer their right of occupancy'.[61] In Amritsar, the hereditary cultivator and the proprietor paid according to the same rates 'both as regards land and water'.[62] Similarly, in Rawalpindi, '*mushakhasa* assessment or *kankūt*' was uniformly applied to proprietors and hereditary cultivators.[63] In Ambala and Ludhiana, the Sikh rulers 'took the same payment and the same proportion of grain from the hereditary proprietor or from the hereditary cultivator or the mere tenant-at-will'.[64]

In addition to the land revenue and cesses and *kamiāna*, the tenants in many parts of the Sikh dominions had to pay *mālikāna* and other proprietary dues. The amount of these dues varied from area to area, depending partly on the strength of the proprietors. In Gurdaspur, *mālikāna* ranged from 10 to 15 per cent of the revenue.[65] The rate of *mālikāna* in Kohat varied from 5 to 10 per cent.[66] In Jalandhar, the tenants paid 5 per cent of the revenue as '*lambardārī* allowance'.[67] In Hoshiarpur, a fifth of the revenue was the maximum rate of *mālikāna*, and the majority of the tenants paid no other dues.[68] In Shahpur, however, the majority made some other payments in addition to *mālikāna* which was 5 per cent of the revenue.[69] In Gujranwala, *mālikāna* was 'the exception not the rule', and rarely exceeded 6¼ per

[61] Edward Prinsep, *SR Sialkot (1865)*, para 375. In Karnal, however, the tenants shared 'equally with the owners in the proceeds of the common lands' such as the sale of firewood or grass, or grazing dues paid by other villagers : J.M. Douie, *SR Karnal-Ambala*, 103.

[62] R.H. Davies, *SR Amritsar (1859-1860)*, para 95.

[63] J.E. Cracroft, *SR Rawalpindi (1864)*, para 298.

[64] R.H. Davidson, *SR Ludhiana (1859)*, para 17. See also, *SR Ambala (1859)*, para 192. Generally, burdens of all kinds were levied 'from all classes alike' : *Gazetteer of Hazara*, 89. See also, *SR Jehlam*, 152; *Gazetteer of Rawalpindi*, 71; *SR Shahpur*, 103; *SR Thanesar*, 49.

[65] R.H. Davies, *SR Gurdaspur (1856-1859)*, para 36.

[66] *SR Kohat*, 89.

[67] R. Temple, *SR Jullunder (1852)*, para 300.

[68] *SR Hoshiarpur (1852)*, para 191.

[69] *SR Shahpur*, 102 & 103.

cent of the produce.[70] In Multan, only a 'small fraction' of the revenue, at the general rate of 2 seers in the maund or 'one-twentieth of the gross produce', was paid to the proprietors.[71] In Gujrat, *biswī* and *mālikāna* dues were altogether 'unknown'.[72] In some parts of the Sikh dominions, the tenants paid numerous 'extra dues': *jholī, kirāya, kiāra, 'amlāna, bhikh, laigadhah, bataliah* and *malba*, for instance.[73] On the whole, *mālikāna* varied from 1½ per cent to 25 per cent of the land revenue and a *ghair-mustaqil* tenant usually gathered half of the produce.[74] It may be added that most of the tenants paid in kind, whether it was revenue and cesses due to the state, or *mālikāna* and *habūbāt* due to the proprietors.[75]

The early British administrators of the Panjab identified three classes of villages in the former dominions of the Sikh rulers on the assumption of three distinct types of tenure : *zamīndārī, pattīdārī* and *bhaiyachāra*. The first designated estate was possessed in full proprietary right by a single owner; the second was meant to cover cases in which land was divided and held 'in severalty' by different proprietors according to ancestral or customary shares; and in the third, land was held 'in severalty' without reference to any ancestral or customary shares. In the *pattīdārī* tenure, share regulated the revenue payable; in the

[70] J.H. Morris, *SR Gujranwala (1860)*, para 33.

[71] *Gazetteer of Multan*, 70.

[72] *Gazetteer of Gujrat*, 78.

[73] *Gazetteer of Multan*, 72-80. These dues were known under the general name of *habūbāt* and were 'essentially voluntary offerings'. Nor were these all taken in any one village, the extent of the taking depending 'entirely on the strength of the proprietor'. For further detail, see Munshi Hukm Chand, *Tārīkh-i-Multan*, 632-35. See also, *Gazetteer of Rawalpindi*, 73; *SR Thanesar*, 48.

[74] *GRAPP (1849-1851)*, See also, *Famine Commission Enquiries Report (1878-1879)*, II, 553 & 570; *SR Kangra*, 228.

[75] The tenants in Multan, for example, held more than half of the cultivated area and paid their revenues in kind for nearly 97 per cent : *Gazetteer of Multan*, 78. Out of 29,146 tenants in Dera Ghazi Khan, only 250 paid revenues in cash : *SR Dera Ghazi Khan*, 81. See also, *Famine Commission Enquiries Report (1878-1879)*, II, 570 & 573-80.

bhaiyachāra tenure, the revenue payable regulated the share.[76]

The appealing simplicity of this classification veiled its inadequacy, but only for some time. Before long, some of the settlement officers began to air their scepticism. It was noticed in the 1860s that:

> In the earlier settlements effected in the Punjab, considerable laxity prevailed in the mode of recording tenures. There were declared to be three classes of tenures : zamindāri, pattidāri and bhaiyachāra. These terms were little understood by the subordinate officers of settlement; the rights and customs prevailing among the people differing perhaps in each estate were little heeded and no record was made of measure of rights which regulated the division of land and the distribution of profit and loss amongst the several village communities, well understood and always acted upon by them. Every estate was declared to be held on one of the three classes of tenure before stated and as it was easy to say that the possession was the standard of every man's right and responsibility the tenure prevailing in the largest number of estates was declared to be bhayachāra.[77]

This classification was imported into the Panjab from the North Western Provinces and its 'original crudity' was increased by its forced application to villages in the former dominions of the Sikh rulers.[78] Denzil Ibbetson, a well-known ethnographer and social anthropologist of the Panjab, thought of this classification as 'practically meaningless'.[79] He was not alone. Many a British administrator of the Panjab pointed out the

[76] Douie, *Punjab Settlement Manual*, 66.

[77] R.P. Nisbet, *SR Gujranwala (1866-1867)*, 61.

[78] Baden Powell, *Land Systems*, II, 621; also, *Indian Village Community*, 356 & 358. In fact, in the case of the Panjab frontier, according to Baden Powell, 'there is a peculiar method of allotting lands, which on the whole cannot really be brought under the definition of either the *pattīdārī* or *bhaichāra*, as these terms are generally understood in Northern India' : *A Short Account of the Land Revenue and its Administration in British India; with a Sketch of the Land Tenures*, 92-93.

[79] *SR Karnal*, 95.

inadequacy of this *zamīndārī-pattīdārī-bhaiyachāra* classification, underlined its inapplicability, or even discarded it.[80]

An evolutionary theory of tenures was put forth by Edward Prinsep, which took into account the variability and complexity of village tenures. He enunciated that collective property always preceded divided property; the clan originated in the tribe, the village in the clan and the joint family in the village, joint ownership of all the members of the community was followed by division of the village into *tarafs*, each forming a section of the commune; each *taraf* or *pattī* was divided into plots, first on ancestral and then on customary shares, and lastly on the basis of possession alone. In the Panjab, the tribe was represented by *qaum* or clan, and the clan by *got*; one single *got* could cover a hundred villages, but also a single village could have 'proprietors of several *gots*'.[81] This theory accounted for the division of villages into *pattīs* or *tarafs*, the existence of the members of different clans in the same village, and the individual proprietor's rights with or without his share in common property of the commune or the *got*.

This conceptualization of village tenures had a close bearing on the conception of the village community in the Sikh dominions. Henry Maine was responsible for underlining 'common kinship' and 'joint ownership' of the village communities in India.[82] This was only one extreme idea, however. The sense of proprietorship among the agricultural community of a

[80] For example, according to one report, 'it is in many cases simply impossible to class a village satisfactorily under any one of the ordinarily recognised tenures; the primary division of rights between the many subdivisions (*tarafs*) of the village following one form, while the interior distribution among the several proprietors of each of these subdivisions follow another form which itself often varies from one division to another' : *Gazetteer of Gujrat*, 53-54. According to another, it is 'by no means uncommon to find different tenures existing side by side in the tarafs of the same village'. In fact, the individual share may not fall within 'the definition of either one of the three standard types' : *Gazetteer of Rawalpindi*, 65 & 66. See also, *Gazetteer of Multan*, 71; *SR Thanesar*, 49.

[81] For Prinsep's Theory of Tenures and some comments on it, see C.L. Tupper (ed.), *Punjab Customary Law*, Vol. II : *Statements of Customary Law in Different Districts*, 50-53. See also, *Gazetteer of Sialkot*, 48-49.

[82] *Village Communities in the East and West*, 175-77.

village, according to Baden Powell, did not necessarily imply common proprietorship : 'The village owners whatever their origins, have a strong sense that they, as a body. . . have the landlord's right over the whole area of the village, arable and waste alike'; but there was never any 'socialistic' or 'enjoyment in common' idea of property.[83] Indeed, there is no evidence in support of communal ownership.[84] On the contrary, there is plenty of evidence in favour of the individual's right to own his share of land. There is much justification in a contemporary's contention that one and the same man was 'usually absolute proprietor and generally the sole cultivator' in the Panjab.[85]

However, the village was generally inhabited by a certain number of persons of common descent, 'forming one large cousinhood, having their own headman, accustomed to joint action and mutual support'.[86] At times, they were strong enough to resist the payment of revenue; occasionally, different cousinhoods could decide their disputes by petty wars against one another without any reference to a superior authority.[87] However, such an agricultural community did not enjoy a pure or exclusive existence in a village. Proprietors belonging to different *gots* and a few *muzāri's* could be the cultivators of land in a village; the 'village community' was never confined to the

[83] *Land Systems* II, 609 & 626 n 2, respectively.

[84] This has been discussed at length by B.R. Grover in 'The Concept of Village Community in North India during the Mughal Age and the Pre-British Era', a paper presented at the Institute of Advanced Study, Simla in 1966 (seen through the author's courtesy). See also, Irfan Habib, *Agrarian System*, 123-24; Satish Chandra, 'Some Aspects of Indian Village Community in Northern India during the 18th Century', *Indian Historical Review*, Vol. I, No. 1, 51.

[85] J.S. Mill, quoted in Romesh Dutt, *Economic History of India*, II, 69. In Multan, in the case of the 'greater number of the bhayachara villages which constituted some 75 per cent of the whole, the village community, in the ordinary acceptation of the term, can scarcely be said to exist; they being for the most part aggregations into a fiscal circle of independent plots of cultivation or 'merely a collection of wells' without 'any community of interest' : *Gazetteer of Multan*, 68.

[86] J.S. Mill, quoted in Romesh Dutt, *Economic History of India*, II, 69.

[87] Barkley, '*Character of Land Tenures*', *RAPD*, 13.

cultivators either. There were also the labourers and artisans (*kamīns*) who assisted the cultivators directly or indirectly and whom the agriculturists regarded as being inferior to themselves.

The professional men like the blacksmith, carpenter, potter, washerman, barber, water-carrier, tailor, cotton-stuffer, cobbler, and the priest were nonetheless necessary to the agricultural families, who paid them a certain allowance of grain per plough for their professional assistance.[88] The need for self-sufficiency was realized through caste cohesion and the hereditary division of labour. In a certain sense, the village community did exist, but it was constituted by the entire population of the village and not by an agricultural brotherhood.

[88] On the average, the blacksmith, the carpenter, the barber and the water-carrier received one maund per plough; the potter, the washerman, the bearer, the sweeper, the guide, the police informer and the musician received 20 seers per plough; the tailor received 15 seers per plough; the cotton stuffer, the cloth stamper, the dyer and the messenger received 10 seers per plough; and the *brāhman* received $\frac{3}{4}$ seer per plough: 'Report on the Revenue System of the Delhi Territory', *Punjab Government Records (1807-1857)*, I, 81. For a comprehensive list of the *kamīns*, see *Gazetteer of Multan*, 82.

9

Conclusion

Though the Sikhs had started occupying territories in the *sūba* of Lahore and the *sarkār* of Sarhind soon after 1750, it took them nearly fifteen years to complete the process of occupation. Gradual expansion continued for another decade, but the country was already divided into a large number of principalities under independent Sikh rulers. The more powerful among them fought for supremacy till Ranjit Singh succeeded in uniting a large number of principalities into a single whole in the Panjab proper. However, his position as a sovereign ruler was in no way different from that of the Sikh chiefs whom he subverted, or failed to subvert.

Politically subordinate but administratively autonomous pockets remained in existence throughout the period of Sikh rule, especially in the hills. The vassals paid tribute but retained substantial control over their territories which were not directly affected by the revenue policies of the Sikh rulers. Ranjit Singh claimed suzerainty over autonomous chiefs often as a prelude to the annexation of their territories, making little distinction between a Sikh, a Muslim and a Hindu chief in this respect. More hill principalities were subverted by him than by all the Mughal emperors put together. Three principalities were annexed during the time of his successors. Nevertheless the number of vassals retained in the hills remained pretty large. Some of the vassal chiefs served not only on military expeditions, but also as *nāzims* and *ijāradārs*. The Jamwal brothers who were the most powerful of all the vassal chiefs of the Sikh rulers, were a creation of Ranjit Singh himself.

Only in the kingdom of Lahore did the need arise to divide conquered territories into provinces over which governors (*nāzims*) were regularly appointed. Each province, like the Sikh principality, consisted of a number of *ta'alluqas* or *parganas*, the two being interchangeable, and a *kārdār* was appointed to look after the administration of a *ta'alluqa*. In many parts of the Sikh dominions, the *ta'alluqa* was further divided into *tappas* for fiscal purposes, each *tappa* consisting of a number of villages. Whereas the *nāzims* and *kārdārs* were frequently transferred from place to place, the *muqaddam*, the *chaudharī* and the *qānūngo* generally remained at one place to assist the *kārdārs* appointed by the rulers.

Among the methods of assessment prevalent in the Sikh dominions, *batāī* and *kankūt* were by far the most important. Fixed cash rates were charged on wells and ploughs in some areas and certain crops were also assessed in cash. The system of *zabt* proper, with fixed cash rates per unit area of a crop, was known in most parts of the Sikh dominions, but its application was limited to a few crops. Different methods of assessment existed side by side in many places and a combination of methods was used at places for a single holding. In *batāī* and *kankūt*, the share of the government could be commuted into cash, but only if the cultivator agreed.

Whatever the methods of assessment, the rates varied from place to place and, in all probability, from time to time, depending on several factors. On the average, the share of the government was 2/5ths of the produce, though in some areas the cultivators paid much more and in others, much less. The percentages or the *in'āms* of officials and intermediaries were normally paid from the share of the government. But the cultivators had to pay certain *abwāb* which varied from area to area. They also paid *kamiāna* to 'village servants'. They were generally able to retain nearly half the produce from their lands. They were often encouraged to extend cultivation through various means, including artificial means of irrigation. Orchards, dates and pastures supplemented the revenues collected from seasonal crops. The total revenues, even from the core dominions, were less than what the government had received during the Mughal times. But this was largely because of the lower rates of assessment prevalent during the Sikh times.

The practice of collecting land revenue through farming (*ijāra*) was prevalent in many parts of the Sikh dominions but at no time did it become the predominant method of revenue collection. Furthermore, when a *nāzim* or a *kārdār* undertook to pay to the royal treasury a fixed sum (*mushakhasa*) from a certain area, the amount of *mushakhasa* was rather close to the actual returns. No *ijāradār* was allowed to determine the method or the rate of assessment, or even the mode of payment, against the wishes of the cultivators. He made his profits within certain limitations.

A substantial part of the land revenue was assigned to the servants of the state in lieu of their salaries. Former rulers and their *jāgīrdārs* were absorbed into the *jāgīrdārī* system evolved by Ranjit Singh. Also, new recruits were picked up for patronage irrespective of their race or religion. The Jat Sikhs formed the largest group without constituting the majority. A considerable portion of the *jāgīr* revenues went to the princes and some prominent individuals or families. The revenues assigned in *jāgīr* on the whole, however, were seldom more than 50 per cent of the total revenues. Though a clear distinction was made between *jāgīr* and *khālisa* lands at any given time, the distinction was not permanent with regard to a given area.

Jāgīrs were often transferred from place to place and a large *jāgīr* was seldom allowed to become one contiguous area. The *jāgīrdār* was allowed to collect revenues from the lands assigned to him either directly or through an agent. For the term of his tenure he was allowed to alienate revenues in favour of others. Disputes between different *jāgīrdārs*, between the *zamīndārs* and the *jāgīrdārs* or between the *jāgīrdārs* and the revenue officials and intermediaries were not uncommon. The property of a deceased *jāgīrdār* was temporarily taken over by the state to settle accounts and to recover arrears, if any. The descendants of a *jāgīrdār* were given preference for service, but there were no hereditary *jāgīrdārs* in the service of the Sikh rulers. When a *pattīdār* was reduced to the status of a *jāgīrdār*, however, his tenure remained permanent and hereditary. Subsistence and *in'ām jāgīrs* oo could be given in perpetuity, or for a lifetime, but they were of inconsequential magnitude.

The *dharmarth* grants made by the Sikh rulers tended to become hereditary even if originally they had not been made in perpetuity. The wasteland brought under cultivation by a grantee always became his property. The Sikh rulers generally confirmed the *madad-i-ma'āsh* grants made by the former masters of the territories they occupied. They gave fresh grants of their own to Sikhs and non-Sikhs alike. The largest share of *dharmarth* grants went to the Sikhs, but not necessarily at the cost of the non-Sikhs. Princes and *jāgīrdārs* followed the example of the rulers and alienated revenues in favour of men and institutions of known sanctity. The majority of such grants appears to have continued to be enjoyed by the grantees even after the prince or the assignee ceased to hold a particular territory. They all tried to ensure that the *dharmarth* grantees received what was granted to them : the land revenue and all other cesses due to the government. Liberal patronage of all religious classes was an expression of the political acumen of the Sikh rulers as well as an expression of their piety and catholicity.

By far the bulk of landed property in the dominions of the Sikhs was held by small proprietors who cultivated their own land in whole or in part. Quasi-proprietary tenures like *mālik-i-qabza* and *adhlāpī* or *chakdār* were existent in some parts of the Sikh dominions. Agricultural land could be donated, mortgaged or sold in accordance with the provisions of the *sharī'at*. *Ta'alluqdārī* rights, in the sense of the claim on the produce of the soil coexisting with other rights, did exist in some parts of the Sikh dominions. In fact, *chahāramī* and *pattīdārī* rights which were analogous to *ta'alluqdārī* rights, were a creation of the Sikh times. However, the proportion of cultivated land covered by the *ta'alluqdārī* tenures was rather small. In terms of numbers and areas involved, the tenants were next in importance to the self-cultivating proprietors. Their formal classification into *maurūsī* and *ghair-maurūsī* was a creation of the British. The Sikh rulers treated them all alike in matters of assessment and collection. If they retained less of the produce than the cultivating proprietors, it was only because of the proprietary dues they had to pay in addition to the land revenue.

In relation to the Mughal, the Sikh agrarian system was marked by both continuity and change.[1] In the administrative sphere, the provincial governor appeared on the scene practically in the time of Ranjit Singh. The old province of Lahore was never revived and the territories conquered in the province of Kabul were never placed under one *nāzim*. With the increase in the number decreased the size of the provinces and the importance of their *nāzims*. The Sikh *ta'alluqa* remained interchangeable with the Mughal *pargana* but, in the core dominions of the Sikhs, the number of *ta'alluqas* was much larger than the number of *parganas* in the Mughal times. Conversely, the sizes of the *ta'alluqas* were not the same as those of the Mughal *parganas*. The Mughal *'āmil* found his counterpart in the Sikh *kārdār* at the *ta'alluqa* level. The division of the *ta'alluqas* into *tappas* or *topes* continued wherever it had been prevalent. The *muqaddam*, the *chaudharī* and the *qānūngo* formed the bed-rock of revenue administration now, as before.

For the assessment and collection of revenues, the Sikh rulers did not introduce any new methods. However, adjustments were made in such a way that a difference of degree is surely discernible in the total picture. In the core areas, the method of *zabt* appears to have been dominant during the Mughal times, though *ghallabakhshī* and *kankūt* were also prevalent at places. By far the dominant methods of assessment and collection during the Sikh times, however, were *batāī* and *kankūt*, though *zabt* was partially applied at many places. Outside the core areas, the older practices were largely retained. The practice of *ijāra* became more prevalent during the Sikh times. But the rates of assessment, on the whole, were lower and the state received a smaller share of the produce.

The system of alienating land revenue in favour of individuals or institutions remained more or less the same during the Mughal and Sikh times. The service *jāgīrs* given by the Sikh rulers were similar even in detail to the *mansabdārī jāgīrs* of

[1] For comparable positions during the Mughal and Sikh times, the reader may consult the works of W.H. Moreland, Irfan Habib, S. Nurul Hasan, Satish Chandra, Noman Ahmad Siddiqi, B.R. Grover and M. Athar Ali, listed in the Bibliography.

the Mughals. The *dharmarth* grants of Sikh rulers were in no way different from the Mughal *madad-i-ma'āsh* grants. However, the proportion of revenues alienated by way of *jāgīr* was smaller than what it had been during the Mughal times and the proportion of revenues alienated by way of *dharmarth* was much larger. Similarly, the porportion of hereditary *jāgīrs* appears to have been much larger during the Sikh times.

Three important classes of the holders of land tenures in the Mughal and Sikh times were the same : the peasant proprietor, the superior owner (*zamīndār* or *ta'alluqdār*) and the tenant. The first was by far the most important. The position of the peasant proprietor improved during the Sikh times in relation to the *ta'alluqdār* and the position of the tenant improved in relation to both the peasant proprietor and the *ta'alluqdār*.

The Sikh ruling classes appear to have received a relatively smaller share of the surplus produce from land. Much of this share was distributed among a considerable number of *sardārs* and *rājas* of more or less equal importance. The peasant proprietor and the tenant were able to enjoy a considerable part of what they produced. There were no signs of any agrarian crisis developing in the kingdom of Ranjit Singh. But after his death in 1839, tension between various groups of *sardārs* and *rājas* came to the surface and their mutual jealousies weakened the state. Their factious rivalries do not appear to have sprung from any socio-economic crisis.

Glossary

The definitions and meanings given in this glossary hold true of the present study. The same terms might have a different connotation at other times and places.

Ābād-kārān : the tenants who acquired the right to occupancy by bringing wasteland under cultivation. See also, *banjar-shigāfān* and *muzāri'ān.*

Abwāb : generally, cesses paid by the cultivator to the officials in addition to the land revenue; also called *kharch* (*ikhrājāt*) *or habūbāt*. The latter term was also used at places for the payments made by the tenant to the proprietor in addition to his share in the produce at a stipulated rate. The items which find mention in the present study, and most of which are included in the glossary, are: *'amlāna, batāliah, begār, bhāra, bhikh, bhūsa, chautara, chilkāna, chobdārī-i-kotwālī, dabīrī, faslāna, gāo-shumārī, haqq-i-khidmat-i-patwārī, jama'bandī, kāh-charāī, kārdārī, kiāra, kirāya. khurāk, laigadhah, langar, mu'āfī-i-chāt, muhaltāna, muhrāna, muhāsilāna, mutassadīāna, nazr-i-kanjan, nazr-i-muharrir, nazr-i-muqaddamī, nazrāna, rasūm-i-qānūngoī, sar-i-chāhī, sar-i-dehī, sarrāfī, shukrāna* and *thānadārī.* This is a collective list of terms used for cesses, without any implication that all of them were levied at any given place or time.

'Adālatī : a touring justice under Sikh rule.

Adhlāpī : a tenure in which a person became owner of half of the land commanded by the well he had sunk, and shared with the original proprietor half the profits and obligations. See also, *chakdār, sildār* and *taraddadkār.*

Ādī Granth : The Sikh Scripture, compiled by Guru Arjun in 1604, containing the compositions of the first five and the ninth Guru and a number of *sants* and *sūfīs.*

Ajnās (pl. of *jins*) : the grains; *ajnās-i-kīmatī* : the grains considered superior, such as wheat, rice, barley and *mūng.*

Ahl-i-kār (*ahlkār*) : an agent ; an official.

Akālī : also called *nihang* : the militant followers of Guru Gobind Singh who regarded themselves to be the guardians of the faith; *singhān-i-akālia* : the *akālī* or *nihang* Sikhs employed in the army of Ranjit Singh and receiving *jāgīrs* from the state.

Akhbārāt : the news-letters.

'Amal-i-Pādshāhān : rule of the (Mughal) emperors.

Amān : literally, protection or peace, and synonymous with *rākhī* (in Panjabi). See also, *rākhī*.

'Āmil : a revenue collector, interchangeable with *kārdār* as the administrator of a *ta'alluqa*.

'Amlāna : a cess paid for the establishment of the revenue collector.

Arāzī-i-maurūsī : the hereditary agricultural lands.

Arbāb : the head-men of *tappas* in the Peshawar region (*'ilāqa*).

Ardās : the Sikh prayer ; *ardāsia* : literally, one who offered *ardās* ; the Sikh priest, officially employed by the Sikh rulers and *jāgīrdārs* for the purpose.

Āsāmī : a tenant ; a cultivator without any proprietary claims. See also, *muzāri'ān*.

Āsāmī-i-qadīm : literally, a tenant of old standing ; an occupancy tenant, coming down from the late 18th century ; also called *qadīmī*. See also, *muzāri'ān-i mustaqil*.

Bairāgī : a member of the *Vaishnava* order of ascetics

Bājguzār : one who pays tribute (*bāj*) ; a tributary ; also called *kharājguzār*.

Bandobast-i mu'āmala : settlement of the revenue payable.

Banjar : the barren or wasteland ; *zamīn-i-banjar uftādah* : land fallen out of cultivation ; *banjar-shigāfān* : those who brought the barren land under cultivation. See also, *abād-kārān* and *muzāri'ān*.

Banwazīrī : the farming of the forest products, particularly in the Kangra hills. See also, *ijāra*.

Bāolī : a large well with stairs descending to the level of the water.

Bār : the upland wasteland between the two river valleys.

Batāī : division of produce between the cultivator and the state ;

also called *ghalla-bakhshī ; batāī-lutāi*: a saying embodying the idea that, from the viewpoint of the state, *batāī* is throwing away much of its share.

Bāz-khwāst : investigation.

Begār : a cess in lieu of unpaid labour ; *kār-o-begār* : forced labour.

Bet : the flood plain of a river.

Bhāī : an epithet generally used for a Sikh formally connected with religious affairs ; also, an epithet of respect.

Bhaiyāchāra : a term used by the British administrators for a tenure in which land was supposed to be held in severalty by different proprietors whose shares were regulated by the revenue payable, and not by the ancestral or customary shares.

Bhāra: a cess for carrying grain to the market ; also called *kirāya*.

Bhet : an offering to a deity; land given in charity.

Bhishtī : a water-carrier.

Bhūsa : a cess for straw for the horses of the revenue collector's establishment.

Bigha : a measure of land generally considered equal to 20 *biswas* or 4 *kanāls*; also ½ of a *ghumāon*; the actual size varying from region to region.

Biswa : a unit area of land consisting of 20 *biswāsīs*, and equal to 1/20th of a *bigha*.

Biswāsī : a unit area of land equal to one square *karam* or 1/20th of a *biswa*.

Biswī : literally, 1/20th, signified 5 per cent of the revenues paid to the *muqaddam* ; also called *lambardārī* or *haqq-i-muqaddamī* or *pachotra*.

Butamār : a tenant whose right was based on having cleared the jungle ; also called *mundamār*. See also, *muzara'iān*.

Chahār Mahāl : the four *mahāl* of Aurangabad, Pasrur, Sialkot and Eminabad ceded to Nadir Shah by the Mughal emperor and later claimed by Ahmad Shah Abdali. See also, *mahal*.

Chahāram : literally, one fourth; the fourth share generally of the produce, and sometimes of the revenues ; *chahāramī* : a holder of the *chahāram ; takhfīf-i-chahārami-i-zamīndāran:*

deduction of a fourth from the government share on account of the remuneration payable to the *chaudharīs* and *muqaddams*.

Chak: the circular wooden frame on which the masonary cylinder of a well is built; *chakdār*: the owner of a *chak* or well, as opposed to the land attached to the well, acquiring certain rights over the produce of the land irrigated from his well. See also, *adhlāpī* and *sildār*.

Chakla: used at places in the Panjab synonymously with a *tope* and thus actually denoted the subdivision of a *tappa*. In the Mughal times, however, introduced as a recognised local division for the first time in the reign of Shah Jahan, it signified an administrative division covering a number of *parganas*.

Chamār : a leather-worker by caste.

Charīkār : a tenant using the bullocks and seeds provided by the proprietor and getting a share of the produce. See also, *muzāra'iān*.

Chaudharī : the hereditary headman of a *tappa* ; *chaudharāī* : the position of the *chaudharī* ; also, perquisites and remuneration associated with that position.

Chaurī : a fly-brush made of the tail of the Yak, and used generally for deities and royalty ; *chaurī-bardār* : the bearer of the *chaurī*.

Chautara : literally, a raised platform (*chabūtra*) ; a cess for the *kotwālī* (police station).

Chauth : one-fourth share of the revenue collected by the Marathas as the price of forbearing from ravaging.

Chhapparband : literally, the one who sets up a hut ; a tenant who settled on the land he had come to cultivate ; a settler. See also, *muzāri'ān*.

Chhāta-bardār : the bearer of the royal umbrella (*chhatra*).

Chhatāk: a measure of weight, consisting of 5 *tolas* and equal to 1/16th of a *ser*.

Chilkāna : a cess to make up the difference between the standard and other rupees.

Cho : an intermittent hill stream.

Chobdār-i-kotwālī : a cess for the gate-keepers (*chobdār*) of the police station (*kotwālī*). See also, *chautara*.

Chukā : an arrangement in which the cultivator undertook to pay a fixed sum of money for the *kharīf* and a fixed quantity of grain for the *rabī'* crop.

Dabīrī : a cess for the writer (*dabīr*) in the revenue collector's establishment.

Daftar-i-mu'allā : the central office.

Daftarī : a record keeper.

Dāl : the pulses.

Dal Khālsa : an *ad hoc* combination of the forces of more than one *sardār* for a specific purpose.

Dām : originally a copper coin, but a money of account under the Mughals ; 40 *dāms* were reckoned as equal to a rupee under Akbar, the ratio in actual practice changing from time to time.

Darbār : the royal court.

Dārogha : a superintendent or head of any organization.

Dastūr-al-'amal : a revenue or administrative manual.

Dastūr-i-sābaq : an old, established practice, *b'dastūr-i-sābaq*: in accordance with the established practice. See also, *qarār-i-qadim.*

Deg : literally, a cauldron, signifying bounty.

Deh : a village or a hamlet ; also called *mauza'*.

Dera : the camp.

Dhādhī : a musician who used to sing in praise of the Sikh Gurus and recount the heroic deeds of the Sikhs.

Dharat : for *haqq-i-dharat*, the ground rent.

Dharmarth : literally, by way of religious duty ; land revenue alienated in favour of a religious personage or institution by a ruler or, acting in his place, by a *jāgīrdār*. In Mughal times, the term most commonly used was *madad-i-ma'āsh,* literally, aid for subsistence.

Dharmsāla : synonymous with *gurdwāra* as a place of Sikh worship ; also a resting place for travellers.

Dherī : a heap or a lot ; the undivided heap of grain.

Dīwān : the head of the finance Department ; a finance officer ; also an honorofic title given to the Hindu nobles who were mostly *khatrīs*.

Doāb : a region lying between two rivers.

Faqīr : used generally for a Muslim mendicant.

Farmān : a royal order.

Farrāsh : the official who looked after the royal tents, floorings, etc.

Faslāna : literally, relating to the harvest or the crop; a cess for the *patwārī* ; also a cess for giving the 'first fruits'.

Fateh : victory.

Faujdār : literally, the official who maintained troops for law and order ; the administrator of a *sarkār* under the Mughals ; used indiscriminately for the Sikh *nāzims* and *pargana* officials ; loosely an administrator.

Gaddī : a throne ; also used for the seat of the head of a religious fraternity ; *gaddī-nashīn* : one who sits on the *gaddī* ; also the reigning chief.

Gadwaī : the bearer of *gadwī* (containing water for washing, the counterpart of the ewer) for a Sikh ruler.

Gāo-shumārī : probably a cess on the heads of cattle in excess of those needed for cultivation and domestic use.

Ghair Maurūsī : literally, non-hereditary ; a tenant at-will ; also called *muzāra'iān-ghair mustaqil.* See also, *muzāra'iān.*

Ghalla : grain ; also the payment of revenues in kind.

Ghalla-bakhshī : see *batāī.*

Ghī : the clarified butter.

Ghumāon : a measure of land, varying in different parts of the Panjab, and consisting of 8 *kanāls* ; also, equal to 2 *bighas* or about an acre.

Ghurchara : literally, a horse-rider ; one of the 'irregular horsemen' of the kingdom of Lahore ; *sawārān-i-ghurcharāha-i-khās* : the *ghurchara* horsemen of Ranjit Singh, organised into a separate regiment and recruited from amongst the aristocracy of the Panjab.

Got : a subcaste ; a subdivision of a clan.

Granthīs : the professional readers of the Granth.

Gumāshta : an assistant or subordinate, generally of a revenue collector.

Gurmata : a unanimous decision arrived at by the Sikhs present before the Gurū Granth Sāhib.

Guzāra : maintenance ; subsistence ; *guzārakhwār* : the recipient of a charity for subsistence.

Habūbāt : generally the dues paid by the tenants to the proprietor in addition to the *mālikāna*. See also, *abwāb*.

Hajjām : a barber.

Hākim : not a precise designation but denoted any high executive officer or an administrator.

Haqq : a right ; a rightful claim ; *haqq-dār* : a tenant holding a certain right. See also, *muzāri'ān*.

Har Mandir : the Golden Temple at Amritsar.

Hāsilāt : the collections (of revenue).

Hatāin : a tenant using the bullocks and seeds provided by the proprietor and getting a share of the produce. See also, *muzāri'ān*.

Hāth : a cubit or a scale of length, measured from the elbow to the tip of the middle finger, or about 18 inches.

Hāth-rakhāi : a tenure in which a village body placed themselves by a fictitious sale or transfer under the protection of a more powerful *zamīndārī* body, generally paying a stipulated amount in return for the protection received. See also, *lakband* and *muzāri'ān*.

Hissadār : a co-sharer.

Hundī : a bill of exchange.

Huzūr : lord or master.

Ijāra : an arrangement in which a certain source of income was placed in the charge of a person on the condition that he would pay a certain stipulated sum to the state in return ; *ijāradār* : a farmer ; also called *mustājjir*.

'Ilāqa : an area, generally inhabited by people belonging to the same tribe, and also treated as an administrative sub-division.

In'ām : literally, a reward ; an assignment of revenue distinct from *jāgīr* and *dharmarth*, and implying the idea of reward ; *in'ām-i-zamīndārī* : the revenue-free lands given to *chaudharīs* and *muqaddams* in addition to their customary commission (generally called *pachotra*).

Jāgīr : an assignment of land revenue in lieu of salary ; *dar-wajah-i-naukarī* : a *jāgīr* for personal service ; *dar-wajah--i-naukrī-i-sawārān* : a *jāgīr* also on account of the maintenance of horsemen ; *jāgīrdārī fauj* : the term used collectively for the horsemen of the *jāgīrdārs*. *Jāgīrdār* : the holder of a *jāgīr* ; an assignee.

Jama' : the aggregate of revenue assessed.

Jama'bandī : the rent roll of a village in which the total estimated yield and the shares of the state and the individual cultivator for each crop and the value of the state's share were entered ; also a cess for the preparation of the rent-roll.

Jama'dār : the leader of a band of uncertain number ; an officer above a *havaldār* in the 'regular' army of the kingdom of Lahore.

Jamā'at : a group of an uncertain number ; *jamā'atdār* : the leader of a group.

Jarīb : the chain or rope for measuring ; a unit of length generally considered equal to 10 *karams*. See also, *zabt*.

Jatha : a group ; *jathadār* : the leader of a group.

Jawār : the maize.

Jhalār : a wheel fixed on the bank of a river, a stream or a canal to draw water for irrigation.

Jholī : one of the *habūbāt* paid by the tenants to the proprietor, and consisting of a small quantity of grain, or nearly 20 *sers* from every 32 *maunds*, for village menials.

Jhūrī : literally a clenched fist, an installation fee paid by the *chakdār* to a proprietor for permission to sink a well on his land, and cultivate it ; also known as *lungī*, *pag* and *saropā*. See also *adhlāpī* and *chakdār*.

Jhūrī-band : a tenant cultivating after the payment of the *jhūrī* to the proprietor who marks out the plot given by tying down the bushes and grass in knots.

Jog : a yoke of bullocks.

Jogī : from *yogī* ; a renunciant belonging to one or another of the twelve Gorakhnāthī orders.

Kachhu Kadmī or *Kadam Kash* : a man who measured the area sown by pacing the sides.

Kāh charāī : the grazing dues.

Kahār : a palanquin-bearer or water-drawer by caste.

Kamblī : literally, blanket ; money paid for safety against plunder.

Kamīn : literally, inferior ; the village workmen such as

sweepers, potters, cobblers, water-drawers, barbers and washermen ; *haqūq-i-kamiāna* : the customary dues paid to them by the cultivators for the services rendered as the village servants. See also, *lāg* and *sep*.

Kāmil : literally, perfect ; a well worked to the maximum with 8 yokes of bullocks.

Kanāl : a measure of land consisting of 20 *marlas* and equal to 1/4th of a *bigha* or 1/8th of a *ghumāon*.

Kanīz : a slave girl.

Kankūt : a method of assessment based on the appraisement of the standing crop by measurement of the land and inspection of the crop ; *kannia* : the professional appraiser of the fields. See also, *khasra-zabt-i-kankūt* and *kachhu-kadmī*

Kār-o-begār : see *begār*.

Karam : a space of 2 steps, used as the basic unit of length equal to 3 *hāths* (cubits) or from about 54 to 66 inches ; also called *Karū*.

Kārdār : an agent ; an official ; a revenue collector of a *ta'alluqa* or a *pargana* ; *kārdārī* : a cess for the *kārdār*.

Kasūr : literally, fractional parts ; a fraction of the produce paid to the one who invested capital as a *chakdār* or *banjar-shigāf* or even as a *sāhukār* in digging a well or bringing barren land under cultivation ; *haqq-kasūr* : the right to a certain amount of grain-fee. See also, *lichh* and *solh-satārī*.

Katra : a market-cum-residential quarter, with its own entrance and internal management.

Khadīna : a paid labourer.

Khalīsa : lands from which revenues were collected directly by the state in contrast to land alienated in *jāgīrs*, *dharmarth*, *īn'ām* or any other kind of the alienation of revenue.

Khālsa : an epithet used for the followers of Guru Gobind Singh, derived from the idea of a direct link between the Sikh and the Guru ; also used for an individual Sikh as well as for the collective body.

Khānqāh : a religious establishment, generally of the *sufi* recluses.

Kharāj : the tribute paid by the vassal to the suzerain ; also called *peshkash* ; *kharājguzār* : one who pays tribute.

Kharch (*ikhrājāt*) : see *abwāb*.

Kharch-i-dhūnī : the expense granted for constant fire.

Kharīf : the autumnal harvest, sown in April-May before the commencement of the rains and reaped in October-November.

Khārij-az-jama' : literally, 'exempt from the payment of land revenue' ; used generally for the *dharmarth* grants.

Kharwār : literally, an ass load, signifying a measure of weight as well as of land in Kashmir. See also, *trak*.

Khasra-i-zabt-i-kankūt : a field book containing the name of the cultivator, description of the crop, dimensions and area of the field, quality of the soil and the estimated yield ; also called *khet-khasra*.

Khatrī : from the Sanskrit *kshatriya* ; a caste to which most of the Hindu revenue officials and other administrators belonged in the Panjab. See also, *dīwān*.

Khidmat : service ; *khidmatgār* : a servant ; an attendant.

Khil'at : a dress of honour, containing articles of constume generally numbering three to twenty-one, including even arms or horses, and bestowed by a superior on an inferior as a mark of distinction ; *khil'at-i-mātamī* : a dress suitable for an occasion of mourning, sent by a superior to an inferior by way of condolence.

Khud-kāshta : literally, self-cultivated ; wastelands given in *madad-i-ma'āsh* became the property of the grantee and were held in hereditary right, the occupant arranging for its cultivation and generally appropriating the entire produce.

Khurāk : a cess for feeding the measurers.

Kiāra : a cess for the green fodder for the horses of the *kārdār*, and generally commuted into grain.

Kirāya : see *bhāra*.

Kohistān : hilly tracts.

Kuhl : a small canal or water course.

Kuhmār : a tenant whose right is based on his having sunk a well (*kuh*). See also *adhlāpī* and *chakdār*.

Lāg : the fees, generally up to 5 per cent of the grains, customarily given by the cultivators to the village menials and artisans for the services rendered ; also called *sep* or *haqūq-i-kamiāna* ; *lāgī* : the recipient of *lāg*.

Lakband : literally, those who girded their waists (on behalf of the proprietors) ; the holders of land without any liability other than that of rendering military service, and were located generally on the border or in disputed territory.

Lākh : a hundred thousand.

Lambardār : the headman of a village, or part thereof called *pattī*; *lambardārī* : 5 per cent of the revenue paid to him by the tenants in his capacity as a *zamīndār* ; See also, *haqq-i-muqaddamī* and *biswī*.

Langar : literally kitchen ; a cess for the kitchen.

Lāngrī : the person incharge of the *langar* of a chief.

Latmār : a tenant who erected embankments. See also *muzāra'-iān*.

Lichh : a grain fee, generally one or two sers in a *maund* or 1/17th of the gross produce, paid by the tenants to the *chakdār* ; also called *kasūr* or *solh-satārī*.

Lichhaīn : the tenant using bullocks and seeds provided by the proprietor and getting a share of the produce after deducting *lichh*. See also, *muzāri'ān*.

Lungī : literally, a piece of cloth worn tied to the waist and flowing down to ankles ; installation fee for digging a well. See also, *jhūrī*.

Madad-i-ma'āsh : literally, aid for subsistence, it was the term most commonly used in the Mughal times for land revenue alienated in favour of a religious personage or institution by a ruler, or acting in his place, by a *jāgīrdār*. See also *dharmarth*.

Mahalla : a quarter in a town.

Mahal : a revenue sub-division under Akbar, usually corresponding with *pargana* ; also applied to a source of revenue, like *mahal-i-singhāra* in Kashmir.

Mahant : the head of a religious order or establishment among the Hindus and *udāsī* Sikhs.

Mājha : the central portion of the Bari Doab, covering the region roughly from Amritsar to Qasur and from Lahore to Bhairowal on the Beas.

Malba : the public fund in a village for common village expenses covering payments of various kinds including perquisites of officials but not the land revenue ; also one of the *habūbāt* paid by the tenant to the proprietor.

Mālguzārī : the payment of land revenue ; also the person or land subject to such payments.

Malik : the title of the hereditary head of a tappa in the Bannu region.

Mālik-i-a'alā or *a'alā mālik* : literally a superior proprietor ; he had a recognised right over land, and claim to a certain share in the produce, usually ranging from 1.5 to 10 per cent.

Mālik-i-adna : literally, inferior proprietor, like *adhlāpī*, *chakdār* and *sildār*.

Mālik-i-qabza : a tenure in which the holder was entitled to full ownership of the land he occupied, but not to any share in the communal rights in the village.

Mālikāna : the proprietary dues paid by the tenant to the proprietor, the amount generally ranging between 1½ to 25 per cent of the land revenue.

Mālwa : that part of the Panjab which is covered by the district of Ludhiana, a large part of the district of Ferozepur and portions of the erstwhile states of Patiala and Nabha ; loosely applied to the whole tract across the Satlej.

Mandī : a market or a particular market for any one commodity.

Mansab : literally, office, position or rank, indicating under the Mughals the status, obligations and remuneration of its holder in the official hierarchy ; *Mansabdār* : the holder of a rank carrying certain fixed remuneration and obligations.

Manwattā : a unit of weight prevalent in Kashmir, said to have been actually of varying weight.

Marla : a measure of land consisting of 9 *sarsaīs* and equal to 1/20th of a *kanāl* or 1/60th part of a *ghumāon*.

Masnad : a seat ; a throne.

Māsha : a unit of small weight consisting of 8 *rattīs* and equal to 1/12th part of a *tola* or 1/80th part of a *chhatāk*. It is generally used for weighing precious metals and stones.

Math : a monastery or a religious establishment.

Maund : a unit of weight consisting of 40 *sers* and seldom standardised for a large area.

Maurūsī : literally, hereditary ; an occupancy tenant. See also, *muzari'ān*.

Mauza' : see *deh*.

Mi'ādī : a tenant for a fixed term. See also, *muzāri'ān.*

Milkīat : the proprietory right; *milkīat-o-mu'āmala* : proprietorship and proceeds.

Mirāsī : a caste of Muslims employed as musicians, bards and genealogists.

Misl : strictly a group of soldiers ; *misldār* : the commandant of a *misl.*

Mistrī : a head artificer.

Mu'āf : the lands exempt from the payment of land revenue ; *mu'āfidār* : the holder of a piece of land exempt from the payment of land revenue.

Mu'āmala : revenue ; *bandobast-i-mu'āmala* : settlement of land revenue.

Muhaltāna : a cess for giving respite or exemption from the payment of land revenue.

Muhar-i-kalān : the great royal seal.

Muharāna : a cess for affixing the seal.

Muharrir : a writer or a clerk.

Muhāsilī : a cess for the field watchman ; also called *muhāsilāna.*

Mujāwir : the keeper of a shrine.

Mukaridār : a tenure in which the holder owned the land he occupied subject to the payment of a fixed amount to the original proprietors. See also, *muzāri'ān.*

Mukhtār-i-kār : an agent or a deputy ; also called *sāhib-i-kār.*

Mulāzmat : service.

Mulla : a Muslim priest and teacher, generally in charge of the mosque in a village.

Mundamār : see *butamār.*

Munshī : a writer or a scribe ; *kār-pardāzān-i-munshiān-i-huzūrī* : the royal scribes.

Muqaddam : the headman of a village, or a part thereof ; *haqq-i-muqaddamī* : the dues paid to the *muqaddam* ; also called *lambardārī* and *biswī* ; *nazr-i-muqaddamī* : a cess for the *muqaddan.* See also *pachotra* and *in'ām.*

Mushakhasa : the assessment of revenue based on the records of collection made in the past.

Mustājjir : see *ijāra.*

Mutafarriqa : miscellaneous.

Mutasaddī : an accountant, an official ; *mutasaddīāna* : a cess for the *mutasaddī*.

Mutrib : a minstrel or a singer.

Muzāri'ān : (pl. of *muzāri'*) : the terms used for the various categories of *muzāri'ān*, mentioned in this study and included in the glossary, are : *ābād-kārān, āsāmī, āsāmī-i-qadīm, banjar-shigafān, būtamār, chārikār, chhapparband, ghair maurūsī, ghair mustaqil, god-kash, haqq-dār, hatāin, hāth-rakhāī, jhūrīband, kuhmār, lakband, latmār, lichhaīn, maurūsī, mundamār, mastaqil-jadīd, mustaqil-purāna, pāhī-kāsht, qadīmī* and *rakh*.

Muzāri'ān i-ghair-mustaqil : tenants-at-will ; also called *ghair maurūsī* by the British administrators.

Muzāri'ān-i-mustaqil : the occupancy tenants ; *mustaqil jadīd* : the persons who had started cultivating land as tenants after 1810 ; *mustaqil purāna* : the tenants who had started cultivating land before 1810. See also, *āsāmī-i-qadīm*.

Nāzim : the governor of a province ; an administrator ; *nizāmat* : an administrative charge ; also, governorship of a province or a primary division in an empire .

Nazr : an offering or a present ; also cesses of various kinds, like *nazr-i-kanjan* : a cess on each well of eight yokes ; *nazr-i-muharrir* : a cess to start weighing; *nazr-i-muqaddamī* : a cess for good harvests.

Nazrāna : the tribute paid by a vassal ; also, paid by an official on a regular basis or on special occasions ; *nazrāna-gīrī* : collection of tribute. See also, *bāj* and *kharāj*.

Nihang : see *akālī*.

Nirkhnāma : the schedule of current rates and prices.

Nirmala sādhs : the ascetics and renunciants belonging to the *nirmala* order among the Sikhs.

Pachotra : a commission of 5 per cent on the revenues collected, received by the *chaudharīs* and *muqaddams* as remuneration for their services. See also, *in'ām, lambardārī* and *biswī*.

Pag : literally, a turban ; an installation fee to the proprietor. See also *jhūrī*.

Pahī-kāsht : a non-resident tenant generally residing in a neighbouring village.

Paibāqī : a term used for the land meant for assignment but not yet assigned in *jāgīr*.

Pālkī-bardār : a bearer of palanquin.

Panch : a member of the *panchāyat* ; the headman of a village or of one of its sub-divisions.

Pandā : a *brāhman* priest, generally with a fixed clientele, and conducting worship at places of pilgrimage. See also, *purohit*.

Pandit : a *brāhman*, whether learned or not.

Pargana : the administrative sub-division of a *sarkar* under the Mughals and of a *sūba* under Ranjit Singh, and thus interchangeable with *ta'alluqa*.

Parwāna : a written order under the seal of a person in power ; *parwāna-nawīs* : the writer of *parwānas*.

Pāthī : the professional reader of a religious book.

Pattā : a deed of lease ; a document given to the revenue-payer, indicating the sum payable by him.

Pattī : a part or portion of a village, generally being the sub-division of a *taraf* ; a share in a village.

Pattīdār : literally, the holder of a share ; used for virtually autonomous co-sharers of the early conquerers reduced later to the position of hereditary *jāgīrdārs*.

Pattīdārī : a definition of the land tenure given by the British administrators in which land was supposed to be divided and held in severalty by different proprietors according to ancestral or customary shares which also determined the revenue payable.

Patwārī : the village accountant ; *haqq-i-khidmat-i-patwārī* : the customary remuneration of the *patwārī* amounting to 1½ anna a rupee or ¼-½ *ser* a *maund*.

Peshkash : see *kharāj*.

Pīrī-o-mīrī : leadership in both the spiritual and the temporal realms associated with the Sodhis, the descendants of Guru Hargobind ; also used for the Sodhis are *sāhib-i jāgīr-o-mulk*: master of *jāgīrs* and territory and *sardārī-o-riyāsat* : leadership and rule.

Pīrzāda : literally, the son of a saint (*pīr*) ; used also for a descendant.

Purohit : a *brāhman* performing social and religious ceremonies for individual families. See also, *pandā.*

Qadīmī : literally, as of old ; an occupancy tenant. See also, *muzāri'ān.*

Qānūngo : a hereditary keeper of the revenue records at the *pargana* or the *ta'alluqa* level ; *qānūngoī* : the office of the *qānūngo* ; the perquisites and remuneration related to it, also called *rasūm-i-qānūngoī.*

Qaum : a clan or caste.

Qarār-i-qadīm : established practice. See also, *dastūr-i-sābaq.*

Qashqa i mulkdārī : a sectarial mark ceremoniously made with sandal wood or red ochre on the forehead of a ruler or a chief on the occasion of his coronation.

Qāzī : an official appointed by the government to administer civil and criminal justice according to the Islamic Law.

Rabābī : one who plays on the *rabāb* (a kind of violin with three strings).

Rabī' : the spring crop generally sown in October-November and reaped in April-May.

Rafīqān : the associates.

Rāgī : a singer, particularly of the verses in the Sikh Scripture.

Rāj-o-khitāb : the title and the territory ; *rāj-o-riyāsat* : autonomous administration of a given territory ; *rāja* : a ruler, generally subordinate; also a title ; *rāja-i-rājgān rāja-i-kalān bahādur* : a title meaning the *rāja* of *rājas*, the great *rāja* (actually the premier vassal chief) ; *rājgī* : the position of a vassal.

Rakh : a tenant receiving food, clothing and some cash twice during the year. See also, *muzāri'ān.*

Rākhī : literally protection ; a transitional arrangement signifying essentially the Sikh chief's claim to a part of the produce from land in return for protection afforded against all other claimants. See also, *amān.*

Rasūmāt (pl. of *rasūm*) : perquisites or commission ; customary payments and gratuities.

Rattī : a unit of small weight equal to 8 grains of rice or 1/8th of a *māsha.*

Razā'nāma : a letter of acceptance usually furnished before assuming an office.

Rozīna : the daily pay or allowance, generally paid in cash ; also called *yaumia*.

Sadābart : a free kitchen that remains open continually.

Sādh : a person devoted to religious pursuits.

Sāhib-i-kār : see *mukhtār-i-kār*.

Sahibān-i-Farānsīs : the French officers of Maharaja Ranjit Singh.

Sāhūkār : a wealthy businessman ; also a money-lender.

Sailāba : the autumnal floods from a river.

Sā'ir : taxes other than the revenues from land ; custom duties.

Sāl b'sāl fasl b'fasl : literally, 'year after year, harvest after harvest' ; in perpetuity ; generally used for the *dharmarth* grants.

Sāliyāna : annual pension or annuity ; land taken up for the whole year.

Samādh : a memorial raised on the place of cremation, generally for persons prominent in one sphere or another.

Sammat : an era ; the Bikramī Era.

Sanad : royal ordinance or any deed or grant or certificate from one in authority.

Sarāi : a resting place for travellers.

Sarbat Khālsa : the entire body of the Khālsa ; the Sikh Panth.

Sardār : a leader ; a Sikh ruler ; a title given to a Sikh noble under Ranjit Singh.

Sarkār : the primary division of a province under the Mughals ; one of the forms of address used for Ranjit Singh.

Sarkār-i-wālā : literally, His Exalted Majesty ; a form of address used for the Maharaja of Lahore.

Saropā : literally, from head to foot ; a dress of honour ; an installation fee paid for permission to sink a well. See, also, *jhūrī*.

Sarrāf : a money-changer or a banker ; one who knows and distinguishes the relative excellence and superiority of different coins.

Sarrāfī : the discount on exchange of coins ; a cess levied at different rates to defray the cost of testing the money paid as revenue.

Sarsāī : the small unit of area in the *ghumāon* system of land measure, equal to one square *karam* of about 1/9th of a *marla*.

Sat-panj-bāra : a rate of assessment on wells according to which 7 rupees per well were paid for the *rabī'* crop and 5 rupees for the *kharīf*.

Sawār : a horseman. See also, *ghurchara*.

Sawāī : an additional fourth part.

Sayyid : a descendant of Prophet Muhammad, especially one of his grandson, Husain, and held venerable by the rulers and people alike.

Sep : generally the grain given for the service rendered by the village artisans and menials ; *sepī* : one who renders the service called *sep* and receives the customary remuneration. See also, *kamīn* and *lāg*.

Ser or seer : a measure of weight varying in different parts of the Panjab, and for different articles but generally reckoned as 1/40th of a *maund* ; *sermanī* : a grain-fee of a *ser* in every *maund* of the produce paid to the superior owner.

Shaikh : the head of a religious fraternity ; the title taken by the descendants of Prophet Muhammad.

Shāl dāgh : income from the shawl industry in Kashmir given in farm. See also, *ijāra*.

Sharī'at : the Islamic Law.

Shī'a : of or belonging to the sect of Ali as the rightful Imām after the Prophet.

Shukrāna : a cess for the rise in prices after commutation of the land revenue into cash, and for adhering to the rate of commutation fixed even when the prices increased.

Sildār : the holder of a proprietary right acquired over the bricks (*sil*) of a well, sunk by him and also over the land commanded by that well. See also, *adhlāpī* and *chakdār*.

Singhāra : the water chestnut, an edible water root.

Solh-satārī : literally, sixteenth-seventeenth, a grain fee, paid by the tenant to the *chakdār*, generally one or two *sers* in a *maund* or 1/17th of the gross produce. See also, *kasūr* and *lichh*.

Sūba : a province or the primary division of an empire ; *sūbadār* : the governor of a province.

Ta'alluqa : literally, a dependancy denoting connection with, or possession of, a given area ; the term was most commonly used under Sikh rule for the administrative unit next to the province, and as such had become interchangeable with *pargana.*

Ta'alluqdārs : the holders of a superior right over land, largely the descendants of former chiefs, *jāgīrdārs, ijāradārs* and other officials ; *ta'alluqdārī* : a small proprietary due. See also, *mālik-i-a'alā* and *zamīndār.*

Tābi'dār : a subordinate ; in service.

Tahsīl : the collection, particularly of the revenues from land. *tahsīldār* : a revenue collector ; also used occasionally for the *kārdār* under Sikh rule.

Takya : a place of repose or the dwelling place of a *faqīr.*

Tappa : the sub-division of the *ta'alluqa* or the *pargana,* containing a varying number of villages. See also, *chakla.*

Taqāvī : literally, strengthening or assisting ; the money advanced to cultivators for implements, seeds and digging wells, etc.

Taraddadī : literally, one who takes the trouble ; a tenure by which the proprietor made over a well in working order on condition that the holder would make all other investment and pay half the produce to the proprietor and half the revenue to the state. See also, *adhlāpī* and *chakdār.*

Taraf : the primary division of a village. See also, *pattī.*

Tegh : the sword, signifying physical force.

Thākurdwāra : a temple dedicated to Lord Vishnu or one of His incarnations.

Thāna : a garrison stationed usually in a newly conquered territory ; a garrison in a fort ; *thānadār* : the commandant of a garrison or of a fort ; *thānadārī* : literally, the office of the *thānadār* ; also a cess for him.

Til : the sesame.

Tirnī : the grazing tax.

Tombū : a promissory note ; also a draft made on a revenue collector.

Topkhāna : the artillery.

Topsāz : the one who casts cannon.

Tope : an administrative unit between the village and the *tappa* in some parts of the Panjab. See also, *chakla.*

Toshākhāna : the royal treasury.

Trak : a unit of weight in Kashmir, said to be equal to about 4½ Lahore *sers* or 1/16th of a *kharwār*.

Udāsī : literally, a renunciant ; viewed traditionally as a follower of Guru Nanak through his son Sri Chand who founded an ascetical order of Sikhs ; *udāsī akhāra* : a religious establishment of the *udāsī* order.

'Ulamā (pl. of *'ālim*) : the learned ; doctors of Islamic Law and theology.

Vakīl : an agent or a deputy ; an envoy.

Vaish : the periodical redistribution of holdings based on the original proprietary shares.

Vaishnava : relating to the worshippers of Lord Vishnu, in His incaranations of Rama and Krishna in particular. See also, *bairāgī* and *thākurdwāra*.

Wābastgān : the relations and dependants.

Wāguzār : exempt from the payment of land revenue.

Wandāī : see *batāī*.

Wāris : a proprietor ; an heir.

Yaumīya : see *rozīna*.

Zabt : a method of assessment based on measurement and applied commonly to perishable and superior crops under Sikh rule ; *kāghaz-i-zabt* : records of the assessment of land revenue by measurement. See also, *khasra-i-zabt-i-kankūt*.

Zambūrak : a swivel or camel gun.

Zamīndār : literally, possessor of the land ; a peasant proprietor also, the holder of a right over a certain share in the produce from land, and as such, also called *mālik-i-a'alā* or *ta'alluqdār*.

Zāminī : a surety or guarantee.

Zila' : used loosely for an administrative unit ; used indifferently for a *ta'alluqa* and its sub-divisions under Sikh rule.

Zīra : the cuminseed.

Bibliography

I. PRIMARY SOURCES

1. English

(i) PUBLISHED OFFICIAL RECORDS

Abbott, S.A., 'Memorandum of the First Eight Years' British Rule in the District of Hoosheearpore from its annexation in 1846-47 to the close of 1853-54', *Selections from the Public Correspondence of the Punjab Administration*, Vol. IV, No. 3, Lahore, 1857.

Anderson, A. & Fagan, P.J., *Report of the Revised Settlement of the Hissar District (1887-1892)*, Lahore, 1892.

Barkley, D.G., 'Character of Land Tenures', *Report on the Administration of the Punjab and its Dependencies (1872-1873)*, Lahore 1873, Part II, pp. 9-16.

Bates, Charles Ellison, *A Gazetteer of Kashmir*, Calcutta, 1873.

Boyd, D.J., *Final Report of the Fourth Regular Settlement of the Sialkot District (1917)*, Lahore, 1917.

Clarke, J., 'The Agriculture of the Rechna Doab', *Selections from the Public Correspondence of the Punjab Administration*, Vol. II, No. 20, Lahore, 1854-55, pp. 57-117.

Dane, Lewis W., *Final Report of the Revised Settlement of the Gurdaspur District (1892)*, Lahore, 1892.

Douie, J.M., *Settlement Report of Karnal-Ambala*, Lahore, 1891.

———, *The Punjab Settlement Manual* (3rd ed.), Lahore, 1915.

Fazal, Cyril P.K., *A Bibliography of Economic Literature Relating to the Punjab*, Board of Economic Enquiry, Punjab, Lahore, 1941.

Fryer, F.W.R., *Final Report on the First Regular Settlement of the Dera Ghazí Khan District (1869-1874)*, Lahore, 1876.

Gordon Walker, T., *Final Report on the Revision of Settlement of the Ludhiana District (1878-1883)*, Calcutta, 1884.

Grant, J.A., *Final Report on the Revision of Settlement of the Amritsar District (1888-1893)*, Lahore, 1893.

Hamilton, G.W., 'On the Tirnee Tax of Jhung', *Selections from the Public Correspondence of the Administration for the Affairs of the Punjab*, Vol. I, No. 9, Lahore, 1853, pp. 103-11.

Ibbetson, D.C.J., *Final Report of the Revised Settlement of the Karnal District (1872-1880)*, Lahore, 1885.

———, *Report on the Census of the Punjab (1881), 3 Vols.*, Calcutta & Lahore, 1883.

Kaul, Hari Kishan, *Final Report of the Second Regular Settlement of the Mianwali District (1908)*, Lahore, 1908.

Kensington, A., *Settlement Report of the Ambala District (1893)*, Lahore, 1893.

Lyall, J.B., *Report of the Land Revenue Settlement of the Kangra District (1865-1872)*, Lahore, 1874.

Maclagan, E.D., *Settlement Report of the Multan District (1901)*, Lahore, 1901.

Montgomery, J.A.L., *Final Report of Revised Settlement of the Hoshiarpur District (1879-1884)*, Calcutta, 1885.

Nisbet, R.P., *Report on the Revision of the Land Revenue Settlement of the Gujranwala District (1866-1867)*, Lahore, 1874.

O'Brien, Edward, *Report on the Land Revenue Settlement of the Muzaffargarh District (1873-1880)*, Lahore 1882.

O'Dwyer, F., *Final Report on the Revision of Settlement of the Gujranwala District (1889-1894)*, Lahore, 1894.

Ousley, G. & Davies, W.G., *Report on the Revised Settlement of the Shahpoor District (1866)*, Lahore, n.d.

Purser, W.E., *Final Report of the Revised Settlement of the Jullundur District (1860-1866)*, Lahore, 1892.

Robertson, F.A., *Final Report of the Settlement of the Rawalpindi District (1880-1887)*, Lahore, n.d.

Roe, C.A. & Purser, W.E., *Report on the Revised Land Revenue Settlement of the Montgomery District (1874)*, Lahore, 1878.

Saunders, L.S., *Report on the Revised Settlement of the Lahore District (1865-1869)*, Lahore, 1873.

Steedman, E.B., *Report on the Revied Settlement of the Jhang District (1874-1880)*, Lahore, 1882.

Thomson, R.G., *A Report of the Second Regular Settlement of the Land Revenue of the Jehlam District (1881)*, Lahore, 1883.

Thorburn, S.S., *Report of the First Regular Land Revenue Settlement of the Bannu District*, Lahore, 1879.

Tremenheere, G.B., 'On the Present State of Agriculture in the Punjab', '*Selections from the Public Correspondence of the Administration for the Affairs of the Punjab*, Vol. I, No. 12, Lahore, 1853, pp. 191-228.

Tucker, H.St. G., *Report on the Settlement of the Kohat District* (*1875-1882*), Calcutta, 1884.

Tupper, C.L., *Punjab Customary Law*, 3 Vols., Calcutta, 1881.

Waston, H.D., *Gazetteer of the Hazara District* (*1907*) Chatto & Windus, London, MCMVIII.

Waterfield, W.G., *Report on the Second Regular Settlement of the Gujrat District* (*1866-1868*), Lahore, 1874.

Wilson, J., *Final Report on the Revision of Settlement of the Sirsa District* (*1879-1883*), Lahore, 1891.

Wynyard, W., Larkins, W.L. & Davies, R.H., *Extracts from Reports on the Settlement of the Pergunnahs formerly comprised in the Thanesar District*, Lahore, 1865.

Published by Authority

Gazetteers of the Punjab Districts (*1883-1884*):

Ambala, Amritsar, Attock (*1907*), Bannu, Dera Ghazi Khan, Dera Ismail Khan, Gujranwala, Gujrat, Gurdaspur (also, *1891-1892*), Hoshiarpur, Jhelum, Jhang, Jalandhar, Kangra, Karnal, Lahore, Ludhiana (*1888-1889*), Montgomery, Multan, Muzaffargarh, Peshawar, Rawalpindi, Shahpur, Sialkot.

General Report upon the Administration of the Punjab Proper for the years 1849-50 & 1850-51, Lahore, 1854.

Imperial Gazetteers of India (*Provincial Series*), *Punjab*, 2 Vols., Calcutta, 1908.

Punjab Famine Commission Enquiries Report (*1878-1879*), 2 Vols., Lahore 1878 and 1879.

Punjab Government Records, Vols. I-VI, Lahore, 1911-1915.

Report on the Census Taken on the 1st January 1855 of the Population of the Punjab Territories, Calcutta, 1856.

Report on the Census of the Punjab (*1868*), Lahore, 1870

Papers connected with the Question of Tenant Right in the Punjab : Selections from Records of the Government of the Punjab, Lahore, 1869, Appendix No. VII : Landlord and Tenant ('during times anterior to British rule') : Extracts from Settlement Reports of 14 Districts :

Barnes, G.C., *SR Kangra (1850-1855)*
Brandreth, E., *SR Ferozepur (?)*
Cracroft, J.E., *SR Rawul Pindee (1864)*
Davidson, H.D., *SR Loodiana (1859)*
Davies, R.H., *SR Amritsur (1859-1860)*
Davies, R.H., *SR Goordaspur (1856-1859)*
Egerton, R.E., *SR Lahore (1858)*
Elphinstone, Capt., *SR Googāira (?)*
Mackenzie, H., *SR Goojrat (1861)*
Melvill, P.S., *SR Hoshiarpur (1852)*
Morris, J.H., *SR Goojranwalla (1860)*
Prinsep, Edward A., *SR Sealkote (1865?)*
Temple, R., *SR Jullundur (1852)*
Wynyard, W., *SR Amballa (1859)*

Selection from Records of the Financial Commissioner's Office, Old series, No. 37 (New series, Nos. 11 & 16).

(ii) UNPUBLISHED OFFICIAL RECORDS

The following records, in particular, in the National Archives of India, New Delhi, have been useful for the chapters on the vassals, the *jāgīrdārs*, the *dharmarth*, the administrative framework, the land revenue and the land tenures :

Foreign/Political Consultation Files

8 August 1838, Nos. 28-29.
28 November 1838, Nos. 50-52.
9 November 1846, Nos. 2185-97.
26 December 1846, Nos. 1169-72 & 598-601.
31 December 1847, Nos. 1829-32, 2185-87, 2213, 2216-18, 2280, 2288, 2292 & 2378.
16 December 1848, Nos. 93-95.
28 March 1849, No. 12.
12 May 1848, Nos. 142-43.
29 December 1849, No. 49A.

14 March 1851, Nos. 113 & 113A, B, C, D, E, F; also, 666-67.
26 September 1851, No. 118.
14 November, 1851, No. 55
12 March 1852, Nos. 95-98.
16 April 1852, Nos. 98 & 99.
30 April 1852, Nos. 99-102.
7 May 1852, Nos. 40-43.
21 May 1852, No. 142.
11 June 1852, Nos. 109-14.
20 August 1852, Nos. 135-38.
27 March 1853, 195-97.
1 April 1853, Nos. 207-17.
29 April 1853, Nos. 128-31.
27 May 1853, No. 214.
22 February 1854, Nos. 191-94.
17 March 1854, Nos. 195-97.
5 September 1856, Nos. 109-15.
25 September 1856, Nos. 243-46.
27 March 1857, Nos. 245-47.

Foreign/Political Proceedings Volumes

26 December 1846, Nos. 639-662.
28 December 1846, No. 1239.
19 March 1847, No. 9.
31 December 1847, Nos. 1808, 2443, 2444, & 2470-75.
28 July 1848, No. 47.
25 August 1849, No. 82.
3 April 1850, Nos. 194 & 280.
1 May 1850, No. 457.
23 August 1850, Nos. 28 & 28A, 30 & 30A, 35, 35A, B & C.
6 September 1850, Nos. 31-31A.
27 September 1850, No. 73A.
22 November 1850, Nos. 117 & 117A.
14 November 1851, No. 45.
19 March 1852, Nos. 67-68.
13 April 1852, No. 100.
30 April 1852, Nos. 92 & 119-21.

11 May 1852, No. 136.
11 June 1852, Nos. 180-81.
18 June 1852, Nos. 181-85.
15 October 1852, Nos. 116 & 122.
7 January 1853, Nos. 219, 221-26, 228, 231-34 & 238-42.
14 January 1853, Nos. 212-17, 218-20, 221-24, 225-27 & 240-42.
27 March 1853, Nos. 201-03.
7 May 1853, Nos. 202, 205 & 228.
27 May 1853, Nos. 202 & 207-08.
10 June 1853, Nos. 217 & 218-20.
17 March 1854, Nos. 195-97.
23 June 1854, Nos. 204-05.
9 January 1857, Nos. 221, 227, 230, 233, 234-35, & 238.
27 March 1857, Nos. 233-37, 239-40, 242-43, 255-56 & 261-62.
1 May 1857, Nos. 413-19 & 459.
25 February 1859, Nos. 172-74.

Foreign/Secret Consultation Files

24 August 1840, Nos. 114-17.
8 April 1842, No. 37.
18 November 1843, Nos. 17, 19, 21, 22 & 26.
27 April 1844, Nos. 172-81.
26 December 1846, Nos. 1236-38 & 1325-27.
30 October 1847, Nos. 95, 110 & 129-30.
31 December 1847, Nos. 129-30 & 195-98.
25 February 1848, No. 60.
31 March 1848, Nos. 66-70.
28 April 1848, Nos. 57-66, 107-09 & 129-30.
26 May 1849, Nos. 68-71.

Foreign/Secret Proceedings Volumes

26 December 1846, No. 1038.
31 December 1847, Nos. 326 & 334-36.
28 January 1848, Nos. 35-75.
29 February 1848, No. 60.
31 March 1848, Nos. 71-150.
28 April 1848, Nos. 67-93.

30 December 1848, Nos. 446-49, 461 & 464.
18 June 1852, No. 99.

(iii) CONTEMPORARY ACCOUNTS

Browne, James, *Browne Correspondence* (ed. K.D. Bhargava), India Records Series, Delhi, 1960.

Burnes, Alexander, *Travels into Bokhara containing the Narrative of a Voyage on the Indus from the Sea to Lahore*, 3 Vols., John Murray, London, MDCCCXXXIX.

Drew, Frederic, *The Jummoo and Kashmir Territories* (reprint). (first published, 1875), Oriental Publishers, Delhi, 1971.

Eden, Emily, *Up the Country* (3rd. ed.), 2 Vols., Richard Bentley, London, 1866.

Forrest, George W. (ed.), *Selections from the Travels and Journals Preserved in the Bombay Secretariat*, Bombay, 1906 (particularly for the *Journals* of Charles Masson).

Forster, George, *A Journey from Bengal to England through Northern Parts of India, Kashmir, Afghanistan and Persia and into Russia (1782-1784)*, 2 Vols., R. Faulder, London, 1798.

Francklin, W., *The History of the Reign of Shaw Allum*, London, 1798.

———, *Military Memoirs of George Thomas*, London, 1805.

Ganda Singh (ed.), 'Early European Accounts of the Sikhs', *Indian Studies: Past and Present*, reprint, Calcutta, 1962.

Garrett, H.L.O. (ed.), *The Punjab—A Hundered Years Ago, as Described by V. Jacquemont and A. Soltykoff*, The Punjab Government Record Office Publication, Monograph No. 18, Lahore, 1935.

Hasrat, B.J. (ed.), *The Punjab Papers : Selections from the Private Papers of Lord Auckland, Lord Ellenborough, Viscount Hardinge, and the Marquis of Dalhousie, 1836-1849 on the Sikhs*, Vishveshvaranand Vedic Research Institute, Hoshiarpur, 1970.

Honigberger, J.M., *Thirty-Five Years in the East and Historical Sketches Relating to the Punjab and Cashmere*, Vol. I, London, 1852.

Hugel, Baron Charles, *Travels in Kashmir and the Panjab* (tr. & ed. T.B. Jervis), John Petheram, London 1845.

Jacquemont, Victor, *Letters From India : Describing a Journey in the British Dominions of India, Tibet, Lahore and Cashmere during the years 1828, 1829, 1830, 1831, undertaken by orders of the French Government* (2nd ed.), 2 Vols., Edward Churton, London, 1835.

Lawrence, H.M.L., *Adventures of an Officer in the Service of Ranjeet Singh* (reprint–first published 1846), 2 Vols., Languages Department Punjab, Patiala, 1970.

Malcolm John, 'Sketch of the Sikhs' (reprint—first published 1812), *The Sikh Religion : a Symposium*, Calcutta, 1958.

Mohan Lal, Munshi, *Journal of a Tour Through the Punjab, Afghanistan, Turkistan, Khorasan and Part of Persia*, Published by the Author, Calcutta, 1834.

Moorcroft W. & Trebeck G., *Travels in the Himalayan Provinces of Hindustan and the Punjab, in Ladak and Kashmir, in Peshawar, Kabul and Kunduz and Bokhara from 1819 to 1825* (reprint—first published 1837), Languages Department Punjab, Patiala, 1970.

Osbrone, W.G., *The Court and Camp of Runjeet Sing, with an Introductory Sketch of the Origin and Rise of the Sikh State*, London, 1840.

Schonberg, Baron, Erich Von, *Travels in India and Kashmir*, 2 Vols., Hurst & Blackett, London, 1853.

Shahamat Ali, *The Sikhs and Afghans*, (reprint—first published 1847), Languages Department Punjab, Patiala, 1970.

Smyth, Carmichael, *History of the Reigning Family of Lahore*, (reprint—first published 1847), Languages Department Punjab, Patiala, 1970.

Thornton, Edward, *A Gazetteer of the Countries adjascent to India on the North West including Sind, Afghanistan, Beloochistan, Punjab*, London, 1844, noticed critically in the *Calcutta Review*, Vol. II, No. 4 (1844), pp. 469-535.

Vigne, G.T., *A Personal Narrative of a Visit to Ghuzni, Kabul and Afghanistan*, London, 1840.

2. Persian

(i) CHRONICLES

Ahmad Shah Batalia, *Tārīkh-i-Hind*, MS, SHR 1291, Khalsa College, Amritsar.

Ahmad Yar, *Shāhnāma-i-Maharaja Ranjit Singh* (ed. Ganda Singh), Sikh History Society, Amritsar, 1951.

Aliuddin, Mufti, *'Ibratnāma*, MS, SHR 1277, Khalsa College, Amritsar.

Amar Nath, Diwan, *Zafarnāma-i-Ranjit Singh* (ed. Sita Ram Kohli), University of the Panjab, Lahore, 1928.

Bakht Mal, *Khālsanāma*, MS, SHR 1659, Khalsa College, Amritsar.

Bute Shah, *Tārīkh-i-Panjab*, MS, SHR 1288 (Daftars I-IV) & SHR 2289 (Daftar V), Khalsa College, Amritsar.

Daya Ram, Pandit, *Shīr-o-Shakar*, MS, SHR 399, Khalsa College, Amritsar.

Ganesh Das Wadhera, *Chār Bāgh-i-Panjab* (ed. Kirpal Singh), Khalsa College, Amritsar, 1965.

———, *Rājdarshinī*, BM. Or 1634 (photostat), Panjab University, Chandigarh.

Hālāt-i-Ahd-i-Maharaja Sahib Singh (anon.), MS, M/937, Punjab State Archives, Patiala.

Haqīqat-i-Binā wa 'Urūj-i-Firqa-i-Sikhān (anon.), SHR 1284 (photostat), Khalsa College, Amritsar.

Khushwaqt Rai, *Tāwārīkh-i-Sikhān*, MS, SHR 1274, Khalsa College, Amritsar.

Kirpa Ram, *Gulābnāma*, MS, M/358, Punjab State Archives, Patiala.

——— *Gulzār-i-Kashmir*, Kohinoor Press, Lahore, 1870.

Muhammad Naqi Peshawari, *Sher Singhnāma*, MS M/327, Punjab State Archives, Patiala.

Nagina Ram Parmar, *Ravi Parkāsh*, 3 Vols., MSS, M/833, M/834 & M/835, Punjab State Archives, Patiala.

Nur Muhammad, Qazi, *Jangnāma*, MS, SHR 1547, Khalsa College, Amritsar.

Raja Ram Tota, *Gulgashta-i-Panjab*, MS, M/790, Punjab State Archives, Patiala.

Sohan Lal Suri, *Umdat-ut-Tawārīkh*, Daftars I-V, New Imperial Press, Lahore, 1887-89.

Sujan Rai, *Khulāsat-ut-Tawārīkh* (ed. Zafar Hasan), Maulvi Abrar Hasan, Muradabad, 1918.

Tahmas Khan, *Tahmāsnāma*, BM, Or 8807 (photostat), SHR 1283, Khalsa College, Amritsar.

Tārīkh-i-Kashmir (anon.), M/1004 (photostat), Punjab State Archives, Patiala.

Tārīkhnāma (a detailed history of Sikh rule in the Panjab with special reference to the period 1839-49), 2 Vols. (anon.), MS, M/413, Punjab State Archives, Patiala.

(ii) DOCUMENTS, ADMINISTRATIVE MANUALS, NEWSLETTERS, ETC.

Bhandārī Collection, Punjab State Archives, Patiala. There are hundreds of official documents in this collection relating to the Sikh and Mughal times.

Bekas, Jawahar Nath, *Dastūr al-'Amal*, MS, Subhanullah Collection, 954/4, Aligarh Muslim University Library, Aligarh.

Chattar Singh Collection, Punjab State Archives, Patiala.

Dastāvezāt-i-Patiala, MS, M/812, Punjab State Archives, Patiala.

Farhang-i-Kārdānī, Abdus Salam Collection, 315/85 F(4), Aligarh Muslim University, Aligarh.

Ghulam Muhammad, *Dastūr al-'Amal*, MS, M/933, Punjab State Archives, Patiala.

Jakhbar Collection: This Collection contains 16 Persian documents belonging to the Jogi *gaddī* of Jakhbar (district Gurdaspur).

Khālsa Darbār Records, Punjab State Archives, Patiala (particularly Bundles B-4 and B-5 which consist of dozens of volumes relating to *jāgīrs* and *dharmarth*).

Khulāsat-us-Siyāq, MS, Subhanullah Collection, 900/15, Aligarh Muslim University Library, Aligarh.

Kitāb-i-Hālāt-i-Jind wa Dastāvezāt (anon.), MS, M/811, Punjab State Archives, Patiala.

Mir Ahmad, *Dastūr al-'Amal-i-Kashmir*, MS, M/829, Punjab State Archives, Patiala.

Nand Ram, Munshi, *Siyāqnāma*, Nawal Kishore Press, Lucknow, 1879.

Narain Das, *Amīr-ul-Inshā* (photostat), M/836, Punjab State Archives, Patiala.

News of the Court of Ranjit Singh, MS, Persian Miscellaneous 65, National Archives of India, New Delhi.

Parwānajāt-i-Chatar Singh wa Sardar Sher Singh Atari, MSS, SHR 1264 & 1265, Khalsa College, Amritsar.

Pehowa Collection : These documents belong to the Jogi establishment of Pehowa near Kurukshetra and have been used by the author through Prof. B.N. Goswamy's courtesy.

Pindori Collection : This collection belongs to the Vaishnava *gaddī* of Pindori (district Gurdaspur) and is much larger than the *Jakhbar Collection.*

Kāghzāt-i-Dharmarth-i-Harnpur, MS, SHR 1279, Khalsa College, Amritsar.

Tārīkh-i-Jāgīrdārān-i-Zila'-i-Ambala, (anon.), MS, M/975, Punjab State Archives, Patiala.

Tilla Gorakh Nath Collection : The original collection is not traceable but summaries of a large number of documents were made available by the present *mahant*, now in Ambala City, to Dr. B.N. Goswamy, and have been consulted by the author through his courtesy.

3. Panjabi

Bhangu, Ratan Singh, *Prāchīn Panth Parkāsh* (4th ed.), Amritsar, 1962.

Ganda Singh (ed.), *Hukamnāmay*, Punjab University, Patiala, 1967.

Gian Singh, Giani, *Tawārīkh Gurū Khālsā*, Part 2 (reprint—first published 1878), Languages Department Punjab, Patiala, 1970.

Kohli, Sita Ram (ed.), *Fatehnāma Gurū Khālsā Jī Dā* (2nd ed.), Languages Department Punjab, Patiala, 1970.

Rao, Ram Sukh, *Jassa Singh Binod*, MS, M/772, Punjab State Archives, Patiala.

———*Bhag Singh Chandarūday*, MS, M/773, Punjab State Archives, Patiala.

———*Fateh Singh Partāp Prabhākar*, MS, M/774, Punjab State Archives, Patiala.

4. Urdu

Bakhtawar Lal, Rai Bahadur Munshi, *Tārīkh-i-Zila'-i-Montgomery*, MS, SHR 1247, Khalsa College, Amritsar.

Beg, Mirza Muhammad Azim, *Tārīkh-i-Gujrat*, Victoria Press, Lahore, 1870.

———*Tārīkh-i-Hazara*, Victoria Press, Lahore, 1874.

———*Tārīkh-i-Jehlam*, Arya Press, Lahore, 1880.

Gopal Das, Rai Bahadur Munshi, *Tārīkh-i-Gujranwala*, Victoria Press, Lahore, 1874.

———*Tārīkh-i-Peshawar*, 5 Vols., Kohinoor Press, Lahore, 1874.

Hukm Chand, Munshi, *Tārīkh-i-Zila'-i-Multan*, New Imperial Press, Lahore, 1884.

Inaitullah, *An Administrative History of the Kalsia State*, MS, M/810, Punjab State Archives, Patiala.

Kahan Singh Balauria, *Tārīkh-i-Rājgān-i-Jammu-wa-Kashmir*, Prakash Steam Press, Lahore, 1929.

———*Tawārīkh-i-Rājputān-i-Mulk-i-Panjab*, Pratap Press, Jammu, 1912.

Kanhaiya Lal, *Tārīkh-i-Panjab*, Victoria Press, Lahore, 1881.

———*Tārīkh-i-Lahore*, Victoria Press, Lahore, 1884.

Muhammad Hasan Khan, Khalifa, *Tārīkh-i-Patiala*, Safir-i-Hind Press, Amritsar, 1878.

Nur Muhammad, Maulvi, *Tārīkh-i-Jhang Sial*, Ahmadi Press, Meerut, 1865.

Radha Kishan, *Tawārīkh-i-Gosha-i-Panjab*, MS, SHR 1251, Khalsa College, Amritsar.

Ramjas, Diwan, *Tārīkh-i-Khāndān-i-'Alīshān Sarkār Ahluwalia Wālī-i-Kapurthala*, MS, M/809, Punjab State Archives, Patiala.

———*Tawārīkh-i-Riyāsat-i-Kapurthala*, Guru Gobind Singh Press, Lahore 1897.

Sarup Lal, Qanungo, *Tārīkh-i-Sikhān-wa-Dastūr al-'Amal-i-Mumālik-Mahfūza*, MS, SHR 522, Khalsa College, Amritsar.

5. Translations

Banerjee, Indubhusan (tr.) 'A Short History of the Origin and

Rise of the Sikhs' (English translation of *Haqīqat-i-Binā-wa 'Urūj-i-Firqa-i-Sikhān*), Supplement to *Indian Historical Quarterly*, XVIII, No. 1, 1942.

Elliot, H.M. & Dowson, John (tr. & ed.), *History of India as told by its own Historians*, (reprint) Vols. VII & VIII, Kitab-Mahal, Allahabad, 1964.

Ganda Singh (tr. & ed.), *The Panjab in 1839-40 : Selections from the Punjab Akhbars, Punjab Intelligence, etc., preserved in the National Archives of India, New Delhi*, Sikh History Society, Amritsar, Patiala, 1952.

Garrett, H.L.O. & Chopra, G.L. (tr. & ed.), *Events at the Court of Ranjit Singh (1810-1817)*, (reprint), The Punjab Government Record Office Publication, Monograph No. 17, Languages Department Punjab, Patiala, 1970.

Giani Lal Singh (tr.) & Fauja Singh (ed.), *Panjab dī Sair* (Panjabi translation of Rai Kali Rai's & Rai Tulsi Ram's Urdu work, *Sair-i-Panjab*, 2 Vols.), Punjabi University, Patiala, 1971.

Goswamy, B.N. (tr. & ed.), *Painters at the Sikh Court : A Study Based on Twenty Documents* (belonging to the artist family of Rajol), Franz Steiner Verlag, Wiesbaden, 1975.

Goswamy, B.N. & Grewal, J.S. (tr. & ed.), *The Mughals and the Jogis of Jakhbar* (a study of 16 Persian Documents of the *Jakhbar Collection*), Indian Institute of Advanced Study, Simla, 1967.

Goswamy, B.N. & Grewal, J.S. (tr. & ed.), *The Mughal and Sikh Rulers and the Vaishnavas of Pindori* (a study of 52 Persian Documents from the *Pindori Collection*), Indian Institute of Advanced Study, Simla, 1969.

Grewal, J.S. (tr. & ed.), *In the By-Lanes of History: Some Persian Documents from a Punjab Town (belonging to The Bhandari Collection*, PSA, Patiala), Indian Institute of Advanced Study, Simla, 1975.

Grewal, J.S. & Indu Banga (tr. & ed.), *Early Nineteenth Century Panjab* (Ganesh Das's *Chār Bāgh-i-Panjab*), Guru Nanak University, Amritsar, 1975.

Grewal, J.S. & Indu Banga, 'Ranjit Singh, the Suzerain' (contains translations of M/503, M/504, M/507 & M/511 of the *Chattar Singh Collection*, PSA, Patiala), *Proceedings Punjab History Conference (1970)*, pp. 70-89.

Gupta, Hari Ram (tr. & ed.), *Panjab on the Eve of the First Sikh War : A documentary study of the political, social and economic conditions of the Panjab as depicted in the daily letters written chiefly from Lahore by British Intelligencers during the period from 30th December 1843 to 31 October 1844* (2nd ed.) Panjab University, Chandigarh, 1975.

Madhav Rao, P. Setu (tr.), *Tahmas Nama*, Popular Prakashan, Bombay, 1967.

Jerrett, H.S. (tr. & ed.), *Ā'īn-ı-Akbarī*, Vols. II & III (revised by J.N. Sarkar), Bibliotheca Indica Series, Calcutta, 1949 & 1948.

Roe, Charles A. (tr.), *A History of the Sialkot District* (Munshi Amin Chand's) Lahore, 1874.

Suri, Vidya Sagar (tr.), *Siyahat-i-Kashmir* (Ganeshi Lal's), Simla 1955.

———*Umdat-ut-Tawarikh*, Daftar III (1831-1839), S. Chand & Co., Delhi, 1961.

———*Umdat-ut-Tawarikh*, Daftar IV (1839-1845), Punjab Itihas Prakashan, Chandigarh, 1972.

II SECONDARY WORKS

1. Books

Abdul Aziz, *The Mansabdari System and the Mughal Army*, (reprint) Idarah-i-Adabiyat-i-Delli, Delhi, 1972.

Abdur Rashid, Sheikh, *Najibuddaulah : His Life and Times*, Aligarh, 1952.

Archer, John C., *The Sikhs*, Princeton University Press, Princeton, 1946.

Athar Ali, M., *The Mughal Nobility Under Aurangzeb* (reprint), Aligarh Muslim University, Aligarh, 1970.

Baden Powell, B.H., *Handbook of the Economic Products of the Punjab, with a Combined Index and Glossary of Technical Vernacular Words*, 2 Vols., Lahore, 1869 & 1872.

———*The Indian Village Community* (reprint—first published 1896), Cosmo Publications, Delhi, 1972.

———*The Land Systems of British India*, 3 Vols., Oxford, 1892.

Baden Powell, B.H., *A Short Account of the Land Revenue and its Administration in British India; with a Sketch of the Land Tenures* (3rd ed.), Oxford, 1913.

Bajwa, Fauja Singh, *Military System of the Sikhs (1799-1849)*, Motilal Banarasidass, Delhi, 1964.

Bal, S.S., *British Policy towards the Panjab (1844-1849)*, New Age Publishers, Calcutta, 1971.

Bamzai, P.N.K., *A History of Kashmir*, Metropolitan Book Co., Delhi, 1962.

Banerjee, Indubhusan, *Evolution of the Khalsa* (2nd ed.), 2 Vols., A Mukherjee & Co., Calcutta, 1962.

Bawa Satinder Singh, *The Jammu Fox : A Biography of Maharaja Gulab Singh of Kashmir (1792-1857)*, Southern Illinois University Press, Carbondale Edwardsville, 1974.

Bedi, K.S. & Bal, S.S. (ed.), *Essays on History, Literature, Art and Culture : Presented to Dr. M.S. Randhawa*, Atma Ram & Sons, Delhi, 1970.

Bhagat Singh, *Sikh Polity in the Eighteenth and Nineteenth Centuries*, Ph.D. Thesis, Punjabi University, Patiala, 1971.

Chhabra, G.S., *Social and Economic History of the Punjab (1849-1901)*, S. Nagin & Co., Jullundur, 1962.

Chopra, B.R., *Kingdom of the Punjab (1839-45)*, Vishveshavaranand Vedic Research Institute, Hoshiarpur, 1969.

Chopra, G.L., *The Panjab as a Sovereign State* (2nd ed.), Vishveshavaranand Vedic Research Institute, Hoshiarpur, 1960.

Cunningham, Joseph Davy, *A History of the Sikhs* (reprint—first published 1849), S. Chand and Co., Delhi, 1966.

Douie, J.M., *The Punjab, North West Frontier Province & Kashmir* (Provincial Geography Series), Cambridge, 1916.

Ganda Singh, *Life of Banda Singh Bahadur*, Khalsa College, Amritsar, 1935.

———*Ahmad Shah Durrani*, Asia Publishing House, Bombay, 1959.

———*Sardar Jassa Singh Ahluwalia* (Panjabi), Punjabi University, Patiala, 1969.

———*A Bibliography of the Panjab*, Punjabi University, Patiala, 1966.

Ghoshal, U.N., *Contributions to the History of the Hindu Revenue System*, Saraswat Library, Calcutta, 1972.

Grewal, J.S., *Guru Nanak in History*, Panjab University, Chandigarh, 1969.

———*From Guru Nanak to Maharaja Ranjit Singh* (Essays in Sikh History), Guru Nanak University, Amritsar, 1972.

———*The Present State of Sikh Studies*, Christian Institute of Sikh Studies, Baring Union Christian College, Batala, 1973.

Grewal, J.S. & Bal, S.S., *Guru Govind Singh*, Panjab University, Chandigarh, 1967.

Griffin, Lepel, *Ranjit Singh* (reprint), Rulers of India Series, Kitab Mahal, Allahabad, 1957.

———*The Rajas of the Punjab* (reprint—first published 1870), Languages Department Punjab, Patiala, 1970.

———*The Minor Phulkian Families* (reprint—first published 1870), Languages Department Punjab, Patiala, 1970.

Griffin, Lepel & Massy, Charles Francis, *The Panjab Chiefs*, 2 Vols., Lahore, 1890.

———*Chiefs and Families of Note in the Punjab*, 2 Vols., (revised by W.L. Canran & H.D. Craik), Lahore, 1909.

Gupta, Hari Ram, *A History of the Sikhs*, Vol. I (2nd ed.), The Minerva Book Shop, Simla, 1952; Vols. II & III, The Minerva Book Shop, Lahore, 1944.

———*Studies in the Later Mughal History of the Panjab (1707-1793)*, The Minerva Book Shop, Lahore, 1944.

Gustafson, W. Eric & Jones, Kenneth W., *Sources on Punjab History*, Manohar Book Service, New Delhi, 1975.

Hasrat, Bikramajit, *Anglo-Sikh Relations (1799-1849)* Vishveshvaranand Vedic Research Institute, Hoshiarpur, 1968.

———*Life and Times of Ranjit Singh*, Published by the Author, Nabha, Punjab, 1977.

Hoti, Prem Singh, *Kanwar Naunihal Singh* (Panjabi), (reprint), Languages Department Punjab, Patiala, 1971.

———*Maharaja Ranjit Singh* (Panjabi), (10th impression), Lahore Book Shop, Ludhiana, n.d.

———*General Hari Singh Nalwa* (8th inpression), Lahore Book Shop, Ludhiana, n.d.

Hutchison, J. & Vogel, J. Ph., *History of the Panjab Hill States*, 2 Vols., Lahore, 1933.

Ibn Hasan, *The Central Structure of the Mughal Empire* (reprint), Munshiram Manoharlal, Delhi, 1970.

Irfan Habib, *The Agrarian System of Mughal India* (*1526-1707*), Asia Publishing House, Bombay, 1963.

Irvine, William, *The Later Mughals*, 2 Vols. (ed. Jadunath Sarkar), M.C. Sarkar & Sons, Calcutta, 1922.

Jha, D.N., *Revenue System in Post Mauraya and Gupta Times*, Punthi Pustak, Calcutta, 1967.

Kapur, Prithipal Singh, *Sardar Jassa Singh Ramgarhia* (*1723-1803*), (Panjabi), Singh Brothers, Amritsar, 1969.

Karam Singh, *Baba Ala Singh* (Panjabi), Tarn Taran, 1918.

Kessinger, Tom G., *Viliayatpur 1848-1968 : An Historical Case Study of Social and Economic Change in a North Indian Village*, Ph.D. Thesis, University of Chicago, 1972 (seen through the author's courtesy).

Khan, Ahsan Raza, *Position of Chieftains in the Mughal Empire During Akbar's Reign*, Indian Institute of Advanced Study, Simla, 1977.

Khilnani, N.M., *The Punjab under the Lawrences*, The Punjab Government Record Office Publication, Monograph No. 2, Simla, 1951.

Khushwant Singh, *A History of the Sikhs*, 2 Vols., Princeton University Press, Princeton, 1963 & 1966.

———*Ranjit Singh, Maharaja of the Punjab* (*1780-1839*), George Allen & Unwin, London, 1962.

Kirpal Singh, *Life of Maharaja Ala Singh of Patiala and His Times*, Khalsa College, Amritsar, 1954.

———*An Historical Account of Bhai Vasti Ram and Bhai Ram Singh*, Khalsa College, Amritsar, n.d.

———*Sardar Sham Singh Atariwala* (Panjabi), Punjabi University, Patiala, 1969.

———*A Catalogue of Persian and Sanskrit Manuscripts*, Khalsa College, Amritsar, 1962.

———*A Catalogue of Punjabi and Urdu Manuscripts*, Khalsa College, Amritsar, 1963.

Kohli, Sita Ram, *Sunset of the Sikh Empire* (ed. Khushwant Singh), Orient Longmans, New Delhi, 1967.

———*Maharaja Ranjit Singh* (Panjabi), Delhi, 1953.

———*Catalogue of Khalsa Darbar Records*, 2 Vols., Lahore, 1919 & 1927.

Latif, Syed Muhammad, *History of the Panjab* (reprint—first published 1889), Eurasia Publishing House, New Delhi, 1964.

Lawrence, Walter Roper, *The Valley of Kashmir*, Kesar Publishers, Srinagar, 1967.

McGregor, W.L., *The History of the Sikhs* (reprint—first published 1846) 2 Vols., Languages Department Punjab, Patiala, 1970.

Maine, Henry Sumner, *Village Communities in the East and West* (7th ed.), John Murray, London, 1895.

Malik, Ikram Ali, *A Bibliography of the Punjab and its Dependencies (1849-1910)*, Research Society of Pakistan, University of the Punjab, Lahore, 1968.

Man Mohan, *A History of the Mandi State*, Lahore, 1930.

Marenco, Ethne K., *The Transformation of Sikh Society*, Heritage Publishers, New Delhi, 1976.

Mathur, Ram Sahai, *History of Raja Gajpat Singh of Jhind*, Typed MS, M/870, Punjab State Archives, Patiala.

McLeod, W.H., *The Evolution of the Sikh Community*, Oxford University Press, Delhi, 1975.

Moreland, W.H., *The Agrarian System of Moslem India*, (reprint) Oriental Books Reprint Corporation, Delhi, 1968.

———*From Akbar to Aurangzeb*, Oriental Reprints, Delhi, 1972.

———*India at the Death of Akbar : An Economic Study*, (reprint), Atma Ram & Sons, Delhi, 1962.

Nijjar, B.S., *Panjab Under the Later Mughals (1707-1759)*, New Academic Publishing Co., Jullundur, 1972.

Nurul Hasan, S., *Thoughts on Agrarian Relations in Mughal India*, People's Publishing House, New Delhi, 1973.

Pannikar, K.M., *Gulab Singh*, Martin Hopkins, London, 1930.

Prinsep, Henry T., *Origin of the Sikh Power in the Punjab* (reprint—first published 1834), Languages Department Punjab, Patiala 1970.

Qureshi, Ishtiaq Husain, *The Administration of the Sultanate of Delhi* (5th ed.), Oriental Books Reprint Corporation, New Delhi, 1971.

———*The Administration of the Mughal Empire*, N. V. Publications, Patna, n.d.

Rao, Suraj Narain, *Cis-Sutlej States (1803-49)*, Ph.D. Thesis,

Panjab University, Chandigarh. 1952.

Ray, Niharranjan, *The Sikh Gurus and the Sikh Society* (2nd ed.), Munshiram Manoharlal, Delhi, 1975.

Rose, H.A., *A Glossary of Castes and Tribes of the Punjab and N.W.F.P. of India* (reprint—first published 1919), 3 Vols., Languages Department Punjab, Patiala, 1970.

Ross, David, *Land of the Five Rivers* (reprint—first published 1883), Languages Department Punjab, Patiala, 1970.

Saran, P., *The Provincial Government of the Mughals (1526-1658)*, (2nd ed.), Asia Publishing House, Bombay, 1973.

Sarkar, Jadunath, *Mughal Administration* (4th ed.), M.C. Sarkar & Sons, Calctuta, 1952.

Satish Chandra, *Parties and Politics at the Mughal Court (1707-1740)*, (2nd ed.), People's Publishing House, New Delhi, 1972.

Sethi, R.R., *John Lawrence as Commissioner of the Jullundur Doab (1846-49)*, The Punjab Government Record Office Publication, Monograph No. 10, Lahore 1930.

———*The Lahore Darbar : In the Light of the Correspondence of Sir C.M. Wade (1823-1840)*, The Punjab Government Record Office Publication, Monograph No. 1, Simla, 1950.

Sharma, Ram Saran (ed.), *Land Revenue in India*, Motilal Banarsidass, Delhi, 1971.

Sharma, Sri Ram, *Mughal Government and Administration* (2nd ed.), Hind Kitabs, Bombay, 1965.

Shejwalkar, T.S., *Panipat : 1761*, Deccan College, Poona, 1946.

Siddiqi, Noman Ahmad, *Land Revenue Administration Under the Mughals (1700-1750)*, Aligarh Muslim University, Aligarh, 1970.

Sinha, N.K., *Ranjit Singh* (3rd ed.), A. Mukherjee & Co., Calcutta, 1968.

———*Rise of the Sikh Power* (3rd ed.), A. Mukherjee & Co., Calcutta, 1960.

Sircar, D.C., *Landlordism and Tenancy in Ancient and Mediaeval India as Revealed by Epigraphical Records*, University of Lucknow, Lucknow, 1969.

Spate, O.H.K. & Learmonth, A.T.A., *India and Pakistan* (3rd ed.), Methuen & Co., London, 1967.

Stamp, L. Dudley, *Asia : A Regional and Economic Geography*,

(10th ed.), London, 1959.

Teja Singh & Ganda Singh, *A Short History of the Sikhs*, Orient Longmans, Bombay, 1950.

Thorburn, S.S., *The Punjab in Peace and War* (reprint—first published 1904), Languages Department Punjab, Patiala, 1970.

Trevaskis, Hugh Kennedy, *Land of the Five Rivers : An Economic History of the Punjab from the Earliest Times to the Year of Grace, 1890*, Oxford, 1928.

Vogel, J. Ph., *Catalogue of the Bhuri Singh Museum at Chamba*, Calcutta, 1909.

Waheedud-ud-din, Fakir Syed, *The Real Ranjit Singh* (4th ed.), Lion Art Press, Karachi, 1965.

Whitehead, R.B., *Catalogue of Coins in the Punjab Museum, Lahore*, Vols. II & III, Oxford, 1914 & 1934.

Wilson, H.H., *A Glossary of Judicial and Revenue Terms* (reprint), Munshiram Manoharlal, Delhi, 1968.

2. Articles

Athar Ali, M., 'The Passing of Empire : The Mughal Case', *Modern Asian Studies*, Vol. 9, No. 3 (1975), pp. 385-96.

———'Provincial Governors Under Aurangzeb', *Medieval India—A Miscellany*, Aligarh Muslim University, Aligarh, Vol. I, pp. 23-60.

———'Provincial Governors Under Shah Jahan', *Medieval India—A Miscellany*, Aligarh Muslim University, Aligarh, Vol. III, pp. 80-112.

Bajwa, Fauja Singh, 'The Misaldari Period of Sikh History', *Panjab Past and Present*, Vol. XI (1977), pp. 88-92.

Bal, S.S., 'The Sikh Struggle for Independence and the Place of Sovereignty in Sikh Polity, 1699-1765', *The Medieval Indian State*, Panjab University, Chandigarh, 1967, pp. 124-40.

Banerjee, S.N., 'Raja Alha Singh and the Marathas', *Proceedings Indian Historical Records Commission*, Vol. XXI (1944), pp. 76-78.

———'The Cis-Sutlej Chiefs Under Maratha Rule', *Proceedings Indian Historical Records Commission*, Vol. XXIII (1946), pp. 69-72.

Dungen, P.H.M., 'Changes in Status and Occupation in Nineteenth Century Punjab', *Soundings in Modern South Asian History* (ed. D.A. Low), Weidenfeld and Nicholson, London, 1968, pp. 59-94.

Ganda Singh, 'Akhbarat-i-Lahaur-o-Multan', *Proceedings Indian Historical Records Commission*, Vol. XXI (1944), pp. 43-46.

———'The Punjab News in the Akhbarat-i-Darbar-i-Mualla', *Proceedings Indian Historical Records Commission*, XXIV (1948), pp. 61-66.

Grewal, J.S., 'J.D. Gunningham and his British Predecessors on the Sikhs', *Bengal Past and Present*, Vol. LXXXIII, Part 2, Serial No. 156 (1964), pp. 101-14.

———'The Character of Sikh Rule', *The Miscellaneous Articles*, Guru Nanak University, Amritsar, 1974, pp. 146-52.

———'Ganesh Das's *Chār Bāgh-i-Panjāb*', *Proceedings Indian History Congress*, Patiala, 1967, pp. 383-92.

———'The Sikh Movement : A Historical Note', *Dissent Protest and Reform in Indian Civilization* (ed. S.C. Malik), Indian Institute of Advanced Study, Simla, 1977, pp. 159-66.

Griffin, Lepel, 'The Law of Inheritance to Chiefship as observed by the Sikhs previous to the Annexation of the Punjab (reprint—first published 1869), *The Panjab Past and Present*, Vol. VI, Part (i) (1972), pp. 141-98.

Grover, B.R., 'Raqba-Bandi Documents of Akbar's Reign', *Proceedings Indian Historical Records Commission*, Vol. XXXVI, Part 2 (1961), pp. 55-60.

———'Nature of Land Rights in Mughal India', *The Indian Economic and Social History Review*, Vol. I, No. 1, 1963, pp. 1-24.

———'Nature of *Dehat-i-Taaluqa* (Zamindari Villages) and the Evolution of the *Taaluqdari* System During the Mughal Age', *The Indian Economic and Social History Review*, Vol. II, Nos. 2 & 3 (1965), pp. 166-78 & 259-89, respectively.

———Presidential Address : Medieval Indian Section, Proceedings Indian History Congress—Calicut, 1976, pp. 1-36.

———'An Integrated pattern of Commercial Life in the Rural Society of North India During the 17th-18th Centuries',

Proceedings Indian Historical Records Commission, Vol. XXXVII, Part 2 (1962), pp. 121-53.

———'The Concept of Village Community in North India During the Mughal Age and the Pre-British Era' (seen through the author's courtesy).

———'The Concept and Evolution of the Village Community in North India under the British Rule during the 19th Century', *Proceedings Indian History Congress*, Vol. II, Chandigarh 1973, pp. 92-93.

Gupta, Hari Ram, 'The First Sikh Coin of Lahore (Nov. 1761)', *Proceedings Indian Historical Records Commission*, Vol. XV (1938), pp. 427-33.

Gupta, P.C., 'A Note on Polier's Manuscript in the India Office Library', *Proceedings Indian Historical Records Commission*, Vol. XXIII, (1964), pp. 15-17.

Gurtej Singh, 'Bhai Mani Singh : In Historical Perspective', *Proceedings Punjab History Conference*, Patiala, 1968, pp. 120-27.

Hutchison, J. & Vogel, J. Ph., 'History of Basohli State', *Journal of the Panjab Historical Society*, Vol IV No. 2 (1916), pp. 77-97.

Indu Banga, 'Ahmad Shah Abdali's Designs over the Punjab, *Proceedings Indian History Congress*, Patiala, 1968, pp. 85-90.

———'Alha Singh : The Founder of Patiala State', *Punjab Past and Present : Essays in Honour of Dr. Ganda Singh* (ed. Harbans Singh & N. Gerald Barrier), Punjabi University, Patiala, 1976, pp. 150-60.

———'Religious Land Grants Under Sikh Rule', *Proceedings Punjab History Conference*, Patiala, 1971, pp. 144-51.

———'The Nature of Sikh Rule', *Proceedings Punjab History Conference*, Patiala, 1972, pp. 60-73.

———'Sikh Revenue Administration : The Framework', *Studies in Local and Regional History* (ed. J.S. Grewal), Guru Nanak University, Amritsar, 1974, pp. 55-85.

———'Agrarian System of Ranjit Singh,' *Proceedings Indian History Congress*, Aligarh, 1975, pp. 321-25.

———'*Mushakhasa* in *Ijāradārī* under Sikh Rule' (to be published in the *Proceedings Punjab History Conference*, Patiala 1978).

Irfan Habib, 'Aspects of Agrarian Relations and Economy in

a Region of Uttar Pradesh during the 16th Century', *The Indian Economic and Social History Review*, Vol. IV, No. 3 (1967), pp. 205-33.

———'The Social Distribution of Landed Property in Pre-British India (A Historical Survey)', *The Indian Society : Historical Probings* (ed. R.S. Sharma), ICHR, People's Publishing House, New Delhi, 1974, pp. 264-316.

Kohli, Sita Ram, 'Land Revenue Administration under Maharajah Ranjit Singh', *Journal of the Panjab Historical Society*, Vol. VII, No. 2 (1919), pp. 74-90.

———'The Records of the Sikh Government in the Punjab Secretariat', *Proceedings Indian Historical Records Commission*, Vol. II (1920), pp. 23-31.

———'A Book of Military Parwanas', *Proceedings Indian History Congress*, Lahore, 1940, pp. 367-71.

Misra, S.C., 'Social Mobility in Pre-Mughal India', *The Indian Historical Review*, Vol. I, No. 1, (1974), pp. 36-43.

Nurul Hasan, S., 'The Position of the Zamindars in the Mughal Empire', *The Indian Economic and Social History Review*, Vol. I, No. 4 (1964), pp. 107-19.

———'Three Studies of Zamindari System', *Medieval India—A Miscellany*, Vol. I, Aligarh Muslim University, Aligarh, pp. 233-39.

———'Presidential Address', *Proceedings Punjab History Conference*, Patiala, 1965, pp. 73-81.

Paras Ram, Hakim, *Tārīkh-i-Mandir-i-Jawālāmukhī* (Collection of articles in Urdu on the Jawalamukhi temple, Kangra), M/922, Punjab State Archives, Patiala.

Qaisar, A. Jan, 'Distribution of the Revenue Resources of the Mughal Empire among the Nobles', *Proceedings Indian History Congress*, Allahabad, 1965, pp. 237-43.

Rodgers, C.J., 'On the Coins of the Sikhs', *Journal of Asiatic Society of Bengal*, Vol. I, Part 1 (1881), pp. 71-93.

Satish Chandra, 'Presidential Address', *Proceedings Punjab History Conference*, Patiala, 1972, pp. 16-25.

———'Some Aspects of Indian Village Society in Northern India during the 18th Century—The Position and Role of the *khud kāsht* and *pāhī kāsht*', *The Indian Historical Review*, Vol. I, No. 1 (1974), pp. 51-64.

Shafi, Ahmad, 'Ahmadshah Abdali : The Last Mohammadan

Invader of India', *Calcutta Review*, Vol. LI, pp. 1-41.

Temple, R.C., 'Coins of the Modern Natives Chiefs of the Punjab', *Indian Antiquary*, Vol. XVIII (1889), pp. 321-41.

Williams, G.R.C., 'The Sikhs in the Upper Doab', *Selections from the Calcutta Review*, Vol. III, Nos. 10 & 11, Parts I-III, pp. 227-42, 228-59 & 332-54.

Index

PERSONAL

PLACES

TERMS